BODIES AS EVIDENCE

GLOBAL INSECURITIES

A SERIES EDITED BY
CATHERINE BESTEMAN AND DANIEL M. GOLDSTEIN

BODIES AS EVIDENCE

Security, Knowledge, and Power

Mark Maguire, Ursula Rao, and Nils Zurawski, editors

DUKE UNIVERSITY PRESS   Durham and London   2018

Designed by Matthew Tauch
Typeset in Minion Pro by Copperline Books

Library of Congress Cataloging-in-Publication Data
Names: Maguire, Mark, [date] editor. | Rao, Ursula,
[date] editor. | Zurawski, Nils, [date] editor.
Title: Bodies as evidence : security, knowledge, and power /
Mark Maguire, Ursula Rao, and Nils Zurawski, editors.
Description: Durham : Duke University Press, 2018. |
Series: Global insecurities | Includes bibliographical
references and index.
Identifiers: LCCN 2018015847 (print)
LCCN 2018019863 (ebook)
ISBN 9781478004301 (ebook)
ISBN 9781478001690 (hardcover : alk. paper)
ISBN 9781478002949 (pbk. : alk. paper)
Subjects: LCSH: Human body. | Biometric identification. |
Crime prevention. | Border security. | Terrorism—Prevention.
Classification: LCC HM636 (ebook) | LCC HM636 .B543 2018
(print) | DDC 364.4—dc23
LC record available at https://lccn.loc.gov/2018015847

Cover art: *Spirit is a bone*, 2013. © Broomberg
and Chanarin. Courtesy of Lisson Gallery,
London and New York.

CONTENTS

INTRODUCTION

Bodies as Evidence

MARK MAGUIRE AND URSULA RAO

Tricksters or fakes, assistants or 'toons, they are the exemplars of the coming community.
—GIORGIO AGAMBEN, *The Coming Community*

In this volume, we propose that evidence is a key problem in the contemporary moment. Today, evidence-based knowledge is everywhere in demand. Indeed, one sees a veritable obsession with measurement, quantification and verification in areas as diverse as medical science, government decision making, global finance and security policy (see Merry 2011). Disturbingly, even the so-called Islamic State issued periodic corporate reports with metrics and key performance indicators, including the number of "knife murders" and "apostates run over" (Shore and Wright 2015, 440). Yet, at the same time, commentators suggest that this is the age of uncertainty, the post-truth era.[1] Thus, between the demand for evidence-based knowledge and the widespread anxiety that the truth is not what it used to be, we find shifting relations of cause and effect, fact and falsehood, the observable and the occluded. We explore these shifting relations in security contexts.

In this volume, we focus on security contexts because problems of evidence are acute there and thus available for critical reflection. We discuss "bodies as evidence" as a way to explore biometric identification, borders and migration control, forensic knowledge, policing, and counterterrorism. By attending to bodies as evidence, we show how security discourses and practices target the body while also contributing to emergent configurations of knowledge and power. This volume, then, provides anthropological perspectives on the great technical, scientific, and expert efforts that characterize the drive to know and manage the complexities of security in the contemporary moment.

Of course, evidence has always been a problem in contexts of security and insecurity and especially in situations when political power must justify the use of force. Today, when so-called realists attempt to excuse imperialism, they often turn back to Thucydides's *Melian Dialogue*, which details the Athenian effort to secure their empire at the expense of a free society. Their "suspicions about the future" justified the brutal suppression of others, while Melian appeals for justice fell on ears attuned differently—"Your hatred is evidence of our power," the Athenian diplomats explained (Thucydides 1998, 404). Ancient Greece certainly provides us with many examples of conflicts that included battles over the truth, but one can find innumerable bodies of evidence buried throughout history. Some evidential regimes are distinctive; at other times, one can detect striking resemblances across cultural and historical lines.[2]

History certainly teaches us that there is a tendency in contexts of war to fabricate a reality in which to act. In the nineteenth century, for example, British interests in Southern Africa advanced through fraudulent "concessions," carpet bagging, chicanery, and, occasionally, genocidal violence. Indeed, historian Robert Blake (1977, 55) describes Cecil Rhodes's annexation of Matabeleland as a giant episode of *suppressio veri*—an attack on reality itself. Blake's description could serve just as well in an account of the pretext for war in Vietnam or the push for "regime change" Iraq. As is well known, in the run-up to the second Gulf War, a White House advisor (probably Karl Rove) dismissed journalist Ron Suskind (2004) because of his emphasis on facts and evidence. The White House insider explained the situation succinctly: "We create our own reality."

It seems, however, that arguments about evidence are becoming even more pervasive today. Dictionaries declared "post-truth" the word of the year in

2016, but it is just one term in a constellation that includes "truthiness," "fake news" and "alternative facts," terms that suggest the erosion of long-trusted evidential foundations. One cannot dismiss this as a hysterical moment in public culture. In Russia, top Putin aid and former theater student Vladislav Surkov—the Kremlin's "gray cardinal"—openly combines Orwellian ideological techniques and performance art. In Great Britain, many of the discussions about Brexit politics center on a loss of faith in "experts from organizations with acronyms" (*Sky News* 2016). However, former White House deputy assistant Sebastian Gorka set out the situation in even clearer terms. During an interview with the BBC he explained, "We are not going to put up with people who believe they have a monopoly on the truth simply because they have sixty years of a letterhead above them" (BBC 2017).

Clearly, the recent U.S. presidential election highlighted the extraordinary shift in public discourse about evidence from the very outset. Anthropologist Maximilian Forte, one of the few public intellectuals to predict the rise of President Donald Trump, emphasized Trump's theatrics during the election campaign:

> Trump often emerges on stage from behind a dark navy curtain. That is a symbolically rich move, and it is a symbolism whose deeper meaning and importance throws others off. . . . This is the puppet master, the man behind the curtain, the campaign donor and buyer of favours and influence, who has suddenly decided to step out into the spotlight, and to not only be seen but to announce his role as a former puppet master. . . . The move is so deeply subversive, that one has to wonder just how many have truly appreciated its import. (Forte 2016)

The U.S. president may be famous for his failure to reference the usual norms of truth telling, but as Forte realizes, his political power operates off a particular, if deeply authoritarian, body-evidence relationship, namely, his "authentic" betrayal of insider knowledge communicated to an audience who "knew it" all along. Evidence takes the form of a trick revealed, as if the Wizard of Oz pulled back his own curtain. And what becomes possible alongside theatrical subversion is the fabrication of a new reality. In this striking and ritualized political performance, then, one sees no truth per se, but, rather, "the play of light and shadow, truth and error, true and false, hidden and manifest, visible and invisible" (Foucault 2014, 17).

Commentators will surely be preoccupied with matters of evidence in politics for years to come, but here our explicit focus is on security contexts. In recent years, there has been steady flow of anthropological publications on security. Many of the contributors to this volume have added considerably to this literature. Ursula Rao (e.g., 2013; see also M'charek, Hagendijk, and de Vries 2013) explores how security manifests itself in efforts to identify the human body using biometric technologies. Daniel Goldstein (2016) and Ieva Jusionyte (2015) study local articulations and contestations of security in their ethnographic work in Latin America and the United States. Gregory Feldman (2012) and Mark Maguire (2014) write about the security apparatuses that are changing policy and policing. Among others, Antonius C. G. M. Robben (2010), Joseph P. Masco (2014), and Joseba Zulaika (2014) examine transformations in international security and warfare and the consequences of those changes. In short, anthropologists have been able to track security as it shifted the sands under people's feet in numerous field sites, and, from this granular level, they have been able to connect to broader transformations, even at the transnational scale.

The contributors to this volume attend to the extraordinary problems of evidence that manifest themselves in security contexts. Biometric security, for example, is precisely an effort to render the body as evidence for identification; and in the realm of counterterrorism, vast and shadowy security apparatuses scour the present and the near future for real and imagined threats. In short, problems of evidence are acute in security contexts, and yet, with just a few notable exceptions (e.g., Masco 2014), anthropologists have not dealt directly with evidence and security. Moreover, the contributors to this volume also attend to the extraordinary emphasis on the body as a source of evidence for and target of intervention. *Bodies as Evidence* moves back and forth between the analyses of different dimensions of the body-evidence relation. The different chapters show how bodies become sources for the production of evidence, the way bodies as evidence are organized and deployed to classify, recognize, and manage human life itself. We describe a circular motion in which bodies are both the origin of evidence and the target of evidence-based interventions. Rooting truth-making routines in new technologies of the body significantly influences notions of self and other, morality and crime, security and threat. Which assumptions and knowledge systems underscore the making of new security cultures? How do they shape who we are, what we do, and how we perceive of ourselves as physical and social beings? Here, we offer answers to these important questions. However, before formulating those answers, we first need to explore anthropology's approach to evidence.

Anthropology and Evidence

It is possible to narrate the history of sociocultural anthropology as a series of battles over evidence. For example, sociocultural anthropologists often teach students that disciplinary history began when heroes from long ago abandoned their university armchairs to gather evidence firsthand in faraway fields. Franz Boas used ethnographic evidence to challenge racism and evolutionism throughout his career. However, Bronislaw Malinowski's *Argonauts of the Western Pacific* offers an even more dramatic mise-en-scène. In the preface, James Frazer yields his armchair to the "young science" before him; then Malinowski ritually dispatches his predecessor for "wholesale generalizations" (Malinowski 1922, viii, 3). This tale of scholarly patricide centers on evidence, and, like all tales, much is omitted. In fact, Malinowski's scientific approach to "collecting, manipulating, and fixing evidence" offers few innovations (Malinowski 1922, 6; cf. Rivers 1912). Disciplinary historian George W. Stocking argues that the "ethnographer's magic" was less a matter of scientific evidence and more about a style of writing and narrative of adventure whereby "experience of the native's experience must become the reader's experience as well—a task that scientific analysis yielded up to literary analysis" (Stocking 1992, 53).

Analysis of the birth of ethnography reveals that anthropologists have long conflated matters of evidence and methodology. Even Matthew Engelke's recent *The Objects of Evidence*, one of the few anthropological volumes on this topic, foregrounds the following question: "How can we turn fieldwork experience—a highly personal, temporally-bound, and inter-subjective method for collecting data—into objects of evidence?" (Engelke 2009, 2; see also Csordas 2004; Hastrup 2004). Interestingly, one of the other volumes on evidence, *How Do We Know?*, is bookended by two contrasting answers to this question. Marilyn Strathern opens by eschewing the all-encompassing and reductive knowledge of other disciplines before flattering the style of analogical reasoning available in anthropology. However, Keith Hart concludes that the whole enterprise is indefensible, riddled with occult practices, and managed by people "who live in constant fear of being found out" (2008, 207).

Yet, social and cultural anthropology has long been open to self-criticism on these matters. The questions that animate recent volumes on this topic are also found in the contributions to James Clifford and George E. Marcus's *Writing Culture*, a response to the crisis of representation that swept the humanities and social sciences during the 1980s in the form of postcolonial and feminist-inspired critiques of objectivism and the rhetoric of authority (e.g., Pratt 1986, 33). This was also an experimental moment, as illustrated by George E. Marcus's early discussion of multi-sited ethnography and Paul Rabinow's approach to studying how contemporary power and knowledge produce milieux or realities in which to act. In this volume, we are also interested in the bodily and evidential foundations of security reality. However, the question remains unanswered: what precisely is evidence in anthropology?

Battles over evidence and methodology have certainly raged throughout disciplinary history, but definitions have always been in short supply. The settlement that most anthropologists have reached is that evidence is not just some*thing*, a quality always-already present in the world; rather, evidence is also a question or argument.[3] In short, it is relational, or as Thomas Csordas argues, "Evidence has to be *of* or *for* something" (2004, 475 [emphasis added]). This relational openness is important, first, because social and cultural anthropology tends to use the label ethnography for a rather ecumenical collection of theories and techniques, and, second, because it is difficult to operate using a single definition of evidence as one studies populations in which other ("local") definitions obtain simultaneously. In his last major book, *Anthropology and History*, E. E. Evans-Pritchard cast the problem of evidence in separate magisteria thus, "Myth and history are in important respects different in character, not just in the degree to which they can be substantiated by appeal to evidence or to the laws of natural science. Hence a story may be true and yet mythical in character, and a story may be false and yet historical in character. . . . Then, myth differs from history in that it is regarded differently by the people to whose culture both belong" (1961, 8). Here, again, we find the secret core of evidence as discovered by anthropologists: evidence is relational. If this is true, then the truth itself becomes, to borrow from political anthropologist June Nash, a "suspect category" (1997, 25).

Perhaps this is an obscene finding, because it resembles so closely the body-evidence relationship uncovered by those who witnessed and recorded the workings of totalitarian regimes. Take for example Aleksandr Solzhenitsyn's harrowing three-volume account of Soviet forced labor camps, *The Gulag Archipelago*, in which the author realizes that "evidence is always relative." Indeed, he describes what passed for a criminal inquiry as a complex interplay between an interrogator's willingness to inflict cruelty, the physical capacity of the victim, and nebulous "moral forces" that included "party sensitivity" (1974, 179). However, it would be a mistake to read Solzhenitsyn as simply documenting the moral relativity of totalitarian wastelands; rather, he appreciates that bodies as evidence are required to hold knowledge and power together. In short, evidence is not a thing-in-itself but, rather, an expression of broader configurations of power and knowledge. Seen in this light, security is a privileged site in which to study matters of evidence. At root, security concerns itself with fixity, certainty, and control, while never fully restraining mutability, uncertainty, and even chaos. The power-knowledge nexus here includes the ability to arbitrate about the usefulness of any information; accordingly the powerful not only establish the right to know but also the terms of "truth," together with the right to obviate, ignore, or obscure. The process of creating evidence is linked to parallel processes of denying alternative knowledge status as evidence or even destroying material that could give alternative testimony.

Jean and John Comaroff are among the first anthropologists to work through matters of evidence and security ethnographically, though their efforts are concerned primarily with crime and policing. Their anthropological writing on the South African postcolony aims to explore the boundaries of post-Enlightenment humanity (see Comaroff and Comaroff 1999, 281). From a purely economic perspective, South Africa certainly offers perspectives on "the enigma of . . . wealth: of its sources and the capriciousness of its distribution, of the mysterious forms it takes, of its slipperiness, of the opaque relations between means and ends embodied in it" (Comaroff and Comaroff 2000, 298). However, the story they tell is larger than that of Voodoo economics after Apartheid. In the post–Cold War era, much of the world expected colonialism and socialist totalitarianism to vanish beneath an expectant wave of liberal democracy, but the perception in many parts of Eastern Europe and Africa is that crime and social disorder followed in the wake of change.[4] Numerous other countries also witnessed the "deregulation of monopolies over the means of legitimate force, of moral orders, of the protection of persons and property" (2004, 2).[5] Thus, in the gaps, interstices, and aporias of the contemporary one finds the flourishing of shadow banking, occult economies, spectral private armies, and deafening demands for security (see also Marcus 1999).

Like Jean and John Comaroff, we see the great technical, scientific and expert efforts that characterize the contemporary drive to secure individual identities, bodies, borders, and all sorts of boundaries as emergent in the mimetic impulses at the heart of modernity: the impulses to fix, define, secure and otherwise make certain a world that seems incapable of fully obliging.

Moreover, modernity also has its obverse in counterfeit versions of modernity, versions where fakes, tricksters, and frauds prevail. The Comaroffs (2004, 13, 15) explain:

> Mimesis has classically been an attribute projected onto Europe's others, of course, marking the distance between civilization and its apprentices, those perpetually deemed "almost, but not quite," the real thing. Times, though, have changed. In the postcolonial era, copies declare independence as commodities and circulate autonomously. The electronic revolution has abetted this by democratizing the means of mechanical reproduction. It has demystified proprietary goods, whose aura can be mass-produced and flogged at a discount. These brazen simulacra, like counterfeit money, expose a conceit at the core of the culture of Western capitalism: that its signifiers can be fixed, that its editions can be limited, that it can franchise the platonic essence of its mass-produced modernity. . . .
>
> Crime *itself* is frequently the object of criminal mimesis. Counterfeit kidnappings, hijack hoaxes, and bogus burglaries are everywhere an expanding source of profit, to the extent that, in the Cape Province of South Africa, where simulated claims are becoming epidemic, a Zero Tolerance Task Group has been created to put a stop to them. . . . The fetish and the fake. Each, finally, fades into the other.

Jean and John Comaroff (e.g., 2006a) continue to explore crime and the law as sites of battles over numbers and nonsense, mimesis and magic, fetishism and fakery. Indeed, they propose that the ethnographer, much like the detective, has always been a participant in these battles, bringing expertise on the elementary truths encoded in nods and winks and the skills to demystify the magical or even the bizarre (see also Boltanski 2014). Again, we make the point that security contexts are particularly good places in which to observe the contemporary. In this volume, we are interested in security rather than the policing of crime, and we are interested in exploring evidence in close detail.

Evidence in the Anthropology of Security

In recent years we have seen a growing body of ethnographic research on security and insecurity. There is already a large and well-respected anthropological literature on violence and warfare, the military and militarism, and increasingly anthropologists have explored security and insecurity by focusing their ethnographic work (rather unsurprisingly) on everyday experiences. In this latter vein, ethnographies often depict security as a violent and disruptive intrusion. Other anthropologists focus their attention on new security assemblages by working adjacent to security expertise (e.g., Maguire 2014). Studying security agencies and expertise is enormously challenging. Access is often limited, if granted at all, and one often finds oneself lost in a dizzying world of paranoia within reason (see Marcus 1999). In the realm of security agencies, multiple layers and partitions separate and divide bodies as evidence and versions of "the truth." Thus, one must understand configurations of power, knowledge, and evidence in order to understand this realm, and especially in order to understand performances of security. It is, for example, only by attending to power, knowledge, and evidence that one can appreciate the conditions for the possibility of security speech-acts (cf. Waever 1995), such as, for instance, the following statement by a key figure in the infamous U.S. Joint Special Operations Command (JSOC): "We're the dark matter. We're the force that orders the universe but can't be seen" (quoted in Whitehead and Finnström 2013, 21).

However, before most anthropologists even get to explore the operations of security in their field site, they spend frustrating hours trying to answer the question: What is security? One quickly discovers that "security" is a semantically vacuous term that refuses definition. One also discovers that neighboring disciplines offer little by way of support. In the liberal philosophical tradition, for example, security is understood as the foundation stone of good government and even civilization itself—it is that which allows other things to happen, such as the flourishing of life (e.g., Mill [1859] 2002). Political scientists, international relations experts, and security studies scholars tend to draw upon this tradition in ways that naturalize security, and yet they still acknowledge that it is an "essentially contested concept"—in other words, it gains content from things other than itself and from how the concept is deployed (see Buzan 1991). How, then, do we grapple with this rascal concept?

Perhaps the very looseness of security is the key to unlocking it anthropologically. Security is not a thing-in-itself; it is, rather, relational, and so too is evidence. Therefore, security discourses and practices gain their solidity by producing their own, self-reinforcing "bodies"—bodies that always threaten to flee upon close inspection. There are many examples that illustrate the suspicious importance of evidence in security contexts. The contributions to this volume cover biometric security, borders and migration control, forensic knowledge, policing, and counterterrorism. In every one of these domains, one sees great efforts to know, target, and make use of the human body; and we see emergent bodies as evidence that result from these great efforts to ground knowledge and thereby secure the contemporary. It is our contention here that *Bodies as Evidence* offers a way to explore security as efforts to fix and make certain a world while never fully closing off mutability, uncertainty, and the potentially chaotic underside of order.

Bodies as Evidence

It is not surprising that in the contemporary moment one sees a resurgent interest in the body as source of knowledge. Advancements in forensic science, DNA decoding, and biometric technology provide new pathways for the recursive reimagining of the social through the body (see M'charek, Hagendijk, and de Vries 2013). New technologies are nesting alongside established ways of scrutinizing the body through visual inspection (see Maguire 2009). Their common goal is fixity, because the extraction of precise information about identity enables history and projects into the future. Of course, feminist scholars have long argued against tendencies in sciences to reify their own models—such as DNA—by first developing the model and then mistaking it for all there is to know about life itself. However, today, the human and social sciences are placing great emphasis on "emergence." Thus, Tim Ingold recently argued that "we can no longer think of the organism, human or otherwise, as a discrete, bounded entity, set over against an environment. It is rather a locus of growth within a field of relations traced out in flows of materials" (2013, 10; see also Foucault 1994).[6] Such relativist accounts of life as dynamic, nonessential, and evolving threaten the self-assured fixity promised in the obsessive focus on bodies by new security technologies.

In this book, we follow the construction of body-evidence. What we know of a person is often the outcome of processes in which social actors are empowered to read cues and make inferences about identity, rights and duties, treatments, security, and insecurity. In a Latourian (1996) sense, anthropologists are often interested in entanglements between bodies, objects, and technology that lead to effectual interpretations. Annemarie Mol (2002) provides an illustrative example. She analyzes the making of atherosclerosis patients during hospital routines. Being an atherosclerosis patient means being a person with pain that can be related to specific kinds of observations gained during diagnostics—visual inspection, touching, measuring of blood velocity or vessel lumen—and postmortem knowledge of atherosclerosis patients underpins this specific knowledge. The process of knowing about atherosclerosis and deciding about treatment is an uncertain journey of pitching together or discriminating between different (at times contradictory) sets of evidence. The processes of gaining knowledge and acting upon it is the result of specific and fateful relations created between patients, doctors, medical data, machines, hospital accounting, and so on. There is, in short, a specific body-evidence regime in operation.

Body-evidence in security contexts may take the form of identity constructions through biometric inspection, treatment decisions following the anamnesis of injured migrant bodies, the dead body as evidence of violent borders, gaps in forensic infrastructure, or evidence for historical truth-telling; then there are the various traces of criminality, and even the tortured body in the War on Terror. We propose that practices of collecting and collating of evidence about bodies shows the visceral dimensions of (in)security. Bodies as evidence (and knowledge-power) inform the processes by which people become migrants, welfare recipients, prisoners, targets, or victims. These fateful classifications inform decisions about treatment, thus creating the abject body of the torture victim, the targeted body of the terrorist, the hungry body of the noncitizen, the hiding body of the "illegal" immigrant, or the dead body at the border. Of course, a number of prominent theorists have foregrounded the body in theories of social order. Taboo breakers and "others" become figures of danger (Lianos and Douglas 2001), and political order creates its own shadow, bodies that do not matter (see also Agamben 1998). However, evidence matters clearly in the sense that processes are required to know people, to categorize, judge, determine, and even cast people out. Evidence is deployed to fix identity and avoid status ambivalence. If bodies can be linked through biometric technology to databases, assorted officials no longer depend on the narratives of untrustworthy others, who might be terrorists, illegal immigrants, beggars, or welfare frauds.

The first chapter in this volume, "The Truth of the Error: Making Identity and Security through Biometric Discrimination," by Elida K. U. Jacobsen and Ursula Rao, deals directly with contemporary security technoscience. During the past two decades, the world has seen a mushrooming of biometric "solutions" to deal with everything from transit through airports to welfare disbursements. Today, India's Unique Identity (UID), or *aadhaar*, scheme is an experiment in biometric security of global significance. Thus far, over one billion people have registered with a system that promises interoperable digital governance and is widely regarded as a model for emulation by other countries. However, for all the images of clean and efficient contact and circulation—and those images certainly saturate media and policy discourse—biometric security also promises to target the unwanted circulations of illegal migrants, criminals, and terrorists by exposing the fraudulent body. Jacobsen and Rao, however, focus specifically on error: the damaged fingers and eyes, and the failure to account for problematic names and unlikely kinships that lead to exclusions as "failure to enroll." Instead of showing a neutral process of registrations, their ethnographic accounts tell of dense cultural processes through which authorities inspect, visualize, and question bodies, together with the numerous ways that Indian residents attempt to work around a system that now offers a passport to spaces and privileges.

Of course, "error" is a technoscientific concept within the field of biometric security: a tolerable margin of error is that which establishes a norm and thereby the truth of one's identity. Jacobsen and Rao therefore propose that error is constitutive of evidence in the aadhaar scheme. In cases of technical failure, due to manual labor or military service rendering a body unreadable, residents must resort to private brokers that operate a black market in biometric enrollments. What's at stake here, between a system that strives for universality through bodily evidence and a population excluded from benefits to which they are entitled, is a modern dream of a stable truth referent. Deploying the concept of a negative space archive, Jacobsen and Rao argue that the body will only act as a truth referent if historical and sociocultural contexts are excluded or at least controlled in the name of neutrality, and thus schemes such as aadhaar will always run the risk of excluding those persons who deviate from the norm. Biometric security thus has deadly consequences: a single older woman who is unreadable, they explain, becomes a marginal person who cannot claim her right to a food allowance, a victim of "good governance."

Biometric registration in India is certainly one of the more extraordinary experiments in governance through security in the contemporary moment. However, there are many more laboratory spaces where new body-evidence relations are emerging. One such laboratory is the Mexico-U.S. border, an uneven zone of securitization in which one finds high-tech military gadgetry and the hostile landscape itself recruited to deter migration. In chapter 2, "Injured by the Border: Security Buildup, Migrant Bodies, and Emergency Response in Southern Arizona," Ieva Jusionyte shows us the ways in which securitization produces new regimes of inclusion and exclusion and associated regimes of evidence. She begins with the shocking description of an injured man literally stuck in the border fence. Based on ethnographic fieldwork with emergency responders on both sides of the border, Jusionyte explores the regimes of power and knowledge that struggle over the contested body of the injured migrant. The increasing securitization of the border results directly in physical harm, as migrants break limbs and suffer from dehydration en route to the United States. But what does it mean to rescue migrants? In ways that are comparable with ongoing debates about emergency care for migrants crossing the Mediterranean (see Amade M'charek in this volume), in southern Arizona we see a redefinition of lifesaving treatment and a revaluation of human life. Migrants who call 911 are redirected to Border Patrol, and emergency responders are expected to differentiate between those deserving of help and "bad guys" who should be placed in custody immediately.

Of course, there are financial and resource allocation implications when Border Patrol or local emergency responders take charge of an injured body, but many decisions rely on the skill of reading signs of the bodies as evidence of illegal entry, or just a "gut feeling." Matters are further complicated because, for example, traffickers force some migrants to carry drugs, blurring handy distinctions between the "good guys" and the "bad guys." In part, Jusionyte's argument is that the broad landscape of securitization is recruiting the skills of emergency responders, but, in part also, we see the different evidence produced by Border Patrol and emergency responders as suggestive of deep cracks and fissures in the realm of human security.

Félix Guattari once imagined a future world of security in which technologies would enable the spread of electronic borders throughout daily life, a world where everyone is expected to be in their "permissible place" (Deleuze 1988, 182). Jacobsen and Rao show us the powerful role of biometrics in India in establishing and sorting norms, access, and exclusions, while Ieva Jusionyte speaks to the violence of external borders and the intractable problems facing those attempting humanitarian responses. In chapter 3, "E-Terrify: Securitized Immigration and Biometric Surveillance in the Workplace," Daniel M. Goldstein and Carolina Alonso-Bejarano contribute further to this discussion. The rapid rise and spread of U.S. "Homeland Security" as an institutional form, as a set of discourses and interventions, involves the conflation of undocumented migrants with potential terrorists and thus produces a vast suspect population. However, the border is no longer where the map suggests it is: Goldstein and Alonso-Bejarano expose E-Verify, a workplace, web-based biometric technology that aims to square the U.S. reliance on cheap immigrant labor with securing the homeland. E-Verify turns the workplace into a space of immigration surveillance by allowing employers to check employees and job applicants against federal data to determine eligibility. In ways similar to the Indian aadhaar scheme, E-Verify promises neutrality and administrative efficiency; however, it delivers new regimes of exclusion and consequent precariousness for those already marginalized. Employers are relatively free to decide whether they should check a worker, which grants them power as immigration decision makers.

Drawing on several years of ethnographic research in New Jersey, Goldstein and Alonso-Bejarano's work shows us the ways in which a biometric (and legal) security infrastructure nests in the material and spatial realities of everyday life. E-Verify contributes to exclusion and to self-disciplining—migrants caution one another as to how to avoid the gaze of the authorities. Indeed, taken in isolation, the ethnographic accounts of migrants' experiences read like descriptions of life under totalitarianism, where the slightest transgression results in dire consequences. "Don't litter," one migrant advises a friend! However, alongside the exclusion and self-disciplining one finds the emergence of shadow populations and, unsurprisingly, fake identities, the consequence E-*Terrify*.

The production of new regimes of evidence in security contexts is certainly striking where biometrics are deployed to manage marginal populations such as migrants. However, biometrics—from the Ancient Greek *bios* and *metron*, denotes the recognizing and measurement of life itself using intrinsic physical or behavioral traits—is closely connected to the contemporary drive for (and obsession with) forensic knowledge. At the Mediterranean borders of Europe, where many thousands of people lose their lives each year, forensic knowledge is both a technoscientific "solution" and a problem. In chapter 4, "'Dead-Bodies-at-the-Border': Distributed Evidence and Emerging Forensic Infrastructure for Identification," Amade M'charek writes about the border security response to dead migrant bodies. Border security deploys high-tech solutions that seek to identify and police the frontiers of the EU with everything from biometrics to surveillance drones. But what of those who die en route? Dead bodies are both evidence of a failed response to a geopolitical crisis and a very specific set of problems of evidence for the forensic infrastructure of identification.

M'charek's detailed discussion of border forensics shows us the uneven distribution of forensic knowledge. In popular consciousness, forensics is an exact science, and police today even complain about the so-called CSI effect whereby the public attribute enormous exactitude to forensics. Of course, in the wake of natural and other disasters that involve residents of wealthy countries, enormous efforts are made to identify remains. Not so with dead bodies at the border. Indeed, the bodies of migrants are a gap in knowledge and infrastructure. The geographical origin of a body is often unclear; there is no reference population against which to check a DNA or even a dental profile. Moreover, because bodies are recovered after long periods in the sea, the epidermis tends to have detached and with that goes the possibility of fingerprinting. "Forensics has to be invented anew," a leading practitioner tells M'charek. What, however, will the emerging forensic infrastructure look like? M'charek argues that the hundreds of dead migrant bodies found at the shores of Europe will offer a new type of evidence for an emerging infrastructure: the dead-body-at-the-border is also evidence of the price paid in human lives for Europe's border management regime.

In chapter 5, "The Transitional Lives of Crimes against Humanity: Forensic Evidence under Changing Political Circumstances," Antonius C. G. M. Robben and Francisco J. Ferrándiz further explore the ways in which forensic evidence and truth-making activities are problematic and yet promise certainty to an uncertain world. Their specific example is forensic knowledge as embedded in public discourses on justice. They deploy two case studies: the recovery of evidence from historical Death Flights in Argentina and Civil War exhumations in Spain, showing the intertwinement of different types of evidence in efforts to reclaim the past and redeem the victims of crimes against humanity. In their analysis, we must also attend to the contested necropolitics of evidence. The early chapters in this volume attest to the drive to know human life in order to secure it and thereby produce an order of things, but the Death Flights in Argentina and civil war in Spain are episodes marked by great efforts to conceal, "disappear," and distort evidence. As Michael Taussig remarked in his analysis of totalitarianism in South America, one sometimes finds "the chaos that lies on the underside of order and without which order could not exist" (Taussig 1986, 4).

In their chapter, Robben and Ferrándiz emphasize the enormous potential of forensic knowledge of the body as a basis for cultural recovery, truth, justice, and reconciliation. However, this emerging infrastructure in Spain and Argentina is not without its problems. Of course, here again we see the CSI effect of overly optimistic impressions of science, but these different cultural and legal contexts also inject politics into ostensibly neutral practices. They conclude that these new body-evidence relations have the capacity to disrupt other ways to mourn, seek justice, and produce the truth without the "truthiness" of forensic science.

While the first five chapters deal with processes of fixing truth via the process of interpreting and manipulating materials and bodies, the remaining four chapters of the volume discuss (in)security produced by bodies of evidence that remain in the shadow of alchemy-like half-knowledge, prediction, gossip, or even lies. Future crime scenarios, classified information, and knowledge gained through spying, torture, or intelligence are mobilized as evidence for real or potential threats that demand action. The not-fully-realized-evidence of threat scenarios blurs the line between reality and delusion, while producing real material effects through targeted intervention or increased policing activities. Here power materializes as the ability to act also on unconfirmed or nonpublic information, creating security regimes that render insecure not only populations but also police officers, soldiers, and judges who must decide which leads to follow in a realm where information fades into fantasy.

Chapters 6 and 7 turn to contemporary policing in Europe and North America. Chapter 6, "Policing Future Crimes," by Mark Maguire, opens with a discussion of the shooting of Michael Brown in Ferguson, Missouri, in 2014 in order to highlight questions of evidence in police encounters with communities. Anthropologists continue to explore and expose the racialized and often-violent dimensions of urban policing around the world. However, the ethnographic focus on encounters that are observable to the naked eye tends to miss larger transformations in international policing that aim to police future events by cancelling them out before they occur. Today, around the world, important experiments are ongoing in what is termed predictive policing—a specific assemblage of anthropological theories, geographical information systems, and data science. Many police forces welcome these technoscientific experiments—seeing them as "silver bullets" (see Robben and Ferrándiz in this volume) targeting intractable problems—while in other jurisdictions these experiments are resisted or reconfigured in interesting ways. For some, predictive policing is a mask disguising older forms of discrimination and profiling. After all, they are based on social data gathering, mapping, and statistical reasoning that carry their own histories and biased assumptions, especially about what is essential or typical in human behavior. However, Maguire proposes that we should approach predictive policing on its own terms: as a technically mediated form of criminal anthropology with its own body of evidence. New algorithmically produced future scenarios create new forms of evidence that position police personnel in a situation of having to contemplate the relevance of computer knowledge and whether indeed it is safe to hand over decision-making responsibly to mathematical models, or retain trust in personal experience and direct sensual data.

Issues about the status of knowledge and its usefulness as evidence are also the central concern for Gregory Feldman in chapter 7, "'Intelligence' and 'Evidence': Sovereign Authority and the Differences That Words Make," an essay on the intelligence gathering of an undercover squad of European police dedicated to tackling human trafficking. These are individuals bonded together as they make real decisions on the ground, and in so doing they produce their own codes of action. These actions show an ethics as police bring intelligence forward as evidence, or they may leave it in its own category of what is known but not necessarily actionable. These are two very different studies of contemporary policing, then, but they are still complementary. For Maguire, predictive policing operates by means of an anthropological theory of human life itself, one sometimes disputed by the evidence of actual police work on the ground. For Feldman, evidence—that thing that police are expected to produce—cannot label the full range of knowledge and practices of policing. Both anthropologists are exploring ways to say more about the in/securities that drive decision making in contemporary policing, more than institutional studies or algorithmic innovations can possibly say.

The final two chapters of this volume concern the so-called War on Terror. In chapter 8, "The Secrecy/Threat Matrix," Joseph P. Masco draws on his recent work on *The Theater of Operations* (2014) to again track the transformation of the U.S. Cold War national security apparatus into the counterterror apparatus. For Masco this transformation represents a shift in the "secrecy/threat matrix" and thus in evidential relations with the world. Masco shows us that evidence is of vital importance in the War on Terror because the "secrecy/threat matrix" renders knowledge and evidence as suspect categories (see Nash 1997, 25). In such a world only affect lives free—fear, desire, and fantasy are the ghosts driving the counterterror machinery.

"If you want to buy, I am selling!" exclaims a desperate prisoner at Guantánamo hoping to escape torture if he offers what the tormentor wished to hear. In chapter 9, "What Do You Want? Evidence and Fantasy in the War on Terror," Joseba Zulaika replays this statement as a way to hammer home the catch-22 of security labor. The observer is caught in a web of delusional narratives produced in reaction to desperate security forces seeking to uncover the secrets of the dangerous Other. The violent search for hidden "truth" is coupled with a culture of secrecy. The state protects its own knowledge and fails not only democracy but also its own desire for accuracy and well-informed decision making. Security agents make decisions based on a threat scenario backed by claims to secret knowledge, knowledge that will forever remain in the shadows and will thus never achieve the status of evidence per se.

The essays by Joseph Masco and Joseba Zulaika bring back to mind the specifics of the presentation made by U.S. Secretary of State Colin Powell in 2003 to justify regime change in Iraq. In front of the United Nations and the world's media, he briefly lifted the veil of secrecy and showed the world the "veil of transparency" instead (West and Saunders 2003, 20), offering fragments of intercepted phone calls, poor-quality images, and inferences, all while intoning, "My colleagues, every statement I make today is backed up by sources, solid sources. These are not assertions. What we're giving you are facts and conclusions based on solid intelligence. . . . This is evidence, not conjecture. This is true. This is all well-documented" (Powell 2003, 2).

To create the knowledge-effect, conflict or inconsistency must be avoided or, if necessary, denied. The demand for transparency is thus accompanied by a new culture of secrecy. And if Joseba Zulaika shows us in this volume the horror of extracting evidence from fantasy through torture, Joseph Masco's work explores the broader body of evidence, information, and secrets that the War on Terror has brought into play, and with it a phantasmagoria of security and fear, real and fake, terror and suspected terrorists. We are reminded thus of early anthropological inquiries. After all, Sir James Frazer's *The Golden Bough* was an effort to explore the human tendency toward "prying into the future" often by "pulling at strings to which nothing is attached" (Frazer [1890] 1994, 734, 55). Indeed, even the more sickening efforts to extract evidence during the War on Terror point directly to the space between truth and fantasy and the work that people might perform in that space. Having read Frazer's book, Ludwig Wittgenstein remarked that a person might stab the effigy of an enemy before battle but they also sharpened their blade—"We act like this and then feel satisfied" (Wittgenstein 1979, 14). Evidence in action brings a particular world into play but not necessarily the truth. As security performs its control over the shadowy phantasmagoria of threats to the world, it brings to light practical actions and evidence-making processes. Indeed, bodies as evidence in security contexts are not necessarily about the truth. As Masco (2014) reminds us, in the contemporary moment the war against terrorists is in fact the "War on Terror," a potentially never-ending conflict with an emotion.

Using evidence as a conceptual tool, all of the chapters in this volume cut to the heart of contemporary (in)securitization. The volume is composed of essays in dialog that show how the body has come to be the bearer and signifier of security itself, and how new bodies of evidence are growing and showing themselves to be powerful and transformative. Although the term "security" is often deployed with terminological inexactitude, this should not excuse it from critical anthropological analysis. Indeed, as we noted at the outset, security and insecurity name proliferating forms of governance and evidential regimes. By turning our attention to bodies as evidence, we are able to show how these ostensibly diverse aspects are indeed connected: the body as reference, as enemy, as carrier of insecurities, as the agent of irritation, and the ever evading and liquid focus of regulation. *Bodies as Evidence* shows that security, and all the politics and measures that surround it, is unthinkable without the content added by bodies. We must consider efforts to categorize the body and hence classify populations, efforts to thus know life itself sufficient to develop discourses on the nature of life and of death and predict how human bodies will behave in the future, and as a consequence rendering some lives as worthy and casting other lives to the insecure margins. The diverse examples in this volume will indeed show that the body is the substance of security and its unruly subject. Each anthropological contribution in this volume takes as its starting point that life will always exceed any assemblage of technologies or any governmental effort to work those technologies. Rather, an anthropological investigation of bodies as evidence—be they classificatory, expert-driven or imponderable—is an inquiry into the foundations of social arrangements. In short, then, conceptually and from the basis of ethnographic discussions of everyday life and experience, this volume will add to the growing literature on anthropology and security but also contribute to the overall bodies of scholarship on security in novel ways.

Notes

1   In their edited volume, *Modes of Uncertainty* (2015), Paul Rabinow and Limor Samimian-Darash explore the central problem of uncertainty in the contemporary moment, especially the forms of uncertainty that one cannot reduce to traditional notions of risk or danger.

2   Francis Fitzgerald (1972) gives us a curious example of what happens when ev-

idential regimes collide: when the first French steamship visited the coast of nineteenth-century Vietnam, the local Mandarins dismissed it as unseen, because their texts indicated that it was just a dragon.

3   For an excellent treatment of the relational qualities of evidence in legal contexts, see Anthony Good's (2007) *Anthropology and Expertise in the Asylum Courts*.

4   Jean and John Comaroff acknowledge the problems of perception versus reality in any discussion of global crime rates, especially seeing as the numbers can be run to different effects. A reasonably reliable summary is given by the United Nations Office on Drugs and Crime (UNODC). The UNODC combine their own data with the World Health Organization's Mortality Database to provide three-year moving average homicide rates across the world from 1955 to 2012. One sees two clear trends. First, homicide is declining in many parts of the world, especially in prosperous societies with low levels of inequality. Second, where homicide levels are increasing, one sees major societal disruption (see UNODC 2013, 35). The point the Comaroffs make is that uneven crime rates and perceptions of criminality all speak to an underlying shift in societal divisions of labor and moral orders.

5   Daniel Goldstein's recent *Owners of the Sidewalk* (2016) shows the extraordinary scale of the "informal economy" in Bolivia—up to 80 percent of the Bolivian population work in informal commerce. *Owners of the Sidewalk* is also about the "informal" security providers that have sprung up in cities and markets.

6   The work of Foucault on the governing of life itself is heavily influenced by his teacher Georges Canguilhem's discontinuous history of science. Thus, "life has led to a living being that is never completely in the right place, that is destined to 'err' and be 'wrong'" (Foucault 1994, 15).

References

Agamben, Giorgio. 1993. *The Coming Community*. Minneapolis, MN: University of Minnesota Press.

Agamben, Giorgio. 1998. *Homo Sacer: Sovereign Power and Bare Life*. Stanford, CA: Stanford University Press.

BBC. 2017. *Newsnight*. February 17.

Blake, Robert. 1977. *A History of Rhodesia*. London: Eyre Methuen.

Boltanski, Luc. 2014. *Mysteries and Conspiracies: Detective Stories, Spy Novels and the Making of Modern Societies*. Cambridge: Polity Press.

Buzan, Barry. 1991. "New Patterns of Global Security in the Twenty-First Century." *International Affairs* 67(3): 432–33.

Clifford, James, and George E. Marcus, eds. 1986. *Writing Culture: The Poetics and Politics of Ethnography*. Berkeley: University of California Press.

Comaroff, Jean, and John L. Comaroff. 1999. "Occult Economies and the Violence of Abstraction: Notes from the South African Postcolony." *American Ethnologist* 26(2): 279–303.

Comaroff, Jean, and John L. Comaroff. 2000. "Millennial Capitalism: First Thoughts on a Second Coming." *Public Culture* 12(2): 291–343.

Comaroff, Jean, and John L. Comaroff. 2004. "Criminal Justice, Cultural Justice: The Limits of Liberalism and the Pragmatics of Difference in the New South Africa." *American Ethnologist* 31(2): 188–204.

Comaroff, Jean, and John L. Comaroff, eds. 2006a. *Law and Disorder in the Postcolony.* Chicago: University of Chicago Press.

Comaroff, Jean, and John L. Comaroff. 2006b. *An Excursion into the Criminal Anthropology of the Brave Neo South Africa.* Berlin: LIT Verlag.

Csordas, Thomas. 2004. "Evidence of and for What?" *Anthropological Theory* 4(4): 73–80.

Deleuze, Gilles. 1988. *Foucault.* Minneapolis, MN: University of Minnesota Press.

Engelke, Matthew, ed. 2009. *The Objects of Evidence: Anthropological Approaches to the Production of Knowledge.* London: Wiley-Blackwell and the Royal Anthropological Institute.

Evans-Pritchard, E. E. 1961. *Anthropology and History.* Manchester, UK: Manchester University Press.

Feldman, Gregory. 2012. *The Migration Apparatus: Security, Labour and Policymaking in the European Union.* Stanford, CA: Stanford University Press.

Fitzgerald, Francis. 1972. *Fire in the Lake: The Vietnamese and the Americans in Vietnam.* Boston: Little, Brown.

Forte, Maximilian. 2016. "Why Donald J. Trump Will Be the Next President of the United States." *Zero Anthropology.* May 4. https://zeroanthropology.net /2016/05/04/why-donald-j-trump-will-be-the-next-president-of-the-united -states/.

Foucault, Michel. 1994. "Life: Experience and Science." In *The Essential Foucault: Selections from Essential Works of Foucault, 1954–1984,* edited by Paul Rabinow and Nikolas Rose, 6–18. New York: New Press.

Foucault, Michel. 2014. *On the Government of the Living: Lectures at the Collège de France, 1979–1980,* edited by Michael Senellart. London: Palgrave MacMillan.

Frazer, James. [1890] 1994. *The Golden Bough: A Study in Comparative Religion.* London: Macmillan.

Goldstein, Daniel. 2016. *Owners of the Sidewalk: Security and Survival in the Informal City.* Durham, NC: Duke University Press.

Good, Anthony. 2007. *Anthropology and Expertise in the Asylum Courts.* New York: Routledge-Cavendish.

González, Roberto J. 2015. "Seeing into Hearts and Minds (Part 2): Big Data, Algorithms, and Computational Counterinsurgency." *Anthropology Today* 31(4): 13–18.

Hart, Keith. 2008. Afterword to *How Do We Know? Evidence, Ethnography, and the*

Making of Anthropological Knowledge, edited by Liana Chua, Casey High, and Timm Lau, 201–10. Cambridge: Cambridge Scholars Press.

Hastrup, Kirsten. 2004. "Knowledge and Evidence in Anthropology." *Anthropological Theory* 4(4): 455–72.

Ingold, Tim. 2013. "Prospect." In *Biosocial Becoming: Integrating Social and Biological Anthropology*, edited by Tim Ingold and Gisli Palsson, 1–21. Cambridge: Cambridge University Press.

Jusionyte, Ieva. 2015. *Savage Frontier: Making News and Security on the Argentine Border*. Berkeley: University of California Press.

Latour, Bruno. 1996. "On Actor-Network Theory: A Few Clarifications." *Soziale Welt* 47: 369–81.

Lianos, Michalis, and Mary Douglas. 2001. "Danger et régression du contrôle social." *Déviance et Société* 25(2): 147–64.

Maguire, Mark. 2009. "The Birth of Biometric Security." *Anthropology Today* 25(2): 9–14.

Maguire, Mark. 2014. "Counterterrorism in European Airports." In *The Anthropology of Security: Perspectives from the Frontline of Policing, Counter-Terrorism and Border Control*, edited by Mark Maguire, Catriona Frios, and Nils Zurawski, 118–39. London: Pluto.

Malinowski, Bronislaw. 1922. *Argonauts of the Western Pacific*. New York: E.P. Dutton.

Marcus, George E, ed. 1999. *Paranoia within Reason: A Casebook on Conspiracy as Explanation*. Chicago: University of Chicago Press.

Masco, Joseph P. 2014. *The Theater of Operations: National Security Affect from the Cold War to the War on Terror*. Durham, NC: Duke University Press.

M'charek, Amade, R. Hagendijk, and W. de Vries. 2013. "Equal before the Law: On the Machinery of Sameness in Forensic DNA Practice." *Science, Technology, and Human Values* 38(4): 542–65.

Merry, Sally Engle. 2011. "Measuring the World: Indicators, Human Rights, and Global Governance." *Current Anthropology* 52(suppl. 3): S83–95.

Mill, John Stuart. [1859] 2002. *On Liberty*. New York: Dover Publications.

Mol, Annemarie. 2002. *C Body Multiple: Ontology in Medical Practice*. Durham, NC: Duke University Press.

Nash, June. 1997. "When Isms Become Wasms: Structural Functionalism, Marxism, Feminism and Postmodernism." *Critique of Anthropology* 17(1): 11–32.

Powell, Colin. 2003. "US Secretary of State's Address to the United Nations Security Council. Reported." *Guardian*. February 5.

Pratt, Mary Louise. 1986. "Fieldwork in Common Places." In *Writing Culture: The Poetics and Politics of Ethnography*, edited by James Clifford and George E. Marcus, 27–51. Berkeley: University of California Press.

Rabinow, Paul, and Limor Samimian-Darash, eds. 2015. *Modes of Uncertainty: Anthropological Cases*. Chicago: University of Chicago Press.

Rao, Ursula. 2013. "Biometric Marginality: UID and the Shaping of Homeless Identities in the City." *Economic and Political Weekly* 48(13): 1–7.

Rivers, William H. R. 1912. "General Account of Method." In *Notes and Queries on Anthropology*, edited by J. L. Myres and B. Freire-Marreco, 108–27. London: Royal Anthropological Institute.

Robben, Antonius C. G. M., ed. 2010. *Iraq at a Distance: What Anthropologists Can Teach Us about the War.* Philadelphia: University of Pennsylvania Press.

Shore, Cris, and Susan Wright. 2015. "Audit Culture Revisited: Rankings, Ratings, and the Reassembling of Society." *Current Anthropology* 56(3): 421–44.

Sky News. 2016. UK Justice Secretary Michael Gove, interviewed by Faisal Islam. June 3.

Solzhenitsyn, Aleksandr I. 1974. *The Gulag Archipelago 1918–1956: An Experiment in Literary Investigation.* New York: Harper and Row.

Stocking, George W. 1992. *The Ethnographer's Magic and Other Essays in the History of Anthropology.* Madison, WI: University of Wisconsin Press.

Suskind, Ron. 2004. "Faith, Certainty, and the Presidency of George W. Bush." *New York Times.* October 17.

Taussig, Michael. 1986. *Shamanism, Colonialism, and the Wildman: A Study in Terror and Healing.* Chicago: University of Chicago Press.

Thucydides. 1998. *The Peloponnesian War,* translated by Steven Lattimore. New York: Hackett.

UNODC (United Nations Office on Drugs and Crime). 2013. *Global Study on Homicide.* New York: United Nations.

Waever, Ole. 1995. "Securitization and Desecuritization." In *On Security,* edited by Ronnie Lipschutz, 46–86. New York: Columbia University Press.

West, Harry G., and Todd Saunders, eds. 2003. *Transparency and Conspiracy: Ethnographies of Suspicion in the New World Order.* Durham, NC: Duke University Press.

Whitehead, Neil L., and Sverker Finnström, eds. 2013. *Virtual War and Magical Death: Technologies and Imaginaries for Terror and Killing.* Durham, NC: Duke University Press.

Wittgenstein, Ludwig. 1979. *Remarks on Frazer's Golden Bough.* Atlantic Highlands, NJ: Brynmill.

Wittgenstein, Ludwig. 1997. *The Philosophical Investigations.* Oxford: Blackwell.

Zulaika, Joseba. 2014. "Drones and Fantasy in U.S. Counterterrorism." *Journal for Cultural Studies* 18(2): 171–87.

ONE

———

The Truth of the Error

Making Identity and Security through
Biometric Discrimination

ELIDA K. U. JACOBSEN AND URSULA RAO

As moderns, our task and our obligation is to be attentive to ways around
knowledge that claims to be universal when it is contingent, unified when it is at
best partial, and autonomous and sovereign when it is dependent and immature.
—RABINOW, *French Enlightenment: Truth and Life*

"This had to be a fraud! Or could you imagine a family with over 100 members?," the quality assurance officer Amit Chatterjee asked rhetorically. What
has happened? The computer at the central data-processing unit of the Unique
Identity Authority of India (UIDAI) showed an error. The automatic filter of
the new biometric registration system highlighted more than 100 individuals as problematic because they had all been authorized by one single Head of

Family (HoF), indicating that this person had proof of being directly related to each individual.

During an interview, he recounted in an animated fashion the story about how their initial astonishment concerning the extent of the fraud had turned into curiosity and, rather than cancelling the enrollments straight away, the team decided to travel to the region and find out what had happened. When they reached the distant border region in Mizoram, in the northeast of India, they found to their surprise the "biggest family in the world," totaling 184 members.[1] "Can you imagine a man with 39 wives?" Amit repeated dramatically and continued to marvel at how enrollment for India's new biometric database has brought the team in touch with even the most remote people of India.

Today many countries are experimenting with biometric identification systems that use smart cards or central databases. With over 1.2 billion enrollments to date, India's *aadhaar* (Unique Identity, UID) is not only larger than any other similar project but is a "frontier case" that will influence developments in other countries, such as Indonesia or Papua New Guinea (Jacobsen 2012; Zelazny 2012; Gelb and Clark 2013b). According to the World Bank, it is also pioneering because it promises to achieve maximum interoperability by linking a national ID program to multiple sectoral interventions, such as welfare projects, security operations, or commercial applications (World Bank 2015). And indeed, the notion of interoperability captures well the ambition of the architects of UID, who launched the project in 2009 to provide a streamlined means of identifying India's entire population and linking millions to national digital networks of information. The system is meant to biometrically enroll all residents of India and give every person a unique twelve-digit identification number (aadhaar number) that is connected to a record containing their personal biometric data—fingerprints, iris scan data, and photograph—and to a skeleton set of social data—name, address, and gender. It can be used for online verification of identity at any time and any place. Proponents of UID are confident that the new technology will solve India's identification crisis by supplying reliable information to public and private service providers about who is who, thus making all transactions transparent and secure. Currently the aadhaar number is required for identification in most official contexts, such as applying for a passport, receiving welfare payments, or getting a bank loan. It can be used for instant activation of a SIM card, purchasing a train ticket, or conducting internet transactions (Bhatia and Bhabha 2017).

India's biometric project is participating in a global shift toward states using new digital technology in the management of population flows. The contemporary world capitalist system not only depends on the rapid flow of people and goods, but also produces heightened concerns over the unwanted movements of illegal migrants, terrorists, or smugglers, persons who may present a threat to national security and prosperity (Fuller 2003). Biometric technology provides automatized surveillance at crucial checkpoints in order to protect spaces of privileged sociality against unwanted entrants—in short, it is a means to separate "bad" flows from "good" flows (Aas 2006; Amoore 2006; Lebovic 2015; Amicelle and Jacobsen 2016). While surveillance studies scholars analyze the increased usage of networked biometric technologies in managing risks and contingencies (Amoore 2006; Muller 2011; Jacobsen 2013; Lidén, Boy, and Jacobsen 2016), development studies literature emphasizes the role and societal effect of biometric technology for creating more efficient and fraud-free welfare states (Rao 2013; Donovan 2015; Singh and Jackson 2017). The introduction of security logic into welfare contests follows on from neoliberal suspicion about wasteful states and worries over inefficient targeting, corruption, and leakage. By tracking goods and people, governments seek to undercut false reporting or "double dipping"—the illegal diversion of limited resources that impoverish states and contribute to distributional injustice. Regardless of whether biometric surveillance systems face inward or outward—that is to say, to include the undocumented or to exclude unwanted foreigners (Breckenridge 2014)—they fulfill a key purpose of making transactions traceable by employing a binary distinction. On the one side, there is the production of the documented person, the wanted traveler, or the needy citizen, which is mirrored on the other side by its opposite: the imposter, the fraud, or the criminal.

The attractive clarity of the binary logic of biometric classifications is disturbed every time technicians or users encounter an error. An error appears as a red warning on the screen when fingerprints are unreadable or recorded data appears as incoherent. The story from Mizoram is a case in point that was resolved positively, unlike many other cases of data errors that have led to rejections of aadhaar registration because applicants wishing to enroll have washed fingers, damaged irises, or unlikely names. The "failure to enroll" has its complement in the "false reject" of verification, another categorical error that does not register in the yes/no logic of automated surveillance. The technically rendered reading of body parts is unable to account for the calluses on the hands of a hardworking farmer wishing to access his or her biometric bank account, or to recognize poverty through the visual inspection of the worn, unbiometrifiable body of a beggar—more to the point, there is no room for the passionate stories of living people. From our ethnographic study of enrollment, we highlight how an individual status as "error" or "success" is, for the people concerned, a (new) form of social positioning that intersects or overwrites who they think they are or can be.

On the one hand, as the Indian project becomes interoperable and omnipresent, an identification error can deny and exclude individuals and families from entitlements and sociality. On the other hand, the new universal ID creates positive affirmations that can justify the undocumented immigrant or attach an address to the homeless laborer. In both cases of the "accept" or "reject," people's stories of living with biometrics demonstrate a contingent and unstable character of identity that may not adhere to the idealized truth of automated surveillance.

In this chapter, we read the ethnography of enrollment and early usage against the technical view of aadhaar as an efficient, reliable, neutral, and dispassionate means of sorting. We look at the acts of (biometric) registration and verification as practices that are founded on the idea of separating the truth from its error or fraud, in order to minimize the occurrences of the latter. In biometric governance, images of fingerprints and irises are "transported" to create certainty in relation to an individual's status, which in turn produces specific nexuses between bodies, persons, and identities that determine people's status vis-à-vis authorities, governments, or service providers. Yet, such "veridiction" of a bodily status takes place not in a valueless space of technological veracity, but rather in a dense social space saturated with visual information and narrative accounts. During biometric registration, and later at checkpoints of verification, the body and the appearance of the individual are continuously being regarded, problematized, and questioned, leading to a maze of visual, social, and technical information that may not cumulate in a coherent conclusion. As operators and users consider different types of evidence and prioritize information, they produce powerful narratives of identity.

The anecdote from Mizoram illustrates how accounting for citizens and giving out unique numbers intertwines judgments of integrity with narratives of identity. The filter of the quality management software picked up the decontextualized enrollment information because it contradicted standard expectations concerning family size, raising suspicion about fabrication and fraud. It could be discounted only when inspectors saw with their own eyes a man who lives with thirty-nine wives. They saw the narrowness of the "margin of error" in the face of the breadth of human sociality. The error demanded additional investigation that led to a final adjudication, fixing a particular truth and revealing the regime of truth production. The aadhaar enrollment system subsequently "knew" this man not only as a unique body, or a male of a certain age, but as a networked person holding the status for being the father and grandfather of over a hundred children and the husband of thirty-nine women. Moreover, in the process of sorting, the man became "abnormal" according to the programed norm of the system.

It is precisely through the negotiated margins of the established "error" that the biometric system produces truth. The system creates a norm against which errors can be measured. Errors are not just technical faults but also a means of producing expert truths about bodies and populations, which further give way to technical intervention and governmental planning. Therefore, rather than the error being an unintended consequence of the biometric system, we argue that the making of "errors" is a constitutive part of the established system of truth making. To evidence this, we begin with the narration of three cases of enrollments that exemplify how biometric technology repositions people in ways that contradict fundamental aspects of their identity. The troubling inconstancies of these biometric encounters provide an entry point for reflections on the social contexts where biometric technology operates and on the truth effects it produces. By truth effect, we mean a powerful statement of what will count as "truth." When truth in the form of biometric reading collides with other accounts or evidence of identity, it places people in a space of tension between error and truth. The negotiation of judgments resulting from biometric reading illuminates troubling exclusions and confirms prior findings that technology and its deployment in social situations produce specific forms of discrimination often along well-established lines of marginalization (Thomas 2014). Moreover, and more fundamentally, we argue that identity and fraud are interlaced categories and, accordingly, destabilize—and ultimately make incongruous—binary identification systems that seek to install a stable form of verification of personal identity by linking data to bodily markers using a yes/no logic.

On Technical Failure

The Dell computer screen is filled with the glaring brown-and-white image of an enlarged iris. The eye blinks, making large black stripes in slow movements on the screen before the image freezes as the eye is captured and quickly stored on the hard disk of the computer. The digitalization of her iris scan, together with fingerprints and facial image, ceremoniously marks the birth of Ananya's digital double. In a few weeks, she will receive a slip of paper that attests to the delivery of her data double, a name given by the Unique Identity Authority of India counting twelve numerical digits. Ananya gets up from the chair (a white plastic chair that had seen better days), adjusts her purple sari, and steps aside for the next one in line, her husband, Polas. He is not so lucky. The facial image is easily captured, but when he places his fingers on the biometric capture box, the computer refuses to agree with the status of his fingerprints. "Error." The letters appear repeatedly on the computer screen. After the third rejection, the young female operator in jeans and T-shirt looks at him. "Sorry, you cannot be registered." Whereas Ananya, his wife, is from East Bengal (today Bangladesh), it just happens to be that Polas himself is Indian. It is thus ironic that she now holds the digital key to potential entitlements by the Indian government, while he is being refused. The aadhaar number that he was attempting to register for would provide him with a proof of identity and address, and he is hoping that it will be an easier means to gain access to rights and entitlements for persons below the poverty line. Polas is a hardworking painter who works ten hours a day for an average wage of three thousand rupees a month (approximately fifty U.S. dollars), painting temple walls with low-quality paint. He works hard, mixing the liquid with his own hands, and oftentimes plucking old paint off temple walls with his bare fingers. No wonder his fingerprints are unreadable.

Technical errors are part of the enrollment process of India's national biometric system. Against the norm of the biometrically readable subject, concerns over the unbiometrifiability of bodies had surfaced before in the heated debates about the feasibility of aadhaar. In a report, Dr. R. Ramakumar, an expert witness before the Lok Sabha Finance Committee, stated that "it has been proven again and again that in the Indian environment the failure to enroll with fingerprints is as high as 15% due to the prevalence of a huge population dependent on manual labour" (Standing Committee 2011, 11). Others argue that the number is negligible (Nilekani and Shah 2015). The answer to the question of how many people might be excluded on account of poor biomaterial remains safely in the dark, since the aadhaar system only counts positively those who are registered and has no category to acknowledge the existence of people who have been rejected. Citizens resist this form of technical neglect by insisting on registration or seeking imaginative solutions. For example, Polas keeps himself busy making calls to his friend who knows a person willing to use creative solutions to enroll people into the aadhaar scheme in exchange for an under-the-table compensation of a hundred rupees by doing night shifts in the basement of one of the older temples in the town. At night, he enters a room filled with half-moldy paper and waits nervously for the computer to come up. Then, in a matter of a few minutes, his eyes are scanned, his picture is taken, and a clause is added regarding his exception that states that it is unmanageable to register more than a single thumbprint. With the enrollment slip in his hand, Polas is hopeful that he will receive his aadhaar card. He is not yet disillusioned as are others who tried enrolling many times to no avail, such as, for example Pratap.

Pratap lives in Hauz Khas in South Delhi with his son and daughter-in-law and their kids. He likes helping them out, but on a specific day in March 2016 he declines to pick up the kids from school because he urgently needs an aadhaar number and has high hopes that the recently opened enrollment center at the new branch of the Citizens' Bank will finally provide him with this new identity. It is his third attempt. The first time he went to a mass enrollment camp. He followed the prescribed routine and waited for his card. After six months, when the card had not arrived, he consulted, like Polas, a private broker who promised to help him in return for a hundred rupees. An online inquiry showed that Pratap's card had been rejected due to a "technical fault." The precise reason remains unclear. The broker took Pratap to another enrollment station, said all will be fine now, and vanished. "It was a rip-off!" Pratap thinks now. In his hand, he holds the enrollment slip of the second attempt that too yielded no positive result. Looking at it, it becomes obvious that the reading showed very low accuracy for several fingers. Might this be the reason for his rejection? Confronted with the question, Pratap shrugs his shoulder and continues his personal story. At this point, he takes off his sunglasses and exposes a missing eye, explaining that he lost it in a battle in Cargill. "I am a wounded soldier and have fought for the nation," he says proudly and without any sentimentality. Next, he takes out his army card and continues, "Here! See! This is the proof! I used to show this everywhere and it was always accepted. Now, no one wants to even see it. They are only interested in the aadhaar card."

Pratap moves forward in line and begins reenrollment. The computer operator records the disability and crosses out one eye in the form. The iris scan of the second eye goes smoothly. However, the fingers pose problems. The machine alerts the operator to a low accuracy rate of 17 to 20 percent for most fingers, and though he repeats the procedure seven times, he can never pass the minimum threshold of 60 percent. Despite the error, Pratap receives a new enrollment slip. Now he has to wait again and hope. It is unclear whether the quality check will eliminate his data once again. Without an aadhaar number, Pratap feels an acute sense of marginalization. The social pressure to produce it at the pension office, the passport office, or the hospital is strong, and not meeting it has effectively devalued his status as a veteran. He is furious and seriously aggrieved that he is no longer seen as what he is: a war survivor and hero who had given his life to the nation. Instead, now he is reduced to being a person without a number.

The Structural Violence of Ungovernable Bodies

In recent years, a burgeoning body of literature has developed sophisticated and fine-grained understandings of the role of citizen-state relations for processes of identity making (van der Ploeg 1999; Hull 2012; Gelb and Clark 2013a, 2013b). State agencies see citizens and engage the population by adopting classifications that distinguish them between insiders and outsiders, citizens and imposters, or deserving and undeserving poor (Scott 1998; Sharma and Gupta 2006). These classifications are put into effect during the operationalization of policies, which structure the experiences of citizens with state representatives and determine their social status and access to resources (Gupta 2012). In a recursive process, citizens accept, reject, or appropriate such categories into personalized narratives, thereby creating social positioning and a sense of self (Corbridge et al. 2005; Hunter and Sugiyama 2014; Markó 2016). This mutually enforced dynamic of identifying and being identified is powerfully illustrated by the earlier narrations.

The housewife Ananya experiences the empowering effect of ownership of an aadhaar number. It relieves her of a tension that had always impacted her life, the fear of being discovered and then dismissed as an illegal migrant. An official proof of existence can act as a protective shield, especially for vulnerable populations for whom it becomes a highly prized commodity loaded with affective value. The homeless citizen shares this fate with the illegalized immigrant. Life on the streets is harsh, and it is aggravated by the hostility of the security personnel guarding gentrified cities (Rao 2013). The vagabond is easily identified and equated with the beggar or the criminal and thus attracts the disciplining intervention of the police force. "If you show them your aadhaar card, they know 'this is an official man' and they leave you alone," explains Bapu, a rickshaw driver from Bihar, concerning the utility of an aadhaar card. He comes to Delhi every year for a few months after the end of harvest season to earn extra income for the household and the farm. In turn, the veteran, who was refused an aadhaar card, experiences a disruption to his sense of personhood. He identifies as a soldier of merit and is lucky to have a document that proves his status and entitles him to a range of state services, among them a pension and free health care. The introduction of the new identity system threatens to interrupt his ability to connect officially to this status and his rights because his body remains illegible in a system that requires vital finger ridges and pure irises. His grievance is of a particular note and different from the alienation experienced by Polas. Pratap strongly feels that he has given his body to the nation and that his ailments are a direct outcome of his sacrifice. The same state that took his health and strength is now demanding a virgin body that should be available for biometric capture. In turn, Polas experiences his sense of marginalization in contrast to his wife, who despite being an immigrant could easily get the new identity document, while he as her supporter could not and thus had his identity as an effective Head of Family questioned in view of the fact that he could no longer be the main applicant on official documents that would benefit him or his family.

At one level, then, these stories illustrate the discriminatory effect of the inclusion/exclusion dyad typically observed in studies on biometric technology; on another level, they reveal the inefficiencies or even absurdities of the binary logic of governance founded on bodily measures. A burgeoning body of literature substantiates the exclusionary effect of biometric governance, ranging from security situations to projects for social inclusion. The finding that technology itself discriminates is complemented by the study of the political economy in which some groups are more likely to be targets of biometric surveillance than others (Kruger, Magnet, and Van Loon 2008). B. Ajana (2012) provides a compelling example by showing how the Iris Recognition Immigration System at airports is "widening the gap" between welcome travelers and unwanted immigrants in the UK border zone, aggravating already substantial inequalities. Those who have access to a biometric passport, who have volunteered their biometric data, and who have established their status as trusted persons and desirable subjects can move without friction through electronic portals, thus bypassing lengthy immigration queues. This preselection filters the attention of officers and narrows it down to "difficult" cases, enhancing airport efficiency and the grip on persons declared to be illegal. In this volume, Daniel M. Goldstein and Carolina Alonso-Bejarano show how biometric surveillance is exercised on specific racialized subjects whose migration status is put to the test. Shoshana Amielle Magnet (2011) analyzes programming and argues that biometric sorting is discriminatory because it builds on established social classification. Bodies are preselected according to stereotypical attributes of race and gender to reduce the size of the data set against which the uniqueness of any particular body is established (see also Pugliese 2010).

These accounts contradict optimistic narratives that biometric technology, in its new iteration as a universally applied system for electronic sorting, is natural and objective, and emerging in a fully emancipated manner that leaves behind the derogative assumptions about colonial subjects as deviant and deceitful that motivated the colonial sciences of anthropometry and dactyloscopy (Sekula 1986; Cole 2001; Maguire 2009). Instead, biometric technology continues to produce the deviant body, even if it is no longer based on a priori negative classification of people through the lenses of race ideology or the criminal justice system. Discrimination in the case of the aadhaar system results from the underlying assumption that biometric technology is universally applicable equally to all human beings and will function regardless of class, status, education, or any other social characteristics. The aadhaar system does not target specific groups for inclusion or exclusion. It does not confirm citizenship like a passport, the right to vote like a voter ID, or the status of a welfare beneficiary as the ration card, the latter being widely used in India by poor people as an identity document. In this sense of delinking the processes of identification from the making of specific identity claims, it differs from most other identity projects in the world and produces the much-praised potential for interoperability. By simply recording the uniqueness of a person, aadhaar establishes what Nanden Nilekani calls a "thin" identity.

A few months after his appointment as chairman, Nandan met K. V. Kamath, then the chairman of ICICI bank, to deliver a presentation about Aadhaar and its uses. At the end of the talk an amazed Kamath declared that the entire scheme boasted of a "diabolical simplicity." Part of the reason for this simplicity was purely practical—if you have to collect 1.2 billion data sets that will be compared against each other every time a resident uses their Aadhaar number it's best to collect the least possible amount of information. Pragmatism also dictates that the path to success is easier if you provide a "thin" solution—one that does not infringe on turf that other government agencies lay claim to. Aadhaar provides a single, clearly defined piece of information—a person's identity—and nothing more. (Nilekani and Shah 2015, 10)

This technical view of aadhaar as simply proving "uniqueness" through biometric identifiers, and as such saying nothing about a person's identity, discounts the fact that in an environment of near universality of aadhaar, owning an aadhaar number in itself becomes a status that can be negatively contrasted to not having one, or being classified as an "error." The discrimination of those not given an aadhaar number is amplified in a context of interoperability, whereby denial at one access point can lead to chains of exclusion. The aadhaar identity is linked to an individual's personal information, and through this, "the UIDAI will be creating a transaction identity for each resident that is both verified and reliable" (UIDAI 2010, 33) because it is transported into a networked system of information exchange. As a powerful truth-telling practice, biometric-based verification thereby renders those bodies/identities that are not readable by the biometric machine into unverifiable and unreliable identities and therefore outside the realm of legitimized knowledge, thereby making them categorically suspicious (Maguire 2009, 13; see also Hristova 2014). These errors of exclusion and inclusion speak to the topic of discrimination. However, they also point to the blind spot of biometric governance that undermines the goal of perfected population management and universal interoperability of services.

The epistemological position underlying the universalizing aadhaar project assumes a specific biometric norm that regards the human body as adhering to this norm of possessing stable markers available for biometric inspection at any time and any place. Such a presumption sets humans up for failure since it ignores that "normality equals activity and flexibility" (Rabinow 1998, 196). In his comparative discussion of Michel Foucault and Georges Canguilhem, Rabinow elaborates the dialectical relation between norm and error. Scientific modernity is invested in the formulation of "the normal" as a stable truth that may guide the interpretation of life and direct the activity of normalizing the deviant through medical interventions or the reform activities of institutions such as the school, the clinic, or the prison. The notion of the normal and the activity of normalizing deny the dynamic power of life that is forever changing and adapting, or, in other words, the artifice of the norm turns life into an error (see also Maguire and Fussy 2016).

So what happens when the normalizing activity of scientifically measuring an apparently stable truth runs up against the multiple mutation of life? It is acknowledged in the calculation of the error margins and is addressed through the continuous work of reclassifying and adapting the categories that may create new frameworks that will, however, continue to clash with endless variations of dynamic life (Bowker and Star 1999; Singh and Jackson 2017). The work of structuring is a site of political and social struggle precisely because it imposes clear boundaries between phenomena. In our case, the lauded simplicity of the aadhaar's biometric measure makes for an especially rigid system since the binary yes/no classification leaves no space for negotiating the error—technical and social—at the margins. Accordingly, Ananya becomes legitimized as a resident despite the lack of official recognition of her status, while Polas and Pratap are now part of an unknowable shadow population outside the gaze of a biometrically enabled state. They exist in what Murray calls the "negative space archive" of biometric governance:

> Common to any introductory drawing class is the negative space drawing exercise. Such a drawing, of a chair, for example, develops not through a focus on the chair, but on the space around and inside the chair (between the legs and the slits in the back). The most well-known version of a negative space drawing depicts either two faces in profile looking at each other or a vase, depending on how one looks at it. Although "negative" space is described in relation to "positive" space (positive space is the shape of the chair as opposed to the shape of the space around the chair), a look at this type of drawing, at these types of spaces, makes clear that making meaning of such a drawing depends on both spaces existing at once. (Murray 2007, 350)

The illegible body of the negative space archive is troubling for a number of reasons. It turns people into "monsters" or aberrations from the norm (Murray 2007), and it creates an ungovernable population along lines that are unpredictable or apparently unmotivated. The error shares a space with fraud, since a person refusing to show his aadhaar number or able to prove her identity biometrically could be an error or a fraud. He or she might be hiding her real identity or not have one. The system accepts and rejects in a manner that remains incomprehensible to citizens and operators alike, and depending on the result determines whether people can enter into relations with state agencies or private industry, buy a service, pay taxes, or receive welfare benefits. While the aadhaar number in most contexts may not be sufficient for claiming a right or conducting a transaction, the lack of it produces a new status as an outsider. The magnitude of the concern clearly emerges when one adds to the issue of unbiometrifiable people the irregularities of the verification processes.

The errors of enrollment are complemented by the exclusions occurring during verification. People routinely using fingerprinting devices find them wanting in situations when they sweat, use cream or oil, or apply henna for decoration (Rao 2017). In winter, stiffness hinders a swift reading of finger ridges, and after-harvest calluses prevent verification; cooking also inflicts burns that often require days to heal. The exclusion is temporary for some and permanent for others. As published regularly in newspapers and discussed in a growing body of scholarship (Murray 2007; Masiero 2016; Singh and Jackson 2017), there is ample evidence of the regularly high exclusion errors caused especially by fingerprinting.[2] The erratic acceptance or rejection of people has massive consequences for governance. Only by ignoring the volatility of this process and its inefficiencies can organizations maintain the semblance of "good governance." Amma's story is a case in point.

Amma is a widow who lives in Southwest Delhi, where the ration office trials biometrically enabled distribution of rations to people living below the poverty line. She is well known in the neighborhood and an acquaintance of the ration shop owner, who had sold to her subsidized grains for more than twenty years. She is the proud owner of an aadhaar number, and though she also signed up for the new biometrically enabled system of ration distribution, she has discovered that the fingerprint reader at the ration shop cannot recognize her finger. She comes every month and fails every month. The procedure is shameful for the shopkeeper, who tries to deflect responsibility for Amma's plight by invoking the need for family solidarity: "I keep telling her to bring a younger relative, but she does not listen." This statement refers to the rule that biometric authentication of any member of family listed on the ration card would be sufficient to verify the entitlement. The elderly woman has two adult sons. Yet, she laments that both have abandoned her. Neighbors report that she is indeed one of the most destitute widows in the locality. The tension between the different ways of knowing the elderly woman cannot be solved. Locally she is considered destitute on two accounts: first, she has no income, and second, there is no male family member to look after her. Being a single elderly widow in India is a curse. Yet, at the ration shop, the pity of neighbors cannot save her. Here she is reduced to an unreadable body who cannot effectively claim her right to food.

Amma's experience of rejection by her sons is exacerbated by the negligence of an uncaring state, deepening her marginalization so much so that it causes discomfort also to her neighbors and the shopkeeper. The stubborn monthly appearance of her visibly neglected, poor, and frail body deflates claims of objectivity attributed to biometric governance. In the official statistics presented on the home page of the Delhi National Food Security, this error hides behind a smoke screen of absent figures. The column intended to list the number of failed biometric verifications has been disregarded, with the explicitly stated purpose to make nontransparent the difference between people who did not wish to and those who could not collect their monthly food ration (Rao 2017). This comforting opacity between people who choose to ignore a service and those who are ignored by the service melts away when shopkeepers, business correspondents, or IT personnel come face-to-face with people and their claims, alternative stories, and paper evidence. In this situation, governments are unable to trace by which logic services are given or refused, and corporations can simply not sell biometrically enabled products to certain customers. Errors from the perspective of the service providers are a perverse inefficiency that translates into a loss of income, governmental opacity, or distributive injustice.

Our focus on life histories demonstrates the way the biometric system produces a sociological margin of error among those who live a particularly harsh life. When the idealized technonorm of the stable and legible body runs up against live bodies—which age, get hurt, or sweat—governance becomes uncertain. While maintenance of biomaterial as well as cleaning and preparing the body can enhance the success of biometric readings, it cannot bring about readings that tally with all the expectations. Life produces an excess of moments, conditions, and instances that cause a breakdown of the body-machine link. The body is or is not what it has become through the life lived by a person. This failure of bodies to comply with a specific technology complicates the effect of biometric technology, and it damages the idealized dream of biometric sorting as a purely technical and thus objective process. The notion of biometric identification as free from human manipulation was, as a matter of course, always going to be a fiction. All processes of sorting are based on classifications. Handing them over to new technical routines might hide the underlying distinctions, but they do not remove discrimination. By highlighting the classificatory work of the "error," we have illustrated the consequences of ignoring the negative space hidden in the archive of India's aadhaar project. Truth emerges through a process of discriminating people who fail in view of algorithmically rendered norms, thereby creating exclusions and blind spots. These mark the background before which some people can be legitimized. The "error" therefore is not the fault of the system or an unpredictable blunder; instead, it serves the purpose of bringing to the light the truth of which bodies pass and which do not.

Conclusion

Eight years after the introduction of aadhaar and the distribution of more than 1 billion aadhaar numbers, the significance of the system cannot be overstated. Officially, aadhaar is a voluntary system, but, in practice, it is difficult especially for the vulnerable to navigate complex bureaucratic systems without this biometric proof of identity. Today, aadhaar is mandatory for welfare schemes, such as access to subsidized rations or propane gas cylinders. The Modi government is ready to make it a required part of the tax return application and even children now need an aadhaar card to get a birth certificate or register at school. The rationale is that building a secure database will serve as a deterrent to fraud and exclude fake identities from any access to state services. The "biometric imaginary" (Donovan 2015, 817) configures biometric surveillance as a necessary, suitable, and effective way of streamlining governance by making transactions transparent (Sarkar 2014). However, rather than solving the identification crises, the deployment of biometric devices produces new worrying ambiguities and thus an alternative disorder.

Here we have been concerned with the production of the universalized norm of biometric identity and the errors that a specific practice of biometric verification produces. The application of biometric technology requires a particular kind of normalized body that may be at odds with the bodies of living people, which constantly adjust, change, or get mutilated over the course of harsh and complicated lives. The rejection of some bodies during the mandated technological rendering creates temporary or permanent exclusions and belies the notion that the national biometric system will treat everyone equally. The life of the unreadable and unverifiable body is, indeed, a life that, albeit filled with experiences that are real, represents nothing in the biometric system. It gets cast aside as flawed and potentially suspicious, while simultaneously acting as a mirror of truth to the biometric system, since unreason is the foundation for reason. The binary sorting of bodies into true and false produces a new foundational truth, where the lives lived in the erroneous margin are judged not only by the nontruth of error—the technical exclusion—but also by the judgment of unruly, unregistrable lives. The unruly life that is judged an error is also filled with images and visualities of the life of unreadable bodies—that is to say, a widow, or man having too large of a family—thus being caught in games of truth and error. By declaring that these erratic results stand in for an objective truth, those who pass, or do not pass, have been brought to the light of governmental reason.

Notes

1   Subsequently the family received substantial amount of public attention. See, for example, Daily Mail Reporter (2011).
2   See, for example, Malhotra (2017); Viswanath (2017); or Venkatanarayanan (2017).

References

Aas, Katja Franko. 2006. "'The Body Does Not Lie': Identity, Risk and Trust in Technoculture." *Crime, Media, Culture* 2(2): 143–58.
Ajana, Btihaj. 2012. "Biometric Citizenship." *Citizenship Studies* 16(7): 851–70.
Amicelle, Anthony, and Elida K. U. Jacobsen. 2016. "The Cross-Colonization of Finance and Security through Lists: Banking Policing in the UK and India." *Environment and Planning D: Society and Space* 34(1): 89–106.
Amoore, Louise. 2006. "Biometric Borders: Governing Mobilities in the War on Terror." *Political Geography* 25(3): 336–51.
Bhatia, Amiya, and Jacqueline Bhabha. 2017. "India's Aadhaar Scheme and the Promise of Inclusive Social Protection." *Oxford Development Studies* 45(1): 64–79.
Bowker, Geoffrey C., and Susan Leigh Star. 1999. *Sorting Things Out: Classification and Its Consequences*. Cambridge, MA: MIT Press.
Breckenridge, Keith. 2014. *Biometric State: The Global Politics of Identification and Surveillance in South Africa, 1850 to the Present*. New York: Cambridge University Press.
Cole, Simon. 2001. *Suspect Identities: A History of Fingerprinting and Criminal Identification*. Cambridge, MA: Harvard University Press.

Corbridge, Stuart, Glyn Williams, Manoj Srivastava, and René Véron. 2005. *Seeing the State: Governance and Governmentality in India*. Cambridge: Cambridge University Press.

Daily Mail Reporter. 2011. "The World's Biggest Family: The Man with 39 Wives, 94 Children and 33 Grandchildren." February 2. http://www.dailymail.co.uk /news/article-1358654/The-worlds-biggest-family-Ziona-Chan-39-wives-94 -children-33-grandchildren.html. [Or see the film by BTV, *YouTube*. Accessed April 11, 2017. https://www.youtube.com/watch?v=WebTR66FJPc.]

Donovan, Kevin P. 2015. "The Biometric Imaginary: Bureaucratic Technopolitics in Post-Apartheid Welfare." *Journal of South African Studies* 41(4): 815–33.

Fuller, Gillian. 2003. "Perfect Match: Biometrics and Body Patterning in a Networked World." *The Fibreculture Journal* 1(December). http://one.fibreculturejournal .org/fcj002.

Gelb, Alan, and Julia Clark. 2013a. "Identification for Development: The Biometrics Revolution." Working Paper 315. Washington, DC: Center for Global Development.

Gelb, Alan, and Julia Clark. 2013b. "Performance Lessons from India's Universal Identification Program." CGD Policy Paper 020. Washington, DC: Center for Global Development.

Gupta, Akhil. 2012. *Red Tape: Incentive Bribe and the Provision of Subsidy*. Durham, NC: Duke University Press.

Hristova, Stefka. 2014. "Recognizing Friend and Foe: Biometrics, Veridiction, and the Iraq War." *Surveillance and Society* 12(4): 516–27.

Hull, Matthew S. 2012. *Government of Paper. The Materiality of Bureaucracy in Urban Pakistan*. Durham, NC: Duke University Press.

Hunter, Wendy, and Natasha Borges Sugiyama. 2014. "Transforming Subjects into Citizens: Insights from Brazil's Bolsa Família." *Perspectives on Politics* 12(4): 829–45.

Jacobsen, Elida K. U. 2012. "Unique Identification: Inclusion and Surveillance in the Indian Biometric Assemblage." *Security Dialogue*, 43(5): 457–74.

Jacobsen, Elida K. U. 2013. "Preventing, Predicting or Producing Risk? India's National Biometric Identification." In *India's Human Security: Lost Debates, Forgotten People, Intractable Conflicts*, edited by Å. Kolås and J. Miklian, 135–48. New York: Routledge.

Kruger, Erin, Shoshana Magnet, and Joost Van Loon. 2008. "Biometric Revisions of the 'Body' in Airports and US Welfare Reform." *Body and Society* 14(2): 99–121.

Lebovic, Nitzan. 2015. "Biometrics, or The Power of the Radical Center." *Critical Inquiry* 41(4): 841–68.

Lidén, Kristoffer, Nina Boy, and Elida K. U. Jacobsen. 2016. "Societal Ethics and Biometric Technologies." SOURCE *Societal Security Network*. Oslo: SOURCE.

Magnet, Shoshana Amielle. 2011. *When Biometrics Fail: Gender, Race, and the Technology of Identity*. Durham, NC: Duke University Press.

Maguire, Mark. 2009. "The Birth of Biometric Security." *Anthropology Today* 25(2): 9–14.

Maguire, Mark, and Pete Fussey. 2016. "Sensing Evil: Counterterrorism, Techno-science, and the Cultural Reproduction of Security." *Focaal* 75(June): 31–44.

Malhotra, Sarika. 2017. "Aadhaar: How People Are Caught in the Middle of Unique Number Web." *Hindustan Times*. March 28. http://www.hindustantimes.com/india-news/aadhaar-how-people-are-caught-in-the-middle-of-unique-number-web/story-SvLmHXdP5zDx5iRwgFLTjI.html.

Markó, Ferenc David. 2016. "'We Are Not a Failed State, We Make the Best Passports': South Sudan and Biometric Modernity." *African Studies Review* 59(2): 113–32.

Masiero, Silvia. 2016. "Digital Governance and the Reconstruction of the Indian Anti-poverty System." *Oxford Development Studies*: 45(4): 393–408

Muller, Benjamin J. 2011. "Risking It all at the Biometric Border: Mobility, Limits, and the Persistence of Securitisation." *Geopolitics* 16(1): 91–106.

Murray, Heather. 2007. "Monstrous Play in Negative Spaces: Illegible Bodies and the Cultural Construction of Biometric Technology." *The Communication Review* 10(4): 347–65.

Nilekani, Nandan, and Viral Shah. 2015. *Rebooting India: Realizing a Billion Aspirations*. New Delhi: Penguin.

Pugliese, Joseph. 2010. *Biometrics: Bodies, Technologies, Biopolitics*. London: Routledge.

Rabinow, Paul. 1998. "French Enlightenment: Truth and Life." *Economy and Society* 27(2–3): 193–201.

Rao, Ursula. 2013. "Biometric Marginality: UID and the Shaping of Homeless Identities in the City." *Economic and Political Weekly* 48(13): 71–77.

Rao, Ursula. 2017. "Writing, Typing, and Scanning: Distributive Justice and the Politics of Visibility in the Era of E-governance." In *South Asian Media and Politics*, edited by S. Udupa and S. McDowell, 127–40. London: Routledge.

Sarkar, Swagato. 2014. "The Unique Identity (UID) Project, Biometrics and Re-imagining Governance in India." *Oxford Development Studies* 42(4): 516–33.

Scott, James C. 1998. *Seeing Like a State*. New Haven, CT: Yale University Press.

Sekula, Aallan. 1986. "The Body and the Archive." *October* 39(Winter): 3–64.

Sharma, Aradhana, and Akhil Gupta, eds. 2006. *The Anthropology of the State: A Reader*. Malden, MA: Blackwell.

Singh, Ranjit, and Steven J. Jackson. 2017. "From Margins to Seams: Imbricating, Inclusion, and Torque in the Aadhaar Identification Project." Paper presented at the 2017 SIGCHI Conference on Human Factors in Computing Systems, May 6–11, Denver, CO. http://infosci.cornell.edu/sites/default/files/p4776-singhA.pdf.

Standing Committee on Finance. 2011. "42nd Report National Identification Authority of India Bill 2010, Part C Evolution of the UIDAI." *PRS Legislative Research*. http://www.prsindia.org/uploads/media/UID/uid%20report.pdf.

Thomas, Owen D. 2014. "Foucaultian Dispositifs as Methodology: The Case of Anonymous Exclusions by Unique Identification in India." *International Political Sociology* 8(2): 164–81.

UIDAI. 2010. *UIDAI Strategy Overview: Creating a Unique Identity Number for Every Resident in India*. New Delhi: Planning Commission, Unique Identification Authority of India.

van der Ploeg, Irma. 1999. "Written on the Body: Biometrics and Identity." *SIGCAS Computers and Society* 29(1): 37–44.

Venkatanarayanan, Anand. 2017. "'The UIDAI System Design Is Flawed': This Man 'Busts' Nandan Nilekani's 9 Claims on Aadhaar." *News Minute*. May 4. http:// www.thenewsminute.com/article/uidai-system-design-flawed-man-busts -nandan-nilekani-s-9-claims-aadhaar-59891.

Viswanath, L. 2017. "Four Reasons You Should Worry about Aadhaar's Use of Biometrics." *Wire*. March 3. https://thewire.in/119323/real-problem-aadhaar -lies-biometrics/.

World Bank. 2015. *Identification for Development (ID4D): Integration Approach*. Washington, DC: International Bank for Reconstruction and Development/ World Bank Group.

Zelazny, Frances. 2012. "The Evolution of India's UID Program: Lessons Learned and Implications for Other Developing Countries." CGD Policy Paper 008. Washington, DC: Center for Global Development.

TWO

———

Injured by the Border

Security Buildup, Migrant Bodies, and Emergency
Response in Southern Arizona

IEVA JUSIONYTE

Introduction: Body on the Line

His body was bisected by the line—*la línea divisora*, the dividing line, is
what many here call the international boundary separating Mexico from the
United States. Unable to move forward or retreat, the man was stuck, trapped
under the border fence on the hill about two hundred yards south of the Mor-
ley pedestrian crossing between Nogales, Sonora, and Nogales, Arizona. That
late afternoon about a decade ago, a group of Mexicans managed to fold up
the metal sheets—formerly used by the military as aircraft landing pads in
the Vietnam War—just enough to be able to crawl onto the U.S. soil. But he
was not among those who succeeded in what the law designates an "illegal
entry." Emergency responders from both sides of the border were dispatched
to the scene to rescue the trapped man.[1]

Temo, one of the volunteer firefighters, the *bomberos*, in Nogales, Sonora, said that when they arrived they found twenty-something-year-old wedged halfway through the fence. His upper body was in Arizona, but his legs—they remained in Sonora. He pleaded with his rescuers, armed with hydraulic tools, popularly known as "the jaws of life," to pull him back into Mexico. He didn't want to end up in the United States, where the Border Patrol was waiting to take him into custody. The bomberos tried, but without success. "We couldn't get him out here [to Nogales, Sonora]. We had to push him over there [to Nogales, Arizona]." "Barefoot." Apparently, when the man got stuck under the fence, he shouted at the passersby to help him out, hoping that someone would pull him back into Mexico. Instead, they stole his sneakers.

"Qué chiste!" What a joke! Temo laughed, telling me about this incident, one among many he has witnessed during his career as an emergency responder on the U.S.-Mexico border. Before joining the bomberos, Temo spent fourteen years volunteering for the Mexican Red Cross. His passion has always been rescue—confined-space rescue, high-altitude rope rescue, water rescue. He was assigned to the central station, the closest firehouse to the border. The day of our interview Temo was on twenty-four-hour shift, and our conversation kept being interrupted by the dispatch calling him on the radio.

How are the marks that security enforcement on the U.S.-Mexico border leaves on the bodies of unauthorized migrants used both as evidence of their victimhood, entitling them to medical care, and their illegality, warranting detention and deportation? This chapter looks at the injured body of the migrant as contested evidence entangled in overlapping, yet divergent regimes of power and knowledge in emergency medical care and security enforcement. Paramedics who work for local fire departments in southern Arizona are often called to help people who bear the direct consequences of increased securitization and militarization of the region: unauthorized entrants who break their legs when trying to jump over the fence or who suffer from severe dehydration and even heat stroke while crossing hazardous desert terrain in an attempt to avoid checkpoints on all northbound roads. The law requires prehospital medical service providers to screen, treat, and stabilize anyone who seeks emergency medical care regardless of her or his legal status. Yet, criminalization of migration and security buildup on the U.S. Southwest border have created tensions between federal, state, and local authorities and taxpaying residents regarding limited resources and uncompensated costs incurred rescuing border crossers. These disagreements have led to a redefinition of access to lifesaving treatment. Unauthorized border crossers who call 911 routinely get redirected to the Border Patrol instead of the local fire and rescue departments. Prior to receiving medical attention, they are often placed into Border Patrol custody and later deported straight from the hospital—if they are taken there in the first place.

I begin this chapter with an overview of research and scholarship on the risks and dangers that unauthorized migrants face when they try to cross the border from Mexico to the United States. The hazards have changed—they have intensified—as a direct consequence of new border security infrastructures and surveillance technologies that the Border Patrol developed and put in place along the international boundary. The U.S.-Mexico border has become the frontline in the "war on drugs" as well as what looks like a "war" on undocumented migration—in fact, from the federal agency's standpoint and often in practice, the two are inseparable. Using data collected during ethnographic research in fire and rescue departments along the Arizona-Sonora border in 2015–16, I discuss how firefighters and paramedics navigate ethical, legal, and political directives when they are called to rescue injured border crossers. The most difficult, and controversial, part of their job becomes the ability to recognize when the scene is safe to treat the patient because it requires emergency responders to make rash distinctions between undocumented migrants, or the "good guys" who deserve help, and drug runners, or the "bad guys" who pose danger to the rescuers themselves and should not be approached until they are in the custody of the Border Patrol. Through repeated encounters with injured border crossers, emergency responders have developed skills to read migrant bodies for evidence, enabling them to make ethical decisions about safe provision of medical care in potentially violent encounters along the border.

Injuries Are Not Accidents

Many life-threatening injuries in the U.S.-Mexico border space are not accidents. Rather, they result from structural conditions created by the escalation of violence and security enforcement in the borderlands. Criminalization of immigration, which took off in the 1990s and was further radicalized by concerns with terrorism in the aftermath of September 11, 2001, led the U.S. government to designate its southwestern border with Mexico as a threat to homeland security, thereby justifying amassing law enforcement resources to protect it and waging in the borderlands what has been likened to "a low-intensity warfare" (Dunn 1996). To deter unauthorized entry, the government has employed a combination of personnel, technology, and infrastructure, which have made crossing the border considerably more difficult.

Present border security policies are traced back to Operation Blockade / Hold the Line in El Paso, Texas, in 1993; Operation Gatekeeper in San Diego, California, in 1994; and Operation Safeguard in Nogales, Arizona, the same year. These strategies focused on fortifying urban areas that had traditionally been the most popular crossing corridors for unauthorized migrants (Nevins 2010). The Border Patrol's strategic plan, which the agency adopted in 1994, was aimed at deterring unauthorized entry by making towns less accessible—building a taller fence that is more difficult to scale without getting seriously hurt and deploying more Border Patrol agents to watch over it. Known as "prevention-through-deterrence," this strategy was expected to redirect migrants toward the inhospitable terrain of the Sonoran Desert, which was "less suited for crossing and more suited for enforcement" (USBP 1994, 7). There would be no need (authors of the plan thought) to install a fence all along the U.S.-Mexico border. Further from the urban areas, the harsh environment itself would serve as an effective barrier and a discouragement. It didn't happen exactly the way the Border Patrol predicted. The difficulty of this life-threatening journey did not dissuade migrants from trying to get across. Many were effectively rerouted away from border towns, as the strategy had intended, and pushed into the desert, creating what scholars have called "the funnel effect" (Rubio-Goldsmith et al. 2006). But they were not deterred. Instead, they learned to adapt to the new circumstances and the increasingly dangerous itinerary.

In response to continuing unauthorized migration through the Sonora-Arizona border, earlier government policies were updated and expanded, first, through the Secure Border Initiative (SBI), and, most recently, by adopting the Arizona Border Surveillance Technology Plan. The most visible and substantial investments in the latest stages of border militarization have been the physical and the so-called virtual wall to separate Mexican and predominantly Mexican American communities on both sides of the international divide (Heyman 2008; McGuire 2013). The U.S. Border Patrol, operating under the Department of Homeland Security, uses advanced technologies of policing and detection, combining remotely operated infrared cameras, heat sensors, tower-mounted radars, and unmanned aerial vehicles (UAVs, such as Predator-B drones). Statistical data is often unreliable in evaluating such measures in terms of their effectiveness at deterring or intercepting drug trafficking and human smuggling into the United States (Isacson, Meyer, and Davis 2013). However, it has been demonstrated that the trend of border militarization that began in the 1990s and escalated after 9/11—including the adoption of "prevention-through-deterrence" as the primary immigration enforcement strategy, the increase in the numbers of the U.S. Border Patrol agents, and the parallel multiplication of the Mexican military—have all added to the escalation of violence and resulted in a border-crossing experience that is extremely dangerous (Cornelius 2001; Rubio-Goldsmith et al. 2006; Jimenez 2009; Doty 2011; Slack and Whiteford 2011; Infante et al. 2012; De León 2015).

Stringent security policies are directly linked to the routinization of migrant deaths. According to a report prepared in 2009 by the American Civil Liberties Union (ACLU), deaths of an estimated 5,607 unauthorized migrants over the last fifteen years were a predictable and inhumane outcome of border security policies (Jimenez 2009, 7–8). Migrants who are trying to cross into the United States are funneled into less policed but more geographically and environmentally difficult desert and mountain areas in Arizona. Increasingly, they have come to rely on guides linked to drug cartels, leading to robberies, kidnapping, physical abuse, and rape (Jimenez 2009, 25). Some get lost or are abandoned by smugglers, especially when they are injured or in distress. Most deaths occur due to environmental factors, primarily from exposure to extreme heat or cold (temperatures can reach over 120 degrees Fahrenheit during summer days and drop below freezing during winter nights) and dehydration, as people typically never carry enough water to sustain themselves on a multiday crossing (De León 2012). Researchers and activists who work with recovering, identifying, and repatriating migrant remains note that besides existing diseases, other common causes of death while crossing the border include blunt force injuries, train and motor vehicle accidents, gunshot wounds, natural disasters, such as fire and drowning in rivers and irrigation canals (Jimenez 2009, 24). Referring to these deaths as a result of "natural causes" or "unintended effects" of "prevention-through-deterrence" deflects official responsibility (Doty 2009).

There are specific patterns of injury and death that can be traced back to border securitization and militarization. For example, drawing on ethnographic and archaeological data from the Undocumented Migration Project in the Sonoran Desert, Jason De León (2012) has shown how material objects that migrants adopt to help them avoid being caught by border enforcement agents—black plastic water jugs, cheap sneakers, darkly colored clothes—act on people's bodies, causing specific types of injuries. By examining "use-wear" of objects that migrants take with them across the border, he argues that border crossing is a well-structured, dangerous, and violent social process (480). Jeremy Slack and Scott Whiteford (2011) have described how migrants are made vulnerable through encounters with the Border Patrol, coyotes, bandits, and traffickers. They note that women, children, and monolingual indigenous migrants face the greatest risk. Wendy Vogt (2013) has discussed injuries experienced by Central American migrants, as their bodies become commodities in the economies of violence and humanitarian aid during their journey across Mexico. Her research in migrant shelters documents stories of mutilation when people fall off the freight trains colloquially known as La Bestia, as well as rape and assault. These occurrences are not accidents—they must be understood as the result of structural, state, and local economies of violence and inequality.

Despite the risks, many migrants make it across the border alive, but because of severe injuries caused by the journey, they are in need of emergency medical care. In addition to heat exhaustion, dehydration, and hypothermia, they suffer spinal fractures and other orthopedic injuries resulting from trying to jump the border fence, friction blisters, intestinal illness from drinking contaminated water in cattle tanks, and major traumas from human smuggling van rollovers and other transportation-related injuries. The close relationship between securitization of the border and increased number of medical emergencies treated by emergency medical services (EMS) is illustrated by the following detail: *Nogales International* reported that when in 2011 the government doubled the height of the border fence in the city, the number of times fire department ambulances transported someone from the border spiked (Prendergast 2013).

To reduce the number of deaths, the Border Patrol created a special Search, Trauma, and Rescue Unit (BORSTAR). Yet the role of BORSTAR is rather controversial because at other times border enforcement agents are the ones responsible for injuring migrants (Jimenez 2009; Isacson, Meyer, and Davis 2013; Martínez, Slack, and Heyman 2013). To mitigate the deadly effects of security policies, humanitarian organizations, such as Humane Borders, Tucson Samaritans, and No More Deaths, among others, took on the task of rescuing unauthorized migrants and providing them first aid (Magaña 2008; Doty 2009). Volunteers build water stations stocked with food, clothing, and first-aid kits and set up medical camps. They also patrol the desert on foot and in vehicles in search for migrants who need help. In situations, when their condition is critical—for example, the border crossers have altered mental status, difficulty breathing, or snake bites—the volunteers try to persuade migrants to allow them to call 911 and transfer them to local medical facilities. Law enforcement officers at Arizona's ports of entry also have prosecutorial discretion, which enables them to consider the person's condition and use humanitarian parole to temporarily admit immigrants for health reasons, even when the patients do not have a passport and a visa allowing them to travel across the border.

But none of them—neither the Border Patrol agents, nor immigrations officers at the ports of entry, nor humanitarian aid volunteers—have the indiscriminate provision of prehospital medical services as the official mandate of their job. In southern Arizona, this task belongs to firefighters, trained as emergency medical technicians and paramedics. The ethical framework that underlies the principles of healthcare distinguishes emergency responders from Border Patrol agents, who, even when trained in first aid, are primarily concerned with enforcing the law. Their affiliation with local governments also sets them apart from humanitarian volunteers who are not accountable to or representative of the state. How do these local public service employees negotiate their seemingly contradictory functions of being part of the state while at the same time rescuing those injured by that state's policies?

Trauma and Ethics of Distinction

Let us return to the scenario recounted in the beginning of this chapter. Although the man who got trapped under the fence in Nogales was not critically injured, his case illustrates the predicament that injured border crossers face when security logic and humanitarian ethics compete and overlap. In the late 2000s, when this incident occurred, emergency responders were regularly dispatched to help people who tried to breech the border fence, which, in turn, mutilated their bodies. The most graphic of these were amputations caused by the sharp edges of the solid steel panels. Usually, they involved fingers that were cut off as border crossers tried to hold on to the top of the fence before jumping to the ground. This created a special type of jurisdictional problem. While the individual was now on U.S. soil, the person's amputated fingers most often fell to the other side, into Mexico. Alex, a Mexican American firefighter and emergency medical technician in Nogales, Arizona, remembers: "In some places they used to have openings at the bottom [of the fence] with grates on them for the water to go through. You could still see across and you could see the fingers and the hands on the other side of the border [in Mexico], and the people were over here [in the U.S.]. Sometimes we would reach over, grab the body part, and put it on ice." The new slatted border wall, installed in 2011, is taller, reaching between eighteen and thirty feet. Those who try to climb over this bollard-style barrier, generally aided by a ladder on the Mexican side, may fall and fracture their legs or their spine. According to the prehospital emergency medical care protocols in southern Arizona, the mechanism of injury (a fall from a height of over twenty feet) qualifies these patients for air transport by helicopter to the University Medical Center in Tucson, the only Level 1 trauma facility in the region.

The fence is not the only mechanism of injury for transgressive migrant bodies. There are other tools in the Border Patrol's infamous "prevention-through-deterrence" package. Policies of securitization and militarization on the U.S.-Mexico border tactically deploy both natural and manmade environments—the weaponized terrain—to enforce the jurisdictional boundary between the two countries. This enforcement brutally manifests on the bodies of those who do not have the required documents allowing them to cross through the designated port of entry. People who walk along the Nogales Wash through the underground tunnel get swept away by the turbulent water and may drown (Glionna 2016); those who clandestinely travel by rail suffer leg amputations if they fall onto the tracks under the moving train (Clark 2011); many have been ejected from vehicles as their drivers tried to escape from the Border Patrol pursuing them on dangerously windy roads at night (Caesar 2009); and even more need medical treatment for dehydration, heat stroke, rhabdomyolysis, or hypothermia when they are exposed to extreme temperatures during the walk across the "hostile" desert terrain in rural areas, hoping to avoid checkpoints permanently installed on all northbound roads (De León 2015). Fire departments follow medical protocols that outline what mechanisms of injury and what signs and symptoms warrant transporting patients by air to the trauma center in Tucson. These are typically critical conditions, in which any delay in surgery may be life threatening. The patient's legal status in the country has no place in medical decision charts.

However, in the border zone, which extends a hundred miles north of the international boundary, policies guiding patient care at fire and rescue departments in different counties and municipalities as well as the discretion of individual first responders affect whether the injuries that unauthorized migrants sustain are read only through a medical or also through a security lens. The law guarantees that anyone who is in critical condition in the United

States has the right to receive emergency treatment. But the border zone is what has been aptly called a "Constitution free zone," where the location's very proximity to the línea divisora, justifies the suspension of Fourth Amendment Rights (Dorsey and Díaz-Barriga 2015, 208).[2] Here, the application of the law is impeded by the physical terrain—remote, rugged, inaccessible— but also by the discourses and practices of state actors. Government agencies that articulate the border zone as "lawless," where its representatives are seen as potentially vulnerable and thus permitted behaviors that would be marked as unlawful elsewhere in the United States, constitute the borderlands as an area endowed with these characteristics (see Pruitt 2014, 208).

The border fence that trapped the Mexican man separates the town of Nogales, Arizona, located in Santa Cruz County and estimated to have just over 20,000 residents, over 90 percent of them Hispanic or Latino, from its sister city, Nogales, Sonora, home to at least 300,000 residents. Together they are known to locals as Ambos Nogales (both Nogales), one community divided by a wall. According to the data provided to me by the Nogales Fire Department in 2015, about 10 percent of all emergency calls that they responded to were related to the border, whether it was to take over critical patients from the Mexican ambulances at one of the ports of entry or to help injured undocumented migrants. "We are not Border Patrol. Since he's on this side of the fence, wherever it is, we had been told to treat that patient," one fire captain explained. A thirty-year veteran of the Nogales Fire Department continued: "With that issue [referring the patient to the Border Patrol], you are making the EMS people become involved with immigration enforcement."[3] Yet he also noted that on those rare occasions when the Border Patrol is not yet on scene—usually they are the ones who find injured border crossers and request an ambulance—emergency responders have to call the Border Patrol because that is the only way for the fire department to receive compensation for the medications and supplies used to rescue, treat, and transport unauthorized migrants. Surprisingly, the federal agents are not eager to take custody of the "undocumented aliens" (UDAs), who, unless they are the guides or drug mules, are low on the Border Patrol's list of priorities. The costs for reimbursing expensive helicopter rides from Nogales to Tucson have strained the federal institution's budget, to an extent that firefighters I interviewed told me about numerous occasions in which the Border Patrol agents were avoiding taking patients into custody. Local emergency responders arrived on the scene to find federal agents standing next to an injured "fence jumper." But as in a badly staged performance, claiming that they had not witnessed what happened nor had video footage to prove an unauthorized entry, agents acted as if they had no proof the person was in the country illegally.[4]

Nowhere is the tension between security politics, healthcare economy, and medical ethics as evident as in Arivaca, an unincorporated community of about seven hundred residents located eleven miles north of the border in southern Arizona's Pima County, which is on a popular transit route through the desert between Nogales and Sasabe, used by undocumented migrants and drug smugglers alike. When I conducted fieldwork there in 2015, Arivaca had two emergency medical responders per shift covering a territory of over six hundred square miles. They were called to rescue migrants who fell into abandoned mine shafts, broke their bones when falling down steep crevices in the desert, or lost a lot of fluids during prolonged exposure to extreme heat. They helped men and women, old and young. But the small fire district with a very low budget could not afford to transport and treat such large numbers of injured migrants, and since Arizona has exhausted Medicare's Section 1011 funds, which allowed them to be compensated for emergency treatment provided to unauthorized border crossers, their only recourse for getting reimbursement for patient care has been through the Border Patrol. Therefore, when called to help undocumented migrants, paramedics ask the Border Patrol to provide a transport authorization request (known as TAR) number, which they include in the patient care reports and which their department later uses to send a bill to the federal agency. A Border Patrol vehicle then follows the ambulance to the hospital, which is often at least an hour away. Unless they are transported by helicopter and need trauma surgery at the University Medical Center in Tucson, patients who are in the Border Patrol's custody are taken to the hospital's southern campus and placed in a special security unit. Once released, unauthorized migrants are processed for deportation.

There is no law that obliges emergency responders to contact the Border Patrol when they provide treatment to unauthorized migrants. Most do it because of financial considerations. Some others ask for agents to provide security because they are concerned about their own safety. But in order to decide whether to call the Border Patrol, firefighters and paramedics must first recognize that their patient is in the country illegally. This recognition is not synonymous with racial profiling, though it often reinforces existing stereotypes. Rather, the skills of decoding coordinates of the call and reading signs of the bodies as evidence of illegal entry develop through years of repeated encounters with injured border crossers, allowing emergency responders to identify those who could cause them harm, such as armed bandits or drug traffickers.

Even far from the international boundary, emergency responders with local experience know with a great degree of confidence when the patient they are treating is an unauthorized border crosser. It comes down to location (on or off the road, home vs. "out there"), time of call (day or night), appearance ("tattered clothing" and the condition of their shoes), and, often, language (Spanish). Commonly, they further distinguish between undocumented migrants and drug smugglers. "We've been around for so long that we know when they are drug runners or when they are just coming to find a job," Carmen, a Hispanic paramedic with the Tubac Fire District, explained to me in 2015. Undocumented migrants "have been out there for days and days." They are often very dehydrated; they are sick. "And most of the drug runners . . . are still kind of clean, they don't stink as bad, and they are hydrated. . . . And of course they have the red lines here, where they carry the [drug] packs. So they'll complain about their shoulders."

In remote rural areas, and particularly when the first responders are female, they call law enforcement for their own safety and, considering that the closest sheriff's deputy can be half an hour to an hour away, the Border Patrol usually shows up first. "It's not the illegals that I am afraid of. It's the drug runners," said Tangye, a female Anglo paramedic and an interim chief of the Arivaca Fire District. "The illegals, they are tired, they are grateful for the help."[5] But paramedics feel less safe in the presence of drug smugglers. "A lot of those people [drug smugglers] carry guns. We don't carry [bullet-proof] vests. We don't carry guns, of course." I spoke to Carmen the day after the press reported that two Mexican nationals (part of a five-man "rip crew" that crossed illegally into the United States seeking to steal drugs from smugglers in the vicinity of the nearby Peck Canyon) had been convicted of murdering Border Patrol agent Brian Terry: "It's not required for us to call Border Patrol—that's not my job. But when you see them there . . . and we don't know what they really want, you just get that gut feeling from some of them that you don't trust them, unfortunately, a lot of them you don't. Especially when you know that they were doing something wrong already. And at night. In the middle of nowhere. We don't have radio service there. We didn't have cell phone service. There's nobody else out there. It's just my partner and I." Carmen said this to explain why, when she and her partner saw a group of people waving at them in a remote canyon, possibly asking for help, they didn't stop the ambulance but called the Border Patrol instead, informing the agents about the situation. She didn't know whether they found the group, nor whether anybody was hurt.

Despite their skills at recognizing types of border crossers, recently emergency medical responders have been struggling to tell them apart. The boundaries separating border crossers into the categories of migrants/patients and smugglers/criminals have been blurred since more migrants are now forced to carry drug loads as a form of payment for the crossing. It's not easy to sort out who is who in the border zone, and rescue workers are torn between their mandate to help anybody and everybody and the number one rule of arriving on an emergency scene: scene safety. Thus, in some departments, paramedics will not respond to areas that are known corridors used by drug and human smugglers without the escort of the Border Patrol, even if this means delaying medical care or compromising its ethics. In this "Constitution-free zone," where invoking security justifies the bending of the laws, more and more often local fire departments are not even contacted to provide emergency medical services to injured border crossers. In 2015, the ACLU criticized Santa Cruz and Pima Counties for violating the Equal Protection Clause of the Fourteenth Amendment when the sheriffs' departments "selectively referred" 911 calls from migrants in distress directly to the Border Patrol, bypassing local first responders.

Uncertain State Actors

Firefighters occupy a legally and ethically ambiguous position vis-à-vis unauthorized migrants that they encounter along the U.S.-Mexico border. As employees of local governments they carry the insignia of power and authority, but they are also witnesses to the human trauma and suffering that federal and state policies cause on the fringes of the post-911 security state. In their work as emergency responders, where they are charged with identifying and treating critical injuries, this task is complicated because firefighters have to read the signs displayed on the bodies of migrants through mismatched ethical and legal lenses and weigh them against their own concerns about personal safety and security.

A firefighter slogan proudly asserts, "We walk where the devil dances," indicating that by the very nature of their job—to rescue, treat, and transport people who are critically ill or injured—first responders live in a routine state of emergency. But they work in zones of risk and rescue that are unevenly produced by broader political and socioeconomic processes. Nowhere is this more visible than on the U.S.-Mexico border, which since the 1990s has become a primary target of the "war on drugs," the criminalization of migration, and the heightened security buildup. A number of policies on federal and state levels—including, but not limited to anti-immigrant legislation (Arizona's SB 1070), the transfer of immigration enforcement to local police departments through 287(g) and the Secure Communities Program, surveillance expansion under the Secure Border Initiative, and multiplying internal Border Patrol checkpoints on the roads leading away from the border—affect the lived experiences of local firefighters and paramedics, both limiting and expanding the scope of their work. On the one hand, it is now more difficult to maintain old commitments between communities on both sides of the border, such as assisting Mexican first responders with large fires and other mass casualty incidents in sister cities divided by the fence (Jusionyte 2015b). On the other hand, as we have seen, first responders are often called to help people who bear the direct consequences of increased border securitization and militarization: migrants who suffer traumatic injuries from trying to jump over the steel wall that separates urban neighborhoods, or who become dehydrated or hypothermic while crossing hazardous desert and mountain terrain in an attempt to avoid detection at checkpoints.

The issue is further complicated by the scarcity of resources in southern Arizona and the rising costs of healthcare in the United States. Researchers have documented how their illegal status in the United States affects migrants' interactions with local government institutions, often limiting their access to vital public resources (Coutin 1999, 2000; Golash-Boza 2012; Menjívar and Abrego 2012; De Genova 2013; Dowling and Inda 2013, among others). In the context of state and local initiatives to police immigrant communities that extend deep into the interior of the country, such as the 287(g) and Secure Communities Program (Coleman 2012; Stuesse and Coleman 2014), they become "entrapped" (Núñez and Heyman 2007). Their precarious position and insecurity prevent them from seeking legal, social, and medical services. This situation is acute in communities adjacent to the border, which, as transit spaces, are characterized by deep ambivalence toward migrants. Residents and local law enforcement personnel often regard migrants in terms of their illegality and reputed association with violence, thereby lacking legitimate claim to rights and limited resources within the communities through which they cross (Vogt 2013). In some areas along the U.S.-Mexico border, calls for medical assistance at the border became "a growing burden" on the finances and resources of fire and EMS departments. This is true beyond Arizona. For example, a fifth of all calls that the Calexico Fire Department in California responded to in 2011—725 emergencies—were associated with the border. Cited in the *New York Times*, Chief Pete Mercado said the department's only ambulance would sometimes make ten trips to the port of entry in a given day: "For many of those, he said, the department is not able to collect payment, while the ambulance is rendered unavailable for other emergencies.... [According to Mercado:] 'We've absorbed the cost for all these years. I can't express how difficult it is.'" During interviews that I conducted with fire officials along the Arizona-Sonora border, many shared these same concerns.

Some organizations criticize the U.S. federal government for shifting responsibility of providing emergency treatment to local authorities, encumbered with shrinking resources, thereby placing disproportionate burden for its security and immigration policies on Southwest border counties.[6] Medical emergencies related to escalating violence and security measures have had significant effects on these communities and local fire departments (Dinan 2013; Jusionyte 2015a). Local first responders—firefighters, EMTs, paramedics—as well as nurses and doctors who work in area hospitals, comply with the Emergency Medical Treatment and Active Labor Act, known as EMTALA.[7] EMTALA requires that hospitals and emergency personnel provide all patients who arrive in an emergency department with mandatory medical screening examinations; stabilize patients before transit if an emergency medical condition exists; ensure patient safety during the transfer process; and treat anyone who needs emergency medical care regardless of income or immigration status.[8] However, my fieldwork confirms what has been underscored by research conducted in other settings: that relationships among incongruous international and state policies, federal law, medical ethics, disposition of frontline healthcare personnel, and "illegal" patients are fraught with tension (e.g., Rosenthal 2007; Willen 2007; Heyman, Núñez, and Talavera 2009; Castañeda 2011; Chavez 2012; Holmes 2012; Marrow 2012; Willen 2012; Holmes 2013; Huschke 2014) and require distinguishing between universalizing *juridical* arguments about formal entitlement to health rights and situationally specific *moral* arguments about deservingness (Willen 2007). These studies examine difficulties that migrants encounter accessing general healthcare services in host countries. Although many of them discuss emergency situations, in which the government mandates provision of lifesaving care to any patient regardless of his or her legal status, they do not focus on medical first responders who work primarily on critical injuries and largely outside of the hospitals. The burden of reading bodies marked by violence and disease as either worthy of immediate help or a potential source of danger for first responders falls on them.

Historically developed within the military, only fairly recently has pre-hospital medicine become a civilian field of healthcare, staffed by paid professionals and volunteers (Haller 1992; Hutchinson 1996; Zink 2006). Since the 1970s their presence in neighborhoods across the United States, often integrated with the fire departments, has become routine. The history of the U.S. fire service written by social historians (Maclean 1992; Chetkovich 1997; Tebeau 2003) traces how firefighters, who risk their lives protecting life and property of others, became cultural icons of heroism, respected as the guardians of the community. The development of rescue squads in particular entails "the melding of men and technology into an efficient, lifesaving machine" (Tebeau 2003, 287), balancing on tensions between rationalism and expressiveness, efficiency and passion, modernity and tradition. Their role in responding to the 9/11 attacks, when 343 firefighters died under the collapsing towers in New York City, has further solidified their iconicity as national heroes in the "war on terror" (Rothenbuhler 2005; Donahue 2011). Politically, administratively, and infrastructurally, fire and rescue departments across the United States have been incorporated into civil defense and federal emergency management systems. Yet recent anthropological studies of homeland security and national preparedness (Lakoff 2007; Collier and Lakoff 2008; Lakoff 2008; Fosher 2009; Masco 2014), though they bring attention to emergency response infrastructures, focus on the broader scale of strategic planning and protection of the body politic against catastrophic events rather than on the lived experiences of people who deal with emergency situations on a daily basis.

As other healthcare workers, prehospital emergency responders fit within the broader category of street-level bureaucrats, who wield considerable discretion in the day-to-day implementation of public programs (Lipsky 1980; Maynard-Moody and Musheno 2003; Proudfoot and McCann 2008). Anthropologists interested in the contemporary state have studied contradictions between the formal and the pragmatic in government bureaucracies, as well as the broader tensions between law and cultural norms (see, among others, Herzfeld 1992, 1997; Feldman 2008; Chalfin 2010; Gupta 2012; Hull 2012; Fassin 2013; Jauregui 2013). In the borderlands these "disemic" processes (Herzfeld 1997) can be acutely visible, as Josiah Heyman's (2000; 2002) extensive research at the ports of entry on the U.S.-Mexico border demonstrates. Emergency responders who rescue unauthorized migrants in southern Arizona also experience conflicts between state policies, on the one hand, and their professional, moral, and ethical obligations, on the other, which places them in an ambiguous position with respect to the law and to the state as political authority (Jusionyte 2015a).

Emergency medical technicians and paramedics have an exceptional status: in their work they disregard questions of legality and criminal background of their patients, which distinguishes them from other agents of the state who are more strictly bound to the law; yet they also occupy a peculiar symbolic and political niche in the national security apparatus. Emergency responders work at the fractures of what Pierre Bourdieu (1994; 1999) calls "the bureaucratic field"—the "splintered space" of the neoliberal state, where the state's "left hand" (in charge of social functions: public education, health, housing, welfare) and its "right hand" (responsible for enforcing the economic discipline: the police, the courts, the prison) are struggling against each other over the definition and distribution of public goods (Wacquant 2010). According to Loïc Wacquant (2010, 201), these two hands are enmeshed in relations of antagonistic cooperation.

Ethnographic data from fieldwork that I conducted in fire and rescue departments on the U.S.-Mexico border shows how this internal struggle unfolds in practice. More and more often first responders, who rescue and treat unauthorized border crossers, are caught between the imperative of the state, or "security logic," and the obligations of medicine, the "humanitarian reason" (Fassin 2012). They operate at the point of friction between border enforcement and social-humanitarian policies. But, as we have seen, their decision making is not limited to this conundrum of laws versus ethics, of the framework of security versus their humanitarian mandate. In remote areas along the U.S.-Mexico border, including the long stretches of the Sonoran Desert—inhospitable territory where the passage north is controlled by narcos and bandits (Martinez 2014)—emergency responders navigate situations that hurt migrants but that also pose danger to those dispatched to rescue the injured. Their concern for safety adds another layer of complexity to an already difficult scenario of violence, security, and rescue that unfolds in the borderlands.

Conclusion

Neither security infrastructure, such as a higher and longer border fence, nor anti-immigrant policies deter unauthorized migrants from attempting to cross the international boundary separating Mexico from the United States. Motivated by prospective employment in agriculture fields, construction industry, or domestic services; seeking to reunite with family members; or fleeing violence and poverty, they continue to breach the security perimeter, despite the government's stepped-up attempts to reinforce it in the aftermath of 9/11. This does not mean that the Border Patrol's strategy of "prevention-through-deterrence" has failed. Although migrants still get across, the buildup of security has made their journey from northern Sonora into southern Arizona particularly dangerous, even deadly. Funneled to travel through the most hazardous physical terrain, usually at the mercy of drug traffickers and bandits who control the routes where the law and its enforcement stretch thin, unauthorized border crossers experience traumatic injury and disease: leg and spinal fractures, amputations, severe dehydration, kidney failure, and rape. The patterns of injuries that migrants incur on the Sonora-Arizona border have been so consistent that they provide evidence of failing immigration and security policies, implicating the state as the perpetrator of violence.

In this chapter I sketched out what happens once unauthorized migrants are subjected to competing ethical and legal mandates that regulate the actions of emergency responders. In southern Arizona, the ill and injured—whether they are long-term residents of towns and ranches or travelers in transit to their destinations farther north—receive prehospital medical care from paramedics employed by the city or county fire departments. Although, as public service workers, they are incorporated into the post-9/11 state apparatus and obliged to follow the political and legal directives that prioritize homeland security over government's social functions, emergency responders understand their mandate to be that of saving lives, regardless of whether the people they rescue, treat, and transport are U.S. or foreign citizens and whether they are in the country with or without the permission of the federal authorities.

However, as the traumatic injuries that migrants experience have become routine while the costs of healthcare in the United States continue to rise, residents in border communities have become concerned about insufficient resources available to provide lifesaving treatment to everyone in need. The federal government, which created the policies and infrastructures that fortified the border, does not have a mechanism to deal with the social and economic effects of "prevention-through-deterrence" on counties and municipalities that provide emergency medical services to those injured by this security strategy. As tensions regarding resources for treating unauthorized migrants in Arivaca, Nogales, and other communities in southern Arizona rise, emergency responders have been forced to participate in immigration policing—their only option for having the federal government pay for the medical services provided to undocumented border crossers has been to call the Border Patrol and ask the federal agents to take their patient into custody.

In this new role, not written into law but widely adopted in practice, emergency responders interpret the signs on the bodies for evidence of illegal border crossing. They note the types and degrees of injuries; they look and listen for social clues; they decode time and space coordinates—all in an attempt to find clues of criminality and pointers of risk. None of these are decisive proof of unauthorized entry or of threat to the safety of firefighters and paramedics, not even when they are sent to remote patches of the borderlands that have fallen under the control of powerful criminal groups and violent bandits. Bodily evidence is not conclusive, and making patient care decisions based on appearances is both ethically and legally problematic. Yet, because of social pressure, financial concerns, and safety considerations, emergency responders who work in the criminalized and marginalized U.S.-Mexico borderlands have learned and now routinely deploy their skills to sort patients into several sociolegal categories, which unofficially complements decision making based on medical protocols. Inadvertently distinguishing the docile bodies of injured migrants from potentially threatening bodies of their guides or from those of drug smugglers further deepens the schism that exists between evidential regimes underlying federal law, medical ethics, and security logics.

Notes

This ethnographic project was supported by grants from the National Science Foundation, the Wenner-Gren Foundation, and the Humanities Scholarship Enhancement Award at the University of Florida.

1   Unless noted otherwise, the stories are based on ethnographic interviews I con-
     ducted with emergency responders during fieldwork in southern Arizona and
     northern Sonora between May 2015 and June 2016.
2   According to Dorsey and Díaz-Barriga (2015), citizens who live in the Rio Grande
     Valley of Texas do not have the right "to be secure in their persons, houses, pa-
     pers and effects," which is a violation of the Fourth Amendment. Border Patrol
     and Texas Department of Public Safety (who now act as the Border Patrol due to
     287[G] legislation) can pull citizens over and search cars without cause.
3   The Border Patrol is usually first on scene, so firefighters and paramedics rarely
     have to decide whether to call them.
4   If the Border Patrol has no documentation (such as camera footage) of an indi-
     vidual entering the country through an unauthorized passage, they don't have
     to take the person into custody, and they often avoid doing so to save costs.
     Firefighters began writing down the badge numbers of agents and the registra-
     tion plate numbers of their vehicles, so that they could later prove that they were
     present, allowing the department to bill the Border Patrol for the call. However,
     at the federal government's request they can no longer take down this informa-
     tion, because that could be "compromising their safety," if, for example, the notes
     were leaked and the media found out which agents were present on scene.
5   No emergency responder I have interviewed has ever been threatened or as-
     saulted by an undocumented migrant.
6   According to a September 2002 report prepared by United States / Mexico Bor-
     der Counties Coalition and MGT of America, "Medical Emergency: Costs of Un-
     compensated Care in Southwest Border Counties," in the early 2000s the costs
     of providing emergency medical care to undocumented migrants reached $200
     million, accounting for an estimated 25 percent of Southwest border hospitals'
     and an undetermined percentage of emergency medical service's (EMS) uncom-
     pensated costs (MGT of America 2002).
7   More detailed information on EMTALA can be found on the website adminis-
     tered by the Centers for Medicare and Medicaid Services (CMS 2012).
8   Another law from 1996, the Personal Responsibility and Work Opportunity
     Reconciliation Act (PRWORA), limits Medicaid benefits for undocumented im-
     migrants to emergency health services and non-Medicaid funded public health
     assistance (such as immunizations, communicable disease treatment).

References

Bourdieu, Pierre. 1994. "Rethinking the State: On the Genesis and Structure of the
     Bureaucratic Field." *Sociological Theory* 12(1): 1–19.
Bourdieu, Pierre. 1999. "The Abdication of the State." In *The Weight of the World:*

Social Suffering in Contemporary Society, edited by Pierre Bourdieu, 181–88. Cambridge: Polity Press.

Caesar, Stephen. 2009. "Rollover Kills 8 in SUV near Sonoita." *Arizona Daily Star.* June 8.

Castañeda, Heide. 2011. "Medical Humanitarianism and Physicians' Organized Efforts to Provide Aid to Unauthorized Migrants in Germany." *Human Organization* 70(1): 1–10.

Chalfin, Brenda. 2010. *Neoliberal Frontiers: An Ethnography of Sovereignty in West Africa.* Chicago: University of Chicago Press.

Chavez, Leo R. 2012. "Undocumented Immigrants and Their Use of Medical Services in Orange County, California." *Social Science & Medicine* 74(6): 887–93.

Chetkovich, Carol. 1997. *Real Heat: Gender and Race in the Urban Fire Service.* New Brunswick, NJ: Rutgers University Press.

Clark, Jonathan. 2011. "Migrant Teenager, Run Over by Train, Has Hope for Recovery of Crushed Foot." *Nogales International.* March 21.

CMS (Centers for Medicare and Medicaid Services). 2012. "Emergency Treatment and Labor Act (EMTALA)." March 26. https://www.cms.gov/Regulations-and -Guidance/Legislation/EMTALA/.

Coleman, Mathew. 2012. "The 'Local' Migration State: The Site-Specific Devolution of Immigration Enforcement in the U.S. South." *Law and Policy* 34(2): 159–90.

Collier, Stephen, and Andrew Lakoff. 2008. "Distributed Preparedness: The Spatial Logic of Domestic Security in the United States." *Environment and Planning D* 26(1): 7–28.

Cornelius, Wayne A. 2001. "Death at the Border: Efficacy and Unintended Consequences of U.S. Immigration Control Policy." *Population and Development Review* 27(4): 661–85.

Coutin, Susan Bibler. 1999. "Citizenship and Clandestiny among Salvadoran Immigrants." *POLAR: Political and Legal Anthropology Review* 22(2): 53–63.

Coutin, Susan Bibler. 2000. *Legalizing Moves: Salvadoran Immigrants' Struggle for U.S. Residency.* Ann Arbor, MI: University of Michigan Press.

De Genova, Nicholas. 2013. "Spectacles of Migrant 'Illegality': The Scene of Exclusion, the Obscene of Inclusion." *Ethnic and Racial Studies* 36(7): 1180–98.

De León, Jason. 2012. "'Better to Be Hot Than Caught': Excavating the Conflicting Roles of Migrant Material Culture." *American Anthropologist* 114(3): 477–95.

De León, Jason. 2015. *The Land of Open Graves: Living and Dying on the Migrant Trail.* Oakland, CA: University of California Press.

Dinan, Stephen. 2013. "Federal Government Leaves Border Towns with Unpaid Ambulance Bills." *Washington Times.* November 12.

Donahue, Katherine C. 2011. "What Are Heroes For? Commemoration and the Creation of Heroes after September 11." *Anthropology News* 52(6): 6.

Dorsey, Margaret E., and Miguel Díaz-Barriga. 2015. "The Constitution Free Zone in the United States: Law and Life in a State of Carcelment." *POLAR: Political and Legal Anthropology Review* 38(2): 204–25.

Doty, Roxanne Lynn. 2009. *The Law into Their Own Hands: Immigration and the Politics of Exceptionalism.* Tucson, AZ: University of Arizona Press.

Doty, Roxanne Lynn. 2011. "Bare Life: Border-Crossing Deaths and Spaces of Moral Alibi." *Environment and Planning D: Society and Space* 29(4): 599–612.

Dowling, Julie, and Jonathan Xavier Inda, eds. 2013. *Governing Immigration through Crime: A Reader.* Stanford, CA: Stanford University Press.

Dunn, Timothy J. 1996. *The Militarization of the U.S.-Mexico Border, 1978–1992: Low-Intensity Conflict Doctrine Comes Home.* Austin, TX: CMAS Books, University of Texas at Austin.

Fassin, Didier. 2012. *Humanitarian Reason: A Moral History of the Present.* Berkeley: University of California Press.

Feldman, Ilana. 2008. *Governing Gaza: Bureaucracy, Authority, and the Work of Rule, 1917–1967.* Durham, NC: Duke University Press.

Fosher, Kerry B. 2009. *Under Construction: Making Homeland Security at the Local Level.* Chicago: University of Chicago Press.

Glionna, John M. 2016. "Arizona Forensic Sleuths Labor to Identify Migrants Who Perished in Sonoran Desert." *Phoenix New Times.* March 9.

Golash-Boza, Tanya Maria. 2012. *Immigration Nation: Raids, Detentions, and Deportations in Post-9/11 America.* Boulder, CO: Paradigm Publishers.

Gupta, Akhil. 2012. *Red Tape: Bureaucracy, Structural Violence, and Poverty in India.* Durham, NC: Duke University Press.

Haller, John S. 1992. *Farmcarts to Fords: A History of the Military Ambulance, 1790–1925.* Carbondale: Southern Illinois University Press.

Herzfeld, Michael. 1992. *The Social Production of Indifference.* Chicago: University of Chicago Press.

Herzfeld, Michael. 1997. *Cultural Intimacy: Social Poetics in the Nation-State.* New York: Routledge.

Heyman, Josiah McC. 2000. "Respect for Outsiders? Respect for the Law? The Moral Evaluation of High-Scale Issues by US Immigration Officers." *The Journal of the Royal Anthropological Institute* 6(4): 635–52.

Heyman, Josiah McC. 2002. "U.S. Immigration Officers of Mexican Ancestry as Mexican Americans, Citizens, and Immigration Police." *Current Anthropology* 43(3): 479–507.

Heyman, Josiah McC. 2008. "Constructing a Virtual Wall: Race and Citizenship in U.S.-Mexico Border Policing." *Journal of the Southwest* 50(3): 305–33.

Heyman, Josiah McC, Guillermina Núñez, and Victor Talavera. 2009. "Healthcare Access and Barriers for Unauthorized Immigrants in El Paso County, Texas." *Family and Community Health* 32(1): 4–21.

Holmes, Seth M. 2012. "The Clinical Gaze in the Practice of Migrant Health: Mexican Migrants in the United States." *Social Science and Medicine* 74(6): 873–81.

Holmes, Seth M. 2013. *Fresh Fruit, Broken Bodies: Migrant Farmworkers in the United States.* Berkeley: University of California Press.

Hull, Matthew S. 2012. *Government of Paper: The Materiality of Bureaucracy in Urban Pakistan*. Berkeley: University of California Press.

Huschke, Susann. 2014. "Fragile Fabric: Illegality Knowledge, Social Capital and Health-Seeking of Undocumented Latin American Migrants in Berlin." *Journal of Ethnic and Migration Studies* 40(12): 2010–29.

Hutchinson, John F. 1996. *Champions of Charity: War and the Rise of the Red Cross*. Boulder, CO: Westview Press.

Infante, César, Alvaro J. Idrovo, Mario S. Sánchez-Domínguez, Stéphane Vinhas, and Tonatiuh González-Vázquez. 2012. "Violence Committed against Migrants in Transit: Experiences on the Northern Mexican Border." *Journal of Immigrant Minority Health* 14(1): 449–59.

Isacson, Adam, Maureen Meyer, and Ashley Davis. 2013. "Border Security and Migration: A Report from Arizona." *Washington Office on Latin America*. December 5. https://www.wola.org/analysis/border-security-and-migration-a-report-from-arizona/.

Jauregui, Beatrice. 2013. "Beatings, Beacons, and Big Men: Police Disempowerment and Delegitimation in India." *Law and Social Inquiry* 38(3): 643–69.

Jimenez, Maria. 2009. "Humanitarian Crisis: Migrant Deaths at the U.S.-Mexico Border." Report by the American Civil Liberties Union of San Diego and Imperial Counties and Mexico's National Commission of Human Rights. ACLU. October 1. https://www.aclu.org/legal-document/humanitarian-crisis-migrant-deaths-us-mexico-border/.

Jusionyte, Ieva. 2015a. "First Responders Want to Help Migrants, but Immigration Policy Gets in the Way." *Guardian*. September 21.

Jusionyte, Ieva. 2015b. "US, Mexico Depend on Each Other in Emergencies." *Arizona Daily Star*. December 10.

Lakoff, Andrew. 2007. "Preparing for the Next Emergency." *Public Culture* 19(2): 247–71.

Lakoff, Andrew. 2008. "The Generic Biothreat, or, How We Became Unprepared." *Cultural Anthropology* 23(3): 399–428.

Lipsky, Michael. 1980. *Street-Level Bureaucracy: Dilemmas of the Individual in Public Services*. New York: Russell Sage Foundation.

Maclean, Norman. 1992. *Young Men and Fire*. Chicago: University of Chicago Press.

Magaña, Rocío. 2008. "Bodies on the Line: Life, Death, and Authority on the Arizona-Mexico Border." PhD diss., University of Chicago.

Marrow, Helen B. 2012. "Deserving to a Point: Unauthorized Immigrants in San Francisco's Universal Access Healthcare Model." *Social Science & Medicine* 74(6): 846–54.

Martínez, Daniel, Jeremy Slack, and Josiah McC. Heyman. 2013. "Part I: Migrant Mistreatment While in U.S. Custody." In *Bordering on Criminal: The Routine Abuse of Migrants in the Removal System*. Washington, DC: Immigration Policy Center.

Martínez, Oscar. 2014. *The Beast: Riding the Rails and Dodging Narcos on the Migrant Trail*. London: Verso.

Masco, Joseph. 2014. *The Theater of Operations: National Security Affect from the Cold War to the War on Terror.* Durham, NC: Duke University Press.

Maynard-Moody, Steven, and Michael C. Musheno. 2003. *Cops, Teachers, Counselors: Stories from the Front Lines of Public Service.* Ann Arbor, MI: University of Michigan Press.

McGuire, Randall H. 2013. "Steel Walls and Picket Fences: Rematerializing the U.S.-Mexican Border in Ambos Nogales." *American Anthropologist* 115(3): 466–80.

Menjívar, Cecilia, and Leisy J. Abrego. 2012. "Legal Violence: Immigration Law and the Lives of Central American Immigrants." *American Journal of Sociology* 117(5): 1380–1421.

MGT of America. 2002. "Medical Emergency: Costs of Uncompensated Care in Southwest Border Counties." Report published by the United States/Mexico Border Counties Coalition, Washington, DC.

Nevins, Joseph. 2010. *Operation Gatekeeper and Beyond: The War on "Illegals" and the Remaking of the U.S.-Mexico Boundary.* New York: Routledge.

Núñez, Guillermina Gina, and Josiah McC. Heyman. 2007. "Entrapment Processes and Immigrant Communities in a Time of Heightened Border Vigilance." *Human Organization* 66(4): 354–65.

Prendergast, Curt. 2013. "Border Ambulance Leaving City with $250k in Unpaid Bills." *Nogales International.* October 25.

Proudfoot, Jesse, and Eugene J. McCann. 2008. "At Street Level: Bureaucratic Practice in the Management of Urban Neighborhood Change." *Urban Geography* 29(4): 348–70.

Pruitt, Lisa R. 2014. "The Rural Lawscape: Space Tames Law Tames Space." In *The Expanding Spaces of Law: A Timely Legal Geography,* edited by I. Braverman, N. K. Blomley, D. Delaney, and A. Kedar, 190–214. Stanford, CA: Stanford University Press.

Rosenthal, Anat. 2007. "Battling for Survival, Battling for Moral Clarity: 'Illegality' and Illness in the Everyday Struggles of Undocumented HIV+ Women Migrant Workers in Tel Aviv." *International Migration* 45(3): 134–56.

Rothenbuhler, Eric. 2005. "Ground Zero, the Firemen, and the Symbolics of Touch on 9/11 and After." In *Media Anthropology,* edited by E. Rothenbuhler, and W. and M. Coman, 176–87. Thousand Oaks, CA: Sage.

Rubio-Goldsmith, Raquel, M. Melissa McCormick, Daniel Martinez, and Inez Magdalena Duarte. 2006. "The 'Funnel Effect' and Recovered Bodies of Unauthorized Migrants Processed by the Pima County Office of the Medical Examiner, 1990–2005." Report by the Binational Migration Institute, University of Arizona, Tucson, AZ.

Slack, Jeremy, and Scott Whiteford. 2011. "Violence and Migration on the Arizona-Sonora Border." *Human Organization* 70(1): 11–21.

Stuesse, Angela C., and Mathew Coleman. 2014. "Automobility, Immobility, Altermobility: Surviving and Resisting the Intensification of Immigrant Policing." *City and Society* 26(1): 51–72.

Tebeau, Mark. 2003. *Eating Smoke: Fire in Urban America, 1800–1950*. Baltimore, MD: Johns Hopkins University Press.

USBP (U.S. Border Patrol). 1994. "Border Patrol Strategic Plan 1994 and Beyond: National Strategy." *Homeland Security Digital Library*. July. https://www.hsdl.org/?abstract&did=721845.

Vogt, Wendy A. 2013. "Crossing Mexico: Structural Violence and the Commodification of Undocumented Central American Migrants." *American Ethnologist* 40(4): 764–80.

Wacquant, Loïc. 2010. Crafting the Neoliberal State: Workfare, Prisonfare, and Social Insecurity." *Sociological Forum* 25(2): 197–220.

Willen, Sarah S. 2007. "Toward a Critical Phenomenology of 'Illegality': State Power, Criminalization, and Abjectivity among Undocumented Migrant Workers in Tel Aviv, Israel." *International Migration* 45(3): 8–38.

Willen, Sarah S. 2012. "How Is Health-Related 'Deservingness' Reckoned? Perspectives from Unauthorized Im/migrants in Tel Aviv." *Social Science and Medicine* 74(6): 812–21.

Zink, Brian J. 2006. *Anyone, Anything, Anytime: A History of Emergency Medicine*. Philadelphia: Mosby Elsevier.

THREE

E-Terrify

Securitized Immigration and Biometric Surveillance in the Workplace

DANIEL M. GOLDSTEIN AND CAROLINA ALONSO-BEJARANO

With the emergence in the United States of what Nicholas De Genova (2007) has termed "the Homeland Security State" and the rise of the undocumented noncitizen as the state's particular object of regulation and control, policy makers and ordinary citizens alike now regard immigration to the United States as a major threat to national or "homeland" security (Chavez 2008; Inda 2011). Especially since the events of September 11, 2001, public discourse and law enforcement conflate undocumented immigrants with "terrorists," constructing them as challenges to the sovereign territory of the United States who invade the country through clandestine border crossings, most notably at the U.S.-Mexico frontier (Miller 2005; Hing 2006). In addition, the undocumented are imagined as a threat to national populations, the "legal" citizens and residents whose interests are imagined to be in direct opposition to those of the undocumented, who are thought to steal U.S. jobs, overtax U.S. social institutions, and contaminate the bodies and minds of U.S. citizens with their diseases and alien ways. All of this is captured in the concept of "illegality," understood not merely as a legal designation but as an "existential condition," identifying a particular kind of person thought to be different from, and threatening to, the social mainstream (Menjívar and Kanstroom 2015, 2; see also De Genova 2002). The illegalization of millions of undocumented people resident in the United States has produced "shadow populations," communities of the undocumented living in distinct and separate worlds made invisible and insecure by immigration law, even as they remain important contributors to U.S. economic production and consumption (U.S. Select Commission on Immigration and Refugee Policy 1981; Chavez 1998; Coleman and Stuesse 2014). U.S. immigration law and its enforcement thus produce an ingenious contradiction, in which the very people who are supposed to be the cause of national insecurity are themselves rendered among the most insecure people in national space.

Meanwhile, in response to the perceived threat posed by the undocumented, legislators have introduced a variety of laws represented as efforts to confront the "problem" of immigration. The most visible signs of these are at international borders, understood as the front lines in the unending war on terror. At these geopolitical frontiers, laws and technologies both old and new effect increased surveillance of foreigners trying to enter the United States, and enable the Customs and Border Patrol to capture and detain those apprehended crossing without authorization (Cornelius 2004; Levi and Wall 2004; Maguire 2009; Maguire and Fussey 2016). Additionally, the focus of immigration law enforcement has expanded from the nation's borders to include the spaces within those borders, part of the "securitization of immigration"— a shift in national security policy that "reconceptualizes security as the collective management of subnational or transnational threats and the policing of borders and the internal realm, rather than just the defense of territory against external attack" (Faist 2002, 9; see also Bigo 2002; Bourbeau 2011). So, even as the U.S.-Mexico border has in recent years been increasingly militarized, with clandestine border crossings becoming ever-more risky and deadly, the policing of daily life in the cities, suburbs, and small towns of the United States has also intensified, incorporating new programs and technologies of detection and screening that allow for greater policing of immigrant bodies and that recruit new segments of the citizen population to enforce immigration law. This raises levels of anxiety and fear among immigrants who drive cars, send their children to school, walk the streets, or work outside the home.

Mathew Coleman and Angela Stuesse (2014) have suggested that we consider these varied forms of immigrant policing—both within and at the edges of national space—in terms of *geopolitics* and *biopolitics,* concepts that scholars of immigration typically differentiate but that here are better understood as working in concert to produce and regulate immigrant shadow populations. Whereas border control is a geopolitical (or, for Coleman and Stuesse, a topographical) system by which transborder movement is regulated (today through a strategy of "prevention through deterrence," which forces immigrants into rougher and more dangerous terrain, intended to discourage immigration; De León 2015), the biopolitical (or topological) regulation of immigrants reaches beyond the specific site of the border, penetrating the interior of the nation and impacting immigrant daily life. Border geopolitics represents a "hard" system of enforcement, involving the building of walls and detention centers and making the United States into a "zone of confinement" (Coutin 2010), contained by razor wire, metal fences, and concrete, and thus ever more difficult to enter (and re-enter). Interior biopolitics, on the other hand, includes "soft" forms of immigrant regulation, unlocalized and immanent, which shape the behavior of undocumented people within the United States while dangling the continual threat of removal. "Soft" tactics of immigrant policing include hindering immigrants' ability to drive to work or to transport their children to school, limiting their "automobility" and making their lives more difficult (Stuesse and Coleman 2014). Immigrants have to alter their behavior to accommodate these interventions; and while some may elect to "self deport" (see Kobach 2008), the majority remain in the shadows, ever-more constrained in their options and liberties. The biopolitics of immigrant control target behavior modification rather than deportation, threatening removal without actually removing anyone: "interior enforcement in the main," Coleman and Stuesse say (2014, 52), "works by using the looming threat of territorial banishment as a result of traffic enforcement and other social reproduction-specific policing, in conjunction with the specter of lethal geopolitical infrastructures like the U.S.-Mexico border, to regulate the ways in which resident undocumented immigrant communities learn to socially reproduce as well as work."

In this chapter, we examine the biopolitical regulation of immigrant behavior through another form of "social reproduction-specific policing," this one centered on the immigrant workplace. Our focus is a web-based biometric technology called E-Verify, which allows employers to determine their applicants' and current workers' eligibility to work in the United States. Since the passage of the Immigration Reform and Control Act (IRCA) of 1986, federal law has prohibited employers from knowingly hiring people not authorized to work in the United States. Meanwhile, lawmakers have struggled to balance the popular demand to protect the nation from the perceived immigrant threat with the demands of U.S. capital, which requires a steady supply of cheap undocumented labor (Zlolniski 2006). E-Verify serves these contradictory interests. An instrument for what is known as worksite employment eligibility enforcement (Newman et al. 2012), E-Verify introduces the threat of deportation into the jobsite by promising to reveal the presence of an undocumented worker to the state. It instills fear in undocumented people, discouraging them from pursuing their rights as workers while granting employers new disciplinary powers to pacify workers who threaten to do so (compare with previous studies, e.g., Heyman 1998; Zlolniski 2003). As a biometric tool, E-Verify deputizes private-sector employers as immigration control officers, empowering them to determine who is and who is not eligible to work and whether or not to expose the ineligible to the gaze of the state (Stumpf 2012). The technology sorts laboring bodies by their legal status, augmenting undocumented workers' vulnerability to exploitation without actually removing them from the space of the United States. At the same time, E-Verify conveys to the citizen public the appearance that the government is "serious" about immigration enforcement. Through E-Verify, the workplace becomes another site of immigrant surveillance and recognition, exploiting undocumented people's "legal nonexistence" to enhance their vulnerability and submissiveness (Heyman 2001; Coutin 2003; Horton 2015). E-Verify signals legislators' compliance with the politically popular goal of deporting all undocumented immigrants while maintaining the increasingly precarious subclass of noncitizen workers required by U.S. business interests.

Scholars of immigration have debated whether immigration law is in fact intended to serve as labor law—that is, whether federal policy on immigration is designed with immigrant impact on labor markets explicitly taken into consideration (see, e.g., Delgado 1993; Heyman 1998). Clearly, E-Verify represents a direct intervention by the U.S. government in the sites where immigrants work; the fact that use of E-Verify is expanding even though the technology fails to achieve its stated objectives (discussed below) suggests that "immigration policies [and, we would add, technologies] that appear self-contradictory and ineffectual . . . are actually quite effective at maintaining a large and vulnerable undocumented work force" in the United States (Gomberg-Muñoz and Nussbaum-Barberena 2011, 367). Furthermore, as our ethnography shows, E-Verify is successful at instilling fear in the undocumented noncitizen—not least of all due to the lack of understanding about E-Verify among the immigrant population—and immigrant workers modify their behaviors in response. E-Verify, it can thus be argued, represents an effective biopolitical tool for a "soft" immigration policing, enacting policy prescriptions and controlling threatening populations through the deployment of biometric technology that gestures to the "hard" enforcement of the geopolitical border and so functions in collaboration with it. E-Verify screens out ineligible workers while neither detaining nor removing them from national space; it inspires fear in the objects of its attention, shaping consciousness and bodily praxis without providing the recognition that might convey rights or underwrite claims for citizenship or national belonging.

E-Verify: Biometric Surveillance in the Workplace

E-Verify, while a relatively recent innovation, is not unprecedented as a form of biopolitical regulation. Beginning in the late 1970s but intensifying in the 1990s, federal authorities expanded policing of the U.S.-Mexico border as its principal strategy to control undocumented immigration into the country (Nevins 2002). The plan was to fortify the border itself through the "hard" technologies of enforcement: stronger and higher fencing across a wider expanse of terrain; increased surveillance through lighting, video cameras, and heat-sensitive detection equipment; and a significant increase in Border Patrol personnel. This approach to immigration control was authorized through federal legislation like the Illegal Immigration Reform and Immigrant Responsibility Act (IIRIRA) of 1996, which criminalized violation of U.S. immigration laws and expanded the range of people who could be deported on the basis of such violations (Dowling and Inda 2013). Already ten years earlier, authorities had begun to turn their attention to the regulation of immigrant life within the territory of the United States itself. Most significant was the Immigration Reform and Control Act of 1986 (IRCA), which Jonathan Xavier Inda (2013, 303) says, "helped set in motion the contemporary practice of targeting 'criminal aliens' for deportation."[1] The act not only increased funding and support for enhanced border enforcement in the U.S. Southwest while authorizing the "expeditious" deportation of "criminal aliens"; it also criminalized the hiring of undocumented workers, imposing sanctions on employers who knowingly employed the undocumented (Rosenblum and Kandel 2011), making the workplace another site of immigrant policing.

In the aftermath of 9/11, the expansion of immigrant regulation into the heartland of the United States intensified (Meissner et al. 2013), a process that Cecilia Menjívar (2014) calls the "insourcing" of the border. This effort was framed by the Department of Homeland Security (DHS) in terms of securing the homeland against terror, which required "developing a 'continuum of border security,' treating the territorial boundaries of the United States and the interior as a seamless security space" (DHS 2010; Inda 2013, 299). One mechanism for this already in place was section 287(g) of the Immigration and Nationality Act of 1965 (added under section 133 of IIRIRA in 1996), which allowed local and state police departments to partner with Immigration and Customs Enforcement (ICE), essentially deputizing them as immigration officers within their own districts. This was supplemented by the program called Secure Communities (2008), the Obama administration's signature immigration control policy, which ran until 2014. Secure Communities allowed ICE to penetrate the ordinary spaces of immigrant life, extending federal reach via technology into local policing jurisdictions (Coleman 2012). Under Secure Communities, all those arrested for any offense were biometrically screened for immigration violations; a positive "hit" for such a violation resulted in ICE issuing a detainer, a request to local authorities that the individual be held for up to forty-eight hours to allow ICE to determine if an order of removal should be issued. Laws and programs such as IRCA and Secure Communities are best understood as biopolitical technologies in societies of control (Deleuze 1992; Coleman and Stuesse 2014). They are regulatory apparatuses through which the everyday lives of people—but especially immigrants of color—are subjectivized for intervention and management, biometrically selected for detention and deportation (Gold 2012), and disposed of for the purification and well-being of the social body.

The employment provisions of IRCA extended the border into the workplace, a process that has intensified through the use of E-Verify. E-Verify is a web-based platform that enables employers to check the work eligibility of job applicants and current employees using the data on the federal I-9 employment eligibility form, which is to be completed by all job applicants at the time of hiring. The system checks individuals against databases of the DHS and the Social Security Administration to confirm that an individual is legally authorized to work, mainly by establishing that they have a valid name and Social

Security number (USCIS 2015). In 2010, E-Verify added a "photo matching" tool, a biometric component intended to provide another layer of certainty to the determination.[2] The E-Verify website is remarkably free of politics, and no reference is made to immigrants or immigration. We have not even been able to find a statement describing what the E-Verify program is intended to achieve. The website does, however, contain a strong privacy statement, rather striking under the circumstances, claiming that "E-Verify is committed to protecting your privacy and civil liberties with the same rigor that DHS places on protecting our homeland" (USCIS n.d.). The intended audience here is clearly citizens, whose "privacy and civil liberties" are apparently threatened by undocumented job seekers stealing their employment opportunities.

Problems with E-Verify abound. The system is often criticized as unreliable because it depends on inaccurate databases, imposes undue financial burdens on employers, and leaves immigrant workers vulnerable to subjective determinations about their legal status (Patel 2010). While the system functions adequately to identify U.S. citizens, noncitizens with work authorization are much more likely to experience false denials of permission to work (Westat 2012). Moreover, other critics of the system argue that its implementation results in employment discrimination based on race or national origin (Liao 2013), as "some employers may be more reluctant to hire any worker who fits whatever profile the employer may associate with undocumented workers" (Good 2013, 4283). Others fear that E-Verify presents an obstacle to the freedom of movement for workers and employers, and subjects many dimensions of U.S. citizens' lives to government control (Harper 2012; Kravets 2013).

At first glance, E-Verify seems to be an effective tool for discouraging employment of the undocumented and for encouraging immigrants to relocate, either to states that don't mandate E-Verify or to another country entirely. However, on closer examination it becomes clear that the technology does little to impact the overall labor market. In Arizona, for example, where E-Verify was first implemented on a statewide scale under the Legal Arizona Workers Act (LAWA), the reduction in the size of the undocumented workforce had no positive corollary for native U.S. workers in terms of employment: Studies found that low-skilled, non-Hispanic, native-born white men in Arizona in fact experienced a 4 percent *lower* employment rate, a decline that the investigators statistically linked to the E-Verify law (Bohn, Lofstrom, and Raphael 2015).[3] In addition, the Arizona law contains a loophole that exempts independent contractors from the E-Verify requirement. Even as they found a significant decline in the number of unauthorized workers holding formal jobs in Arizona, Bohn, Lofstrom, and Rafael (2015) also noted an 8 percent increase in "self-employment" among unauthorized workers, suggesting that many of the people forced out of the formal sector found work in an expanding informal sector (Lofstrom, Bohn, and Raphael 2011; Menjívar and Enchautegui 2015). As these jobs tend to contain fewer wage and benefits guarantees, the resulting situation is all the more precarious for unskilled, undocumented workers and their families, many of whom remain in Arizona in conditions of augmented vulnerability and invisibility. The effect of mandated E-Verify in Arizona appears to be a deepening of precarity for marginal workers; overall, "there is evidence that undocumented workers are being pushed further to the periphery of the labor market in the wake of" the move to E-Verify and other forms of enhanced immigrant policing (Hall and Greenman 2015, 407).

Notably, E-Verify augments the employer's role as a frontline enforcer of immigration policy while posing little risk to the employer of the undocumented. As with IRCA before them, E-Verify laws contain sanctions (including fines and loss of business license) for employers who don't use the technology or who hire the undocumented; in practice, again as with IRCA, these stipulations of the law are rarely enforced. In Arizona, E-Verify compliance among employers remained "spotty" five years after it became mandatory in the state, with only 43 percent of employers enrolled in the system, and only 19 percent among businesses employing fewer than five people (Henke 2013). Virtually none of the noncompliant employers had been sanctioned. Legal scholars (e.g., Lee 2009) speculate that the state prefers to ignore employer violations of the law in exchange for the role that employers now play in identifying undocumented immigrants for removal. The result of this collusion between state and private enterprise is that employers have become "immigration decision makers," free to decide whether or not to run employees through the E-Verify system and thereby reveal their presence to the authorities. This is a one-way street, however: "unencumbered by fear of being punished, employers can threaten to report workers for removal, whereas workers do not possess any similar ability to blow the whistle on employers" (Lee 2009, 1105–6). Undocumented workers, of course, are not "unencumbered by fear"; to the contrary, the threat of being run through E-Verify is often enough to cow a worker seeking her rights under federal labor law, which protects all workers regardless of immigration status (Hall and Greenman 2015). The vulnerability of undocumented workers to the threat of exposure is further heightened during difficult economic times (which, incidentally, tend to coincide with upticks in the passage of harsh employment laws [Ellis et al. 2014]), when employers gain even greater leverage over their workers due to the scarcity of other local options (Menjívar and Enchautegui 2015). As Sarah Horton (2016) has noted, employers can also create "denounce-ability" in their workers by requiring them to work under someone else's identity papers, making them vulnerable to charges of "identity theft," a situation only worsened by the threatened use of E-Verify (see also Stuesse 2010). These facts demonstrate the negative impact of E-Verify on workers, who are discouraged from organizing or making demands on employers who could threaten them with deportation. Employers, meanwhile, benefit from enhanced control over more disciplined workers, and enjoy the lower costs associated with the shift to a more informal workforce.

E-Verify, then, combines the "hard" federal threat of jail and removal with the "softer" state incitement to hide, relocate, or self-deport. Although E-Verify is not technically about immigrant removal, the existence of the militarized border, though not locally present, is a persistent reminder of the precarious situation of the undocumented and the potential for deportation if they step out of line. Fear and anxiety are the common responses to this situation, feelings that are intensified by the crosscutting, mutually reinforcing laws across legal scales: "Federal laws control who comes in and who is expelled, and policies at the state and local levels shape how immigrants live once they are in the country, in effect, complementing each other. Indeed, a key feature of the U.S. immigration regime today is its multilayered character, composed of federal, state, and local legislation with each layer magnifying the power and control of the other layers" (Menjívar and Enchautegui 2015, 111). E-Verify in this context operates in conjunction with other laws and practices to push undocumented workers out of the legal employment market and into underground settings where they are even more exploitable. The terror and anxiety found in such settings is typical of what one might expect to find among the "shadow populations" of the United States.

"The Dream Will Turn into a Nightmare": E-Verify in Hometown

Our ethnographic analysis of E-Verify and its effects is based in a place we call "Hometown, NJ" a pseudonym that resonates ironically with the ubiquitous "homeland security" agenda, and indexes the Bruce Springsteen song "My Hometown." (Springsteen was born and raised in central New Jersey.)

Hometown is a small borough with a population of about 15,000 residents. Over the course of four years (2011–2015), we engaged in a research project in activist anthropology, a disciplinary stance and mode of conducting research that is explicitly collaborative and constructive in its approach (for a small sample of the literature, see Speed 2006; Hale 2008; and Stuesse 2015). Thus, the research questions and methodology were developed in consultation with local advocacy organizations and with undocumented immigrants themselves, and were designed to focus on issues of particular concern to them in order to develop understandings that would serve the community in its struggles. We trained local individuals to participate in data collection, and two undocumented women became particularly close, serving as paid collaborators in the project. Using an ethnographic methodology of qualitative data collection, our four-person team (the authors of this chapter and two undocumented residents of Hometown) recorded over 100 individual and focus-group interviews and wrote thousands of pages of field notes describing our daily activities of participant-observation. Additionally, the four of us worked as volunteers in two local advocacy organizations, participating in the day-to-day work of legal advocacy and assisting people to cope with the challenges of living undocumented; Goldstein served for two years on the executive committee of one of these organizations.

New Jersey is an interesting state in which to study immigration, in part due to its history as a collection of autonomous municipalities, complicating any attempt to generalize about the state as a whole.[4] In terms of immigration law, some New Jersey towns are highly securitized, with restrictive municipal ordinances that limit undocumented immigrants' ability to work, rent property, or own businesses, while others are "sanctuary cities" that exhibit a welcoming stance toward immigrants. The state is thus a patchwork of contiguous and sometimes overlapping political, legal, and social milieus through which immigrants move in the course of their daily rounds of work, school, socializing, and home. For immigrants, this patchwork is particularly critical in terms of immigration law: as discussed above, state and municipal laws operate in concert with federal law, and there is a substantial degree of variation across localities (Provine and Varsanyi 2012; Menjívar and Enchautegui 2015). New Jersey is a popular destination for immigrants arriving to the United States. On a per capita basis only California and New York have larger nonnative populations; New Jersey ranks fourth in the nation (after Nevada, California, and Arizona) in the percentage of its workforce that is undocumented (Fine et al. 2014), and as a whole it is a relatively tolerant state as far as immigration law is concerned. The state legislature, for example, has consistently voted against requiring E-Verify statewide (initiatives to mandate its use failed in the legislature in 2008, 2010, 2012, and 2014). But there is substantial variation across municipalities, a fact to which undocumented workers must attend as they travel between jobs or simply shop for groceries in an unfamiliar town.

Floating like an island in the middle of a vast suburban sea of what used to be farmland, Hometown Borough is a close-packed cluster of colorful wood-frame houses and stone storefronts centered around an old Town Hall. Parts of Hometown look like classic middle America. There is a historic Main Street, a stately courthouse with white pillars fronting a trim green lawn, and many beautiful old homes with porch swings and American flags. Not far from the Jersey Turnpike and the Garden State Parkway, Hometown is a bucolic place for commuters to reside, an escape from the workday in New York City. More recently, Hometown has also emerged as an ideal place for the settlement of undocumented immigrants who live in the borough and work in the surrounding suburbs. Indeed, a predominantly white town where racial minorities were almost exclusively African American until the mid-1990s, in the past twenty years Hometown has seen a so-called "illegal invasion" (Kelsey 2007) and is now about 50 percent Latino (mostly Mexicans, but also Peruvians, Guatemalans, and others).

Relations between Hometown residents and the newcomers have not historically been cozy. In January 2004, a group of local residents and Latin American immigrants filed a suit in federal court against the borough on behalf of its Latino day laborers. The suit argued that an antiloitering ordinance passed in 2003 prohibiting workers from congregating in public spaces to wait for work was unlawful. In April 2004 a federal judge ruled in the plaintiffs' favor, stating that the borough was violating Latino workers' right to seek employment. In the aftermath, Hometown Borough has become a relatively safe place for immigrants to reside. The people—Latino, African American, and white—who came together to fight the municipality subsequently formed Casa Hometown, an immigrant rights advocacy organization that offers various services to immigrant workers and their families in central New Jersey. The police no longer harass workers in the muster zone, and the municipality has ceased its midnight "home inspections" intended to surprise people crowded into unauthorized housing. Many of the undocumented people we know in Hometown express a strong sense of security about living there. They try to avoid unnecessary contact with the police and with situations that might bring them unwanted exposure to the federal immigrant detection system, but many of them believe that "as long as you don't go breaking the law the police will leave you alone."[5] Many others express a surprising confidence in the local authorities and even told us about instances in which they called the police on someone else (in most cases a *patrón* who refused to pay them their salary at the end of the day), arguing that the police are there to protect their rights as well.

But Hometown Borough is part of the New Jersey patchwork of municipalities, and the policies and politics of one town have implications for others. Hometown Borough is an island in the sea of Hometown Township, the neighboring town that completely surrounds the Borough of the same name. Or, to mix metaphors, Hometown Borough is the hole in the Township's donut, and the two places couldn't be more different (compare with Coleman's [2012] work in North Carolina communities). Whereas Hometown Borough (in the aftermath of the federal lawsuit and the changing demographics that followed) is now relatively tolerant of immigrants and is less than 40 percent white, Hometown Township is 85 percent white and immigrants are only welcome insofar as they are there as contracted laborers. Immigrant residents of the Borough do not like to enter the Township for fear of being stopped by the police on any imaginable pretext. Driving with a broken taillight, for example, or riding with too many people in the car, or riding a bike on the sidewalk, or "loitering" (i.e., waiting for work in the parking lot of a convenience store) can be enough to get you arrested. And once you are arrested, you are fed into the ICE computer, and from there it is a short step to detention and deportation.[6]

Nor do people entirely trust the police of Hometown Borough. Despite some people's willingness to call the police in emergencies, other immigrant residents of Hometown are less trusting, adopting a range of behavioral self-monitoring techniques to limit their contact with the authorities and so minimize the risk of detection, detention, and deportation. Some of these self-disciplinary practices are learned passively through observing other immigrants, or one's parents and friends. Others are explicitly taught. Experienced immigrants instruct new arrivals on how to comport themselves to avoid detection. A Mexican immigrant named Mayer says that when he first came to Hometown, his cousin taught him the rules.[7] Don't drink, he told him, because alcohol can make you noisy, or violent, and either way the cops may be called. Don't go to parties for the same reason. Don't shoplift—it may seem like a small thing, but if you are caught you can be deported. Don't go out after dark, when your presence on the street may attract attention. Make sure not to litter. And so on. Undocumented workers learn the regulatory geography of the New Jersey patchwork and know in which towns they are safer and in which they are more in danger of detection (e.g., through more aggressive policing practices). The emphasis in all of these trainings, both formal and informal, is preparedness, a message echoed locally by workers at Casa Hometown and at the national level by organizations like the National Day Laborer Organizing Network (NDLON) and Domestic Workers United (DWU).

Despite their best efforts to avoid detection, undocumented residents of Hometown—like undocumented people nationwide—have recently begun to encounter new forms of regulation in the workplace through the imposition of E-Verify, which can electronically invade spaces that immigrants previously perceived as "safe." New Jersey does not require employers to use E-Verify, but many elect to use it for the benefits it grants them as employers, as discussed above. This creates another quasi-legal patchwork overlaid atop the jurisdictional patchwork that already constitutes the political geography of the state, though one that is harder for potential workers to identify and map out in their self-disciplining. The challenge lies in anticipating whether or not they will be screened upon applying for a job, or whether or not their current employer might decide to adopt E-Verify and require worker screenings. Of course, many undocumented people do have documents. Some of these documents are fakes that people purchased upon their arrival in the United States, and which enable them to pay income and Social Security taxes, but more often people borrow or buy the papers of a citizen or legal resident, sometimes giving a percentage of their earnings to the owners of the documents (Horton 2015).[8] Indeed, acquiring someone else's valid papers can be seen as a rational response to the possibility of encountering E-Verify in the workplace, though this strategy is not without risks. As one interviewee told us, "a solution to [E-Verify] is to buy someone's Social Security number. But then that can be even worse because using someone else's Social is a crime. If you are caught, the dream will turn into a nightmare."[9]

The fear of encountering E-Verify comes partly from not knowing if a fake or purchased Social Security number is adequate to the test of the biometric database. Although E-Verify is not explicitly designed to deport undocumented immigrants, people who spend their lives in fear of immigration authorities and deportation are threatened by a program that requires them to present their Social Security card to their employer and risk being "outed" as undocumented. Silvia, a longtime undocumented resident of Hometown, described the fear she felt when asked by her employer of thirteen years to present her Social Security card so her information could be entered into E-Verify; she told us that she "became very afraid of immigration. After thirteen years it was a difficult decision to present my papers."[10] Silvia decided not to quit her job but instead submitted the fake Social Security card she bought twenty years ago, right after arriving in Hometown. Miraculously, her Social Security number was accepted by the system and she was able to keep her job. But the terror and anxiety she felt in the encounter were very real.

Not everyone is as lucky as Silvia, though. Many people lose their jobs once their data is processed; others simply resign when asked for their papers. Losing their jobs due to E-Verify further destabilizes people's employment security, pushing them into more insecure situations as they choose to remain in New Jersey. People in Hometown describe how their encounters with employment eligibility verification forced them to move from one job to the next, changing positions each time an employer threatened to use E-Verify, or to search for jobs where the employer wouldn't be using the technology. Clementina, another undocumented resident of Hometown, recently got a job working at a fast-food restaurant. Fortunately, she says, this restaurant does not use E-Verify; but the nearby McDonald's does, and many of her friends at that place fled their jobs in advance of being screened. As in Arizona, where LAWA has pushed many undocumented workers out of formal jobs and into the informal economy, New Jersey residents also move from formal, full-time jobs to contracted, temporary work. These jobs usually consist of domestic or construction day labor and are significantly more precarious than the stable—if barely adequate—biweekly paychecks offered by more formal employers.

Informal workers are especially vulnerable to wage theft and on-the-job injuries, a situation made even more precarious by the use of E-Verify. Flavio, a longtime Hometown resident who works as a day laborer doing construction, was fired by his boss after having a work accident. This is not an uncommon occurrence: employers often deny workers their right to compensation for work injuries by dismissing them, believing that the worker will not pursue her or his rights for fear of being exposed as undocumented. E-Verify makes this practice even easier to employ. As Flavio said: "[My boss] told me I wasn't fired due to my accident. He said he is now using E-Verify and I needed to show him my Social if I wanted to keep my job."[11] Regardless of his undocumented status, Flavio knew he had the right to receive compensation after his work accident, but his employer's request for a valid Social Security Card was enough to discourage him. "People told me it was just an excuse to fire me," Flavio told us, "but I decided to leave things at that and look for another job."

These feelings of insecurity and anxiety are not only linked to the fear of being detained and deported, but to economic worries as well. Although deportation figures largely in the scholarly literature on immigration, economic insecurity is a powerful force shaping the behaviors and politics of undocumented immigrants. Juana, who lost her job at a fast-food restaurant due to E-Verify, told us, "this really affected me both emotionally and economically. I have three kids and I had a good job that helped me provide for them. I now have to start from zero and get used to a totally different job. I was making sixteen dollars an hour. Going back to making eight dollars an hour deeply affects me and my family. . . . I didn't [even] receive any compensation from my employer after working for her for seventeen years."[12] And this was not only her loss, Juana says. In her own words, "with E-Verify we lose because we can't provide for our families, employers lose because they won't have people to work for them, and the state [of New Jersey] loses because even if we have fake papers we still pay taxes every month. If we Hispanics stop paying taxes, New Jersey has much to lose."[13]

The fear that accompanies E-Verify is intensified by people's lack of knowledge of the legal system, and the resulting uncertainty and confusion further contribute to people's insecurity. Apart from the NGO Casa Hometown and some private law offices, there are few venues for undocumented people in Hometown to learn about immigration policies and laws. As a result, they are often confused as to what exactly E-Verify is. Clementina, for example, associates the McDonalds' workers "Fight for $15" campaign for a higher minimum wage with the company's use of E-Verify: "They got rid of all of their undocumented immigrants and now people working for 7 dollars an hour have papers and are asking for their rights."[14] Not coincidentally, Clementina associates E-Verify with the loss of or inability to claim workers' rights. Another interviewee named Roberta told us that "E-Verify is a tool for deportation. It is a law that allows cops to ask for your papers at any point."[15] When we asked Yuri if she's ever had to deal with E-Verify, she proceeded to tell us a story about her place of employment, a local nursery and garden center, being raided by ICE: "E-Verify sent my employer an email saying they'd be checking everyone's papers and then they showed up at my work asking for our documentation. Two months later ICE agents returned and demanded that the employer fire twenty-one of us whose Social Security numbers turned out to be false."[16] What is interesting about this story is that E-Verify is unrelated to physical ICE raids (though it is connected to what have been called "silent raids," in which ICE electronically audits employer records to identify undocumented workers; see Menjívar and Enchautegui 2015, 109). What Yuri perceived to be E-Verify was a routine workplace raid, probably (as her employer ventured) in response to a disgruntled former employee's finger-pointing. Within the complex network of local and national immigration legislation that undocumented people in Hometown have to navigate on a daily basis, E-Verify takes on a life of its own in the minds of the people it targets. In this context, E-Verify, like the highly securitized U.S.-Mexico border, does not keep people away from Hometown but rather makes them more afraid—and therefore more prone to exploitation and abuse.

Conclusion

The border, as mentioned, has been insourced or interiorized, so that it is now everywhere in the United States, an immanent frontier of politics and control situated not merely at the edges but inside the body of the nation. But as our ethnography shows, the border has also been interiorized within the bodies of undocumented people themselves. Authorities seeking to manage the immigrants' presence in the United States have targeted their internal worlds for disciplining, deploying sophisticated regulatory regimes to terrorize undocumented people and thus influence their behavior (compare with Willen 2007). This terror is all the more intense as these regulatory technologies become increasingly pervasive in daily life.

E-Verify is one technology by which this interiorization is accomplished. It is part of the biopolitics of immigrant policing, a form of "soft" regulation that pushes undocumented people into shadow populations and underground economies, where they are made even more vulnerable, their labor rendered even cheaper and more accessible to the needs of U.S. capital, their ability to demand their rights as workers inhibited. As Ruth Gomberg-Muñoz and Laura Nussbaum-Barberena have observed (2011, 366; citing Delgado 1993, 58), "cheap labor is not necessarily docile labor," and E-Verify as a biopolitical instrument is effective in generating worker docility. The production of terror is critical in this regard: Through technologies such as E-Verify, the state can penetrate the inner world of the undocumented immigrant to effect a particular policy outcome by inducing fear of deportation within the subject and causing them to make choices that appear to be agentive but are in fact highly overdetermined. In this, E-Verify and other immigration-related technologies, laws, and programs are not unlike other forms of neoliberal governmentality (Inda 2013), which strive to inculcate particular subject dispositions marked by qualities of self-regulation and individual responsibility—here, the immigrant is even expected to become the primary actor responsible for her own removal.

Although the securitization of immigration is a phenomenon of the twenty-first century, the political power of fear has a long history as part of the public discourse about immigration in the United States (Ngai 2004). Indeed, if fear of the terrorist, criminal, undocumented immigrant has been mobilized in the United States to rally support for the increasing securitization and interiorization of the U.S. border, fear of detention and deportation has also been mobilized to keep the noncitizen and her family in place. But if technologies such as E-Verify are intended to terrify, they are also unlikely to make the undocumented give up the promise of finding prosperity for themselves and their families in the United States. What this reveals, however, are the ways in which state-sponsored security discourses and programs cultivate fear among all segments of the population, citizen and undocumented alike, contributing to a climate of racism, uncertainty, and despair with which everyone must cope.

Notes

1   "Criminal aliens" is the term used by immigration authorities to refer to an undocumented immigrant who has been convicted of a felony or misdemeanor (Inda 2013, 293).

2   There has been some debate in the media about whether or not E-Verify actually constitutes a biometric program, given that it largely relies on name and Social Security number to establish a person's identity. Others argue that these are indeed biometrics, and the inclusion of the photographic requirement seems to obviate any doubt. For more, see Jason Green (2013) and David Kravets (2013).

3   Unfortunately, this study (like most of the other studies reviewed in preparing this chapter) does not provide data on the employment effects of LAWA on other categorical population groups (e.g., African Americans, Native Americans). This seems to be something of a pattern with strictly quantitative analyses of E-Verify.

4   For a comprehensive history of New Jersey, see Maxine Lurie and Richard Veit (2012).

5   Field notes.

6   Although federal policy under the Priority Enforcement Program (PEP), which went into effect in July 2015, is now intended to target only the most dangerous or criminal immigrants, the decision on whether or not to process a detainee through ICE remains at the discretion of local or state police and judges. Thus, in a place such as Hometown Township, it is likely that detention and deportation rates will remain similar to what they were under Secure Communities.

7   All names are pseudonyms, to protect the identities of our undocumented research collaborators.

8   These facts run contrary to the common belief that the undocumented do not pay taxes on their salaries. On the contrary, undocumented workers pay billions of dollars annually in income taxes using false documents or those of other people, including Social Security taxes to which they will later have no claim (American Immigration Council 2011). Many undocumented workers also have a legitimate Individual Taxpayer Identification Number (ITIN) that they receive from the government and with which they pay income taxes.

9   Interview, Hometown Borough, September 23, 2014.

10   Interview, Hometown Borough, September 23, 2014.

11   Interview, Hometown Borough, September 18, 2014.

12   Interview, Hometown Borough, October 10, 2014.

13   Interview, Hometown Borough, October 10, 2014.

14   Interview, Hometown Borough, September 18, 2014.

15   Interview, Hometown Borough, September 18, 2014.

16   Interview, Hometown Borough, October 22, 2014.

References

American Immigration Council. 2011. "Unauthorized Immigrants Pay Taxes, Too: Estimates of the State and Local Taxes Paid by Unauthorized Immigrant Households." *American Immigration Council.* April 18. https://www.american immigrationcouncil.org/research/unauthorized-immigrants-pay-taxes-too.

Bigo, Didier. 2002. "Security and Immigration: Toward a Critique of the Governmentality of Unease." *Alternatives* 27: 63–92.

Bohn, Sarah, Magnus Lofstrom, and Steven Raphael. 2015. "Do E-Verify Mandates Improve Labor Market Outcomes of Low-Skilled Native and Legal Immigrant Workers?" *Southern Economic Journal* 81(4): 960–79.

Bourbeau, Philippe. 2011. *The Securitization of Migration: A Study of Movement and Order.* London: Routledge.

Chavez, Leo. 1998. *Shadowed Lives: Undocumented Immigrants in American Society.* 2nd ed. Fort Worth, TX: Harcourt Brace.

Chavez, Leo. 2008. *The Latino Threat: Constructing Immigrants, Citizens, and the Nation*. Stanford, CA: Stanford University Press.

Coleman, Mathew. 2012. "The 'Local' Migration State: The Site-Specific Devolution of Immigration Enforcement in the U.S. South." *Law and Policy* 34(2): 159–90.

Coleman, Mathew, and Angela Stuesse. 2014. "Policing Borders, Policing Bodies: The Territorial and Biopolitical Roots of U.S. Immigration Control." In *Placing the Border in Everyday Life*, edited by Reece Jones and Corey Johnson, 33–63. Farnham, UK: Ashgate.

Cornelius, Wayne A. 2004. "Controlling 'Unwanted' Immigration: Lessons from the United States, 1993–2004." Working Paper Number 92, Center for Comparative Immigration Studies, University of California at San Diego.

Coutin, Susan B. 2003. "Borderlands, Illegality, and the Space of Non-Existence." In *Globalization under Construction: Governmentality, Law, and Identity*, edited by Richard Perry and Bill Maurer, 171–202. Minneapolis, MN: University of Minnesota Press.

Coutin, Susan B. 2010. "Confined Within: National Territories as Zones of Confinement." *Political Geography* 29(2): 200–8.

De Genova, Nicholas. 2002. "Migrant 'Illegality' and Deportability in Everyday Life." *Annual Review of Anthropology* 31: 419–47.

De Genova, Nicholas. 2007. "The Production of Culprits: From Deportability to Detainability in the Aftermath of 'Homeland Security.'" *Citizenship Studies* 11(5): 421–48.

De León, Jason. 2015. *Land of Open Graves: Living and Dying on the Migrant Trail*. Berkeley: University of California Press.

Deleuze, Gilles. 1992. *Postscript on Control Societies: Negotiations 1972–1990*. New York: Columbia University Press.

Delgado, Hector. 1993. *New Immigrants, Old Unions: Organizing Undocumented Workers in Los Angeles*. Philadelphia: Temple University Press.

DHS (Department of Homeland Security). 2010. *Endgame: Office of Detention and Removal Strategic Plan, 2003–2012*. Washington, DC: DHS.

Dowling, Julie A., and Jonathan Xavier Inda. 2013. Introduction to *Governing Immigration through Crime: A Reader*, edited by Julie A. Dowling and Jonathan Xavier Inda, 1–36. Stanford, CA: Stanford University Press.

Ellis, Mark, Richard Wright, Matthew Townley, and Kristy Copeland. 2014. "The Migration Response to the Legal Arizona Workers Act." *Political Geography* 42: 46–56.

Faist, Thomas. 2002. "Extension du Domaine de la Lutte: International Migration and Security before and after September 11, 2001." *International Migration Review* 36(1): 7–14.

Fine, Janice, Anastasia Mann, David Tulloch, and F. Scott Bentley. 2014. *Meet the Neighbors: Organizational and Spatial Dynamics of Immigrant New Jersey*. New Brunswick, NJ: Rutgers Immigrant Infrastructure Mapping Project, Eagleton Program on Immigration and Democracy, Eagleton Institute of Politics, Rutgers University.

Gold, Steve. 2012. "Border Control Biometrics and Surveillance." *Biometric Technology Today* (July/August): 9–11.

Gomberg-Muñoz, Ruth, and Laura Nussbaum-Barberena. 2011. "Is Immigration Policy Labor Policy? Immigration Enforcement, Undocumented Workers, and the State." *Human Organization* 70(4): 366–75.

Good, Michael. 2013. "Do Immigrant Outflows Lead to Native Inflows? An Empirical Analysis of the Migratory Responses to U.S. State Immigration Legislation." *Applied Economics* 45(30): 4275–97.

Green, Jason. 2013. "The Immigration Bill Does NOT Create a Biometric Database of All Adult Americans." *Daily Beast*. May 13.

Hale, Charles R. 2008. Introduction to *Engaging Contradictions: Theory, Politics, and Methods of Activist Scholarship*, edited by Charles R. Hale, 1–28. Berkeley: University of California Press.

Hall, Matthew, and Emily Greenman. 2015. "The Occupational Cost of Being Illegal in the United States: Legal Status, Job Hazards, and Compensating Differentials." *International Migration Review* 49(2): 406–42.

Harper, Jim. 2012. "Internal Enforcement, E-Verify, and the Road to National ID." *Cato Journal* 32(1): 125–37.

Henke, Joe. 2013. "5 Years after Being Made Mandatory, E-Verify Still Spotty." *Inside Tucson Business* 22(31): 1.

Heyman, Josiah. 1998. "State Effects on Labor Exploitation: The INS and Undocumented Immigrants at the Mexico–United States Border." *Critique of Anthropology* 18(2): 157–80.

Heyman, Josiah. 2001. "Class and Classification at the United States–Mexico Border." *Human Organization* 60(2): 128–40.

Hing, Bill Ong. 2006. "Misusing Immigration Policies in the Name of Homeland Security." CR: *The New Centennial Review* 6(1): 195–224.

Horton, Sarah. 2015. "Identity Loan: The Moral Economy of Migrant Document Exchange in California's Central Valley." *American Ethnologist* 42(1): 55–67.

Horton, Sarah. 2016. "Ghost Workers: The Implications of Governing Immigration through Crime for Migrant Workplaces." *Anthropology of Work Review* 37(1): 11–23.

Inda, Jonathan Xavier. 2013. "Subject to Deportation: IRCA, 'Criminal Aliens,' and the Policing of Immigration." *Migration Studies* 1(3): 292–310.

Kelsey, Richard. 2007. "Mayor's Missteps over Years Have Hurt Hometown Borough." *News Transcript* (New Jersey). November 7.

Kobach, Kris W. 2008. "Attrition through Enforcement: A Rational Approach to Illegal Immigration." *Tulsa Journal of Comparative and International Law* 15(2): 155–63.

Kravets, David. 2013. "Biometric Database of All Adult Americans Hidden in Immigration Reform." *Wired*. May 10.

Lee, Stephen. 2009. "Private Immigration Screening in the Workplace." *Stanford Law Review* 61: 1103–46.

Levi, Michael, and David S. Wall. 2004. "Technologies, Security, and Privacy in the Post-9/11 European Information Society." *Journal of Law and Society* 31(2): 194–220.

Liao, Gening. 2013. "The Misuse of E-Verify and Employer Liability for National Origin Discrimination." ABA *Journal of Labor and Employment Law* 28(3): 417–35.

Lofstrom, Magnus, Sarah Bohn, and Steven Raphael. 2011. *Lessons from the 2007 Legal Arizona Worker Act*. San Francisco: Public Policy Institute of California.

Lurie, Maxine N., and Richard Veit, eds. 2012. *New Jersey: A History of the Garden State*. New Brunswick, NJ: Rutgers University Press.

Maguire, Mark. 2009. "The Birth of Biometric Security." *Anthropology Today* 25(2): 9–14.

Maguire, Mark, and Peter Fussey. 2016. "Sensing Evil: Counterterrorism, Techno-Science, and the Cultural Reproduction of Security." *Focaal* 75: 31–44.

Meissner, Doris, Donald M. Kerwin, Muzaffar Chishti, and Claire Bergeron. 2013. *Immigration Enforcement in the United States: The Rise of a Formidable Machinery*. Washington, DC: Migration Policy Institute.

Menjívar, Cecilia. 2014. "Immigration Law beyond Borders: Externalizing and Internalizing Border Controls in an Era of Securitization." *Annual Review of Law and Social Science* 10: 353–69.

Menjívar, Cecilia, and María E. Enchautegui. 2015. "Confluence of the Economic Recession and Immigration Laws in the Lives of Latino Immigrant Workers in the United States." In *Immigrant Vulnerability and Resilience: Comparative Perspectives on Latin American Immigrants during the Great Recession*, edited by María Aysa-Lastra and Lorenzo Cachón, 105–26. New York: Springer.

Menjívar, Cecilia, and Daniel Kanstroom. 2015. Introduction to *Constructing Immigrant "Illegality:" Critiques, Experiences, and Responses*, edited by Cecilia Menjívar and Daniel Kanstroom, 1–36. Cambridge: Cambridge University Press.

Miller, Teresa A. 2005. "Blurring the Boundaries between Immigration and Crime Control after September 11th." *Boston College Third World Law Journal* 25(1): 81–124.

Nevins, Joseph. 2002. *Operation Gatekeeper: The War on "Illegals" and the Remaking of the U.S.-Mexico Boundary*. New York: Routledge.

Newman, Benjamin J., Christopher D. Johnson, April A. Strickland, and Jack Citrin. 2012. "Immigration Crackdown in the American Workplace: Explaining Variation in E-Verify Policy Adoption across the U.S. States." *State Politics and Policy Quarterly* 12(2): 160–82.

Ngai, Mae M. 2004. *Impossible Subjects: Illegal Aliens and the Making of Modern America*. Princeton, NJ: Princeton University Press.

Patel, Shelly Chandra. 2010. "E-Verify: An Exceptionalist System Embedded in the Immigration Reform Battle between Federal and State Governments." *Boston College Third World Law Journal* 30(2): 453–74.

Provine, Doris Marie, and Monica W. Varsanyi. 2012. "Scaled Down: Perspectives on State and Local Creation and Enforcement of Immigration Law." Introduction to the Special Issue of *Law and Policy* 34(2): 105–12.

Rosenblum, Marc R., and William A. Kandel. 2011. *Interior Immigration Enforcement: Programs Targeting Criminal Aliens.* Washington, DC: Congressional Research Service.

Speed, Shannon. 2006. "At the Crossroads of Human Rights and Anthropology: Toward a Critically Engaged Activist Research." *American Anthropologist* 108(1): 66–76.

Stuesse, Angela C. 2010. "What's 'Justice and Dignity' Got to Do with It? Migrant Vulnerability, Corporate Complicity, and the State." *Human Organization* 69(1): 19–30.

Stuesse, Angela C. 2015. "Anthropology for Whom? Challenges and Prospects of Activist Scholarship." In *Public Anthropology in a Borderless World*, edited by Sam Beck and Carl A. Maida, 221–46. New York: Berghahn.

Stuesse, Angela, and Mathew Coleman. 2014. "Automobility, Immobility, Altermobility: Surviving and Resisting the Intensification of Immigrant Policing." *City and Society* 26(1): 51–72.

Stumpf, Juliet P. 2012. "Getting to Work: Why Nobody Cares about E-Verify (And Why They Should)." UC *Irvine Law Review* 2: 381–414.

USCIS (U.S. Citizenship and Immigration Services). n.d. "Our Commitment to Privacy." *E-Verify.* Accessed August 15, 2015. http://www.uscis.gov/e-verify /about-program/our-commitment-privacy.

USCIS (U.S. Citizenship and Immigration Services). 2015. "E-Verify User Manual." Washington, DC: USCIS.

U.S. Select Commission on Immigration and Refugee Policy. 1981. "Out of the Shadows: The Rule of Law Applied." In *US Immigration Policy and the National Interest: Staff Report of the Select Commission on Immigration and Refugee Policy*, 631–64. Washington, DC: The Commission.

Westat. 2012. "Evaluation of the Accuracy of E-Verify Findings." In *Report Submitted to the US DHS*. Rockville, MD: Westat.

Willen, Sarah S. 2007. "Toward a Critical Phenomenology of 'Illegality': State Power, Criminalization, and Abjectivity among Undocumented Migrant Workers in Tel Aviv, Israel." *International Migration* 45(3): 8–38.

Zlolniski, Christian. 2003. "Labor Control and Resistance of Mexican Immigrant Janitors in Silicon Valley." *Human Organization* 62(1): 39–49.

Zlolniski, Christian. 2006. *Janitors, Street Vendors, and Activists: The Lives of Mexican Immigrants in Silicon Valley.* Berkeley: University of California Press.

FOUR

"Dead-Bodies-at-the-Border"

Distributed Evidence and Emerging Forensic Infrastructure for Identification

AMADE M'CHAREK

The so-called Arab Spring began in Tunisia in 2010 with a wave of pro-democracy protests. In March of the following year, in the company of my young daughter (Aziza) and my best friend we went to visit my father in the town of Zarzis in the south of the country. Upon arriving, in the morning, and being curious about the changes that had taken place, I suggested driving to the city. My father came running, urging us to take blankets, matresses, water, and bread with us. I frowned. "Well, you see, we have all these refugees from Libya and they need help." Together we started filling our small van with stuff from our house. At the next store we bought bread and water.

Arriving in the city center, we first visited a school where hundreds of men, guest workers from Egypt who had to leave Libya, were hanging around waiting to hear whether there would be a flight home. Outside, local Tunisians were carrying huge pots with the lunch meal inside the school. After delivering half of the goods, we drove further to a cultural center nearby. Many more people were hanging around—apparently tired or restless. We entered the center and we found ourselves in the main theater room—filled with men: sleeping, walking about, or having conversations in a dim voice.

I quickly found myself in an animated discussion with a growing group of men, first talking about the situation in Libya, then in Tunisia, but soon they addressed a question to me in a harsh tone: where is the international community? A local Tunisian wondered why local people were the sole caregivers for the refugees. The open discussions about politics were new to the ear, but the problem of refugees within the international order was already evident.[1]

In Europe, attention quickly turned away from political transformations, justice, or democracy and toward concerns over security. Indeed, the world watched as the hopes of the Arab Spring crashed on the rocks of European shores in the form of the bodies of refugees fleeing disruption and violence. In large part, security concerns drive the European response to the refugee crisis: efforts to secure Europe using various identification technologies, from travel documents to surveillance drones. However, EU border control also includes humanitarian policies and aspirations, and, between border security and human security, we find the problem of the dead migrant's body. Over the past number of years, several thousand persons have perished en route to Europe. On the one hand, the dead bodies are a problem of evidence in the context of forensic identification. On the other hand, the dead bodies are the evidence of failed politics and policy. In this chapter I attend to the emergent forensic infrastructure surrounding dead-bodies-at-the-border, and explore the ethics of care for borders and for bodies-at-the-border in contemporary Europe. In this sense, the chapter resonates with and pushes further the line of reasoning about surveilling injured migrants extended by Ieva Jusionyte in this volume.

I propose that when encountering dead-bodies-at-the-border, forensics as it stands offers a messy and contingent set of logics, tools, methodology, and devices. The analysis of an emerging forensic infrastructure and of its selected deployment for identifying migrants' bodies offers a different but important perspective on the human crisis unfolding in the Mediterranean. This chapter discusses who is included or excluded from processes of identification, and explores the significant points of contestation and the measures used to protect the EU border against transgressions by the bodies of Others. I show how the refugee crisis has shifted the focus of hegemonic political discourse in the EU away from the vulnerabilities of migrants or even citizens to the vulnerability of borders. The obsession with borders-at-risk produces a division between living and dead migrants. While Europe includes the living through biometric surveillance and a system for the stringent management of identities, dead bodies are often left unattended or are quickly buried. They appear as illegitimately stretching the limited resources of receiving countries. Moreover, their stages of decomposition challenge the wisdom of forensic science, while their significant numbers challenge current border protection regimes. The dead body then is not just a provocation, or reminder of the human crisis, but an active participant in processes of rethinking what counts as evidence and what evidence might unfold about concrete histories and more general the human condition.

Vulnerable Borders

One month after the commencement of the "Arab Spring," the European external border control agency, FRONTEX, sent out a press release headed "Hermes 2011 starts tomorrow in Lampedusa" (FRONTEX 2011). Joint Operation Hermes began when FRONTEX responded to a request by the Italian government for assistance in dealing with the Mediterranean migration crisis. One of the roles taken on by FRONTEX was the surveillance of vessels carrying migrants on the open seas and measures to prescreen intercepted migrants. The joint operation also involved Europol, the European police agency, which helped the Italian authorities to identify possible criminals among those who reached the Italian coasts (Carrera et al. 2012). Immediately, one could see a blending of the categories of migrant and criminal. An Italian governor even argued that they were "illegal, *clandestine*, wearing brand-name sneakers and Western looking jackets and holding mobile phones in their hands" and thus should not be considered eligible for international protection (Campesi 2011, 6).

Giuseppe Campesi (2011) has argued that the initial emergency was "fabricated" by Italy in order to draw on EU assistance. However, the EU embraced the emergency to implement far-reaching policies for the future management of the European borders. One of the policy aims was to upgrade the Schengen

Information System (SIS) to allow for new EU-wide automatic biometric entry/exit monitoring (within the EU). Another far-reaching technology aimed at the external borders of Europe is EUROSUR, introduced in the late 2013 as

> a pan-European border surveillance system with three main objectives: a) to reduce the number of irregular migrants entering the EU undetected, b) to reduce the number of deaths of irregular migrants by saving more lives at sea, and c) to enhance the internal security of the EU as a whole by contributing to the prevention of cross-border crime.
>
> EUROSUR could form a "system of systems" giving all the Member States' border-control authorities access to a secure and decentralized information-sharing network resulting in a full picture of events at the EU external borders. (FRONTEX 2012)

The Mediterranean border is the testing ground for this *system of systems*. On May 30, 2013, the Greens in the European Parliament issued a press release to coincide with the Parliament and European Council agreement on EUROSUR:

> The general focus of the EUROSUR system [aims] to seal off Europe's borders, using intrusive new technologies (like drones and satellites). This skewed approach to immigration misses the point. EUROSUR aims to prevent refugees even setting off from North Africa towards Europe, with cooperation agreements with countries in the region either established or planned to ensure this. In practical terms, this means the EU is effectively shifting its borders to countries that lack an asylum system and may not even be signatories to the Geneva Convention. (Keller 2013)

The Greens proposed that the monitoring system under EUROSUR could be used to come to the rescue of refugees in distress at sea, which would at least give the system a human face, so they argued. However, EU governments did not accept this proposal. While EU Member States will have to inform each other and FRONTEX if they are aware of refugees in distress, there is no requirement to increase the use of patrol boats in areas that are dangerous for refugees. This makes it clear that refugees are configured primarily as a threat, while Europe and especially the European borders are increasingly perceived as vulnerable entities in need of protection.

The current configuration of migrants and borders is undergoing more radical change in response to the Syrian refugee crisis. In December 2015 the European Commission proposed a far-reaching "Border Package" in the form of the European Border and Coast Guard, also called "the Agency" (European Commission 2015). The tasks of the Agency, which by now has become the synonym for FRONTEX, go beyond the management of the external borders: it will have its own equipment and huge resources, such as a 1,000 permanent staff members, aimed at identifying and addressing weak spots in the borders. The Agency, as the commission conceives it, will have a dazzlingly broad mandate, jeopardizing the sovereignty of individual Member States. This is the very reason that some Member States (especially in the southern and eastern areas of Schengen) have blocked the proposal. In practice, this meant that the proposal had to be watered down in some ways.[2] However, the general direction of the proposal, especially seen in the light of current public debates in the wake of the terrorist attacks on Paris and Brussels, was assured, and it was thus implemented in October 2016. Critics have argued that the proposal is protecting borders rather than people (Online Focus 2015). However, it is also important to acknowledge that border management regimes are not simply about exclusions but also implicate European citizens. One of the mandates of the Agency is the intensification of the systematic surveillance of European citizens entering *and* exiting the Schengen Area. At the border, biometric passport data may be compared to various databases, from the Schengen Information System and the Interpol Stolen and Lost Travel Documents Database to relevant national systems. The rationale for this? "It is estimated that five thousand EU citizens have traveled to conflict zones and joined terrorist groups such as ISIS. When they have come back to Europe, some of these returning foreign fighters have been involved in recent terrorist attacks" (European Commission n.d.). While the proposal concerns all European citizens, its focus today is certainly on the ethnic Other. This is explicit in the press release announcing the proposal for the Agency: "In response to the recent tragic attacks in Paris and the growing threat from foreign terrorist fighters, the Commission has swiftly taken action to accelerate work and implementation of measures under the European Security Agenda. Today's proposal responds to the need to reinforce security controls at the EU's external borders" (European Commission 2015). This measure will inevitably lead to ethnic profiling. Because whereas the checks at airport will be comprehensive, it is advised that "if, however, systematic checks at certain land or sea borders would have a disproportionate impact on the flow of traffic . . . Member States can, based on risk assessments, decide to carry out only targeted checks" (European Commission n.d.).

Obviously economic concerns, and one could say property rights, are made dominant over civil rights, that is, the rights of citizens to be treated equally by state authorities. More generally, casting the borders as vulnerable leads to a particular framing of the problems that have been surfacing in the Arab world and Europe since the early 2011. As a result, the border has become the matter of concern: the prime locus for managing the people wanting to enter Europe as well as those who are already in it, including European citizens. This focus on the border has taken a perverse bend in the deal between the EU and Turkey. While the policy language was about "providing better care for the refugees and improving the management of the stream of people," it is common knowledge that on the ground in Turkey the situation for refugees from Syria has been devastating (FRONTEX 2011). Rather than a concerted effort to improve the shelter and lives of refugees, the deal can be seen as an example of the externalization of the problem, that is, the problem of leaky European borders.

However, the problem resists externalization and is coming back at us in the form of recurrent media reports and, importantly, the bodies of people who have died in their attempt to reach European territory. They are the material evidence of a failed politics. As silent witnesses, they cannot be subjected to the surveillance and governance of refugees. Their presence is a transgression in two senses. While they trespassed the border, they also announce EU's politico-ethical failure.

Waste at the Border

In order to introduce the problem of people dying at the borders of Europe, I wish to ponder waste as an interesting object of evidence. Waste is precisely interesting because in its material form it mediates between various entities and worlds that tend to be kept apart, such as the living and the dead migrants, Europe and its Others, care and surveillance. Waste is not simply a residue in need of expelling, but rather a recursive process and thus symbolically and materially involved in the management of social relations; what is turned into "rubbish tends to have the ability to return" (Hetherington 2004, 159). Here I want to attend to waste in the form of a collection of well-known objects that index specific relations and resist divides that are constantly performed when thinking about the refugee crisis through the lens of borders.

In February 2016, I was in Thessaloniki (Greece) on a research visit. At the time, between thirteen and fourteen thousand people were trapped in Ido-meni Camp, a site to which we had not been granted access. Instead, we were taken on a guided tour to a freshly opened camp just outside Thessaloniki. As we were walking around, apart from the endless numbers of taxis ready to take refugees for extremely high prices to the border, everything seemed disturbingly normal. The camp was reminiscent of a camping site, where children were playing or being entertained while adults were hanging around, chatting or smoking cigarettes. I spotted a typical, golden-colored first aid blanket on the track in front of my feet. It was simply litter, laying about. Waste. All of a sudden, and with incredible force, the aluminum blanket ar-ticulated the purpose of the place, providing refuge for people who had fled their countries. This power of litter made wonder about the work that waste is doing in the context of the so-called refugee crisis. From that moment on, I started to notice waste pictured in newspapers. Alongside the blankets, the orange-colored life jacket has now assumed an iconic force. These jackets, which are bought in their thousands in cities in Turkey and Libya, are now found on the beaches of Europe. I encountered a third instance of waste as I was doing fieldwork in the south of Tunisia. When I was at the office of the Tunisia Association for Fisheries and standing in front of a wall covered with pictures portraying dramas on the sea, I found myself staring at a picture that showed driftwood from the wreckages of boats used to transport refugees. At this moment, Slah Eddin M'charek, a leading figure in that association, de-scribed a nearby island littered with driftwood, all from the shipwrecks. Slah Eddin told me first about the countless times that he and fisherman returned to the port just after sailing out, because rather than catching fish they would end up rescuing people from drowning. He also told me about the numer-ous bodies that they found in the sea over the years. "You can smell the dead bodies from 800 meters or so," he explained. "It is now getting better because the coast guard is doing a much better job, but the number of bodies that we were seeing and the smell. It was just horrible. I can't describe the smell. Just repulsive." So this is another instance of waste, namely smell.

One could say that these instances of waste are merely traces that require oral testimonies or authoritative voices as to reveal a convincing story of what happened. However, waste is also material evidence when it comes to borders and bodies.[3] It is evidence of European borders and the bodies of people who did not make it into Europe. Waste also speaks to a methodological aspect of forensics. Not simply as a scientific (objectifying) method of ordering and connecting traces to events. Eyal Weizman, Tavares Paulo, and Susan Schuppli (2010) have suggested viewing forensics as the art of bringing evidence in front of the forum. Here I want to expand this proposition by suggesting to view forensics as the *art of paying attention*—a way of pausing with material traces and attending to the ways they hold desperate places and times together. Material traces thus do not simply represent something that has become invisible—for example, bodies that have sunk to the bottom of the sea—but are devices that are active, performative. Waste folds in itself various practices that through forensic attention can be unfolded and taken into account. It might thus invite us to ponder movements and circulations of humans and things as well as the ways in which those circulations have been halted (M'charek 2016). With Kevin Hetherington (2004; see also De León 2015) we could think of waste as an *absent presence*. What then are the absences that are folded into the presence of waste? Here I want to discuss three absences, but there are many more to ponder. One of the absences marked by the first aid blanket is the *work of care* that has been ubiquitous during the refugee crisis. Whereas state institutions seem surprised and reactive, citizens, in more or less organized fashion, reached out to refugees and extended care. This work of care and the scale on which it operates tend to be invisible (e.g. Puig de la Bellacasa 2011). Although I do not wish to romanticize care, because there are also enough examples in refugee camps and elsewhere where it has become problematic, its politics cannot be underestimated. The first aid blanket is a material evidence of care for people on the move. It is also material evidence of another version of care, namely, the care for the border. As indicated above, numerous political actors cast the borders of Europe as vulnerable and in need of more care. In this way, the blanket brings into proximity the care for borders and the care for bodies that could not be stopped by, or could not even make it to, the border.

Whereas the blanket could be seen as evidence of care for that which cannot be quantified in monetary terms, namely, life, the orange life jacket I want to briefly suggest, folds in itself the economics of human trafficking and of illegality. The piles of the jackets left behind testify to the incredible amounts of money that people have paid in their attempts to reach Europe. As Ruben Andersson (2014) argues, illegality is not only the product of border management regimes but is also productive of myriad entrepreneurial and economic relations. Attending to the life jacket—although it is paradoxically an object that is close to the individual body, and one that could be seen as an exemplary representation of that which is good—might, because of its visible excess (the piles and piles of these orange objects), point us to the economic costs and revenues at stake. The life jacket thus holds together different values: the value of life and the economic value of migration.

Similarly, one might approach smell as waste and as evidence of death. It folds in itself both the high number of deaths as well as the attempts to prevent people from dying, such as search and rescue operations of Mare Nostrum, the efforts of NGOs such as Sea Watch, or the work of coast guards in different countries. Smell brings together bodies in a pertinent and visceral way. It brings together dead and living bodies. The bodies of dead migrants and of those who aim at stopping them from dying. The rest of this chapter is devoted to a discussion of the deaths at the border.

According to the Deaths at the Borders Database, 3,188 people died attempting to reach Europe between 1990 and 2013.[4] However, these numbers have increased dramatically since the uprising in the Arab world, and especially with the devastating ongoing war in Syria. The International Organization for Migration (IOM) estimates that between 2011 and June 2016, at least thirteen thousand people died or went missing. And, again, the numbers went up dramatically in the second half of 2016. In a recent report, Médecins Sans Frontières (MSF) shows that people are taking the deadliest route to Europe, namely, crossing the Mediterranean basin from Libya to Italy, due to a lack of other safer options (Médecins Sans Frontières 2016).

However, the large number of people dying in the sea is by no means new. For years, fishermen and other local people in Italy, Greece, Spain, as well as in Tunisia, Libya, and Morocco confronted the human tragedy of failed migration. Data show an increasing number of shipwrecks, but accurate figures on the bodies that wash ashore are hard to come by. As the Amsterdam-based migration scholars Tamara Last and Thomas Spijkerboer argue, "There is a general paucity of information about those who have died attempting to cross the southern external borders of the European Union (EU) without authorization, especially when compared with the amount of data generated about the arrival, interception, rescue, detention and deportation of migrants—statistics that can serve to justify funding and intensification of border control" (Last and Spijkerboer 2014, 85). The lack of reliable information hinders policy makers or makes it possible for them to avoid the issue. As Leanne Weber (2010) argues, the lack of official numbers contributes to the acceptance of border-related deaths through a regime of self-evidence, suggesting this is a "natural" consequence of certain processes or even individual choices. As Tamara Last and Thomas Spijkerboer (2014) show, popular interest in and increasing public awareness of migrant deaths in the Mediterranean are rather recent. A case in point is the shocking picture of the dead body of three-year-old Aylan Kurdi, found on a Turkish beach, which sparked a global outcry over the tragedy unfolding in the Mediterranean basin. Indeed, the international media attention led to the boy's identification. But what of the identities of the thousands and thousands other dead people? As Iosif Kovras and Simon Robins (2015) have argued, while living migrants are some of the most heavily monitored individuals in the EU, dead migrants seem to merit almost no attention from the authorities. Thus, little has been said or done about the identities of the dead. Who are these people?

Dead-Bodies-at-the-Border

To whom do the dead-bodies-at-the-border belong? Although shipwrecks with high numbers of casualties constantly make the headlines in European media, and though this has contributed to a general framing of the refugee crisis as a humanitarian crisis, attention directed at the deaths tends to fade quickly. The question of who the dead are has thus received surprisingly little attention.[5] I raised this issue with representatives of the United National High Commissioner for Refugees (UNHCR) and MSF while in the south of Tunisia. Upon questioning about the contribution of MSF to the management of bodies, Fadi Khatib, the coordinator of MSF in Zarzis, kept elaborating on the first-responder training that his organization gives to local fishermen, together with training on hygiene and the use of protective suits and gloves. "Of course," it occurred to me during this interview, "your concern is with the living; with public health, the prevention of infectious diseases that bodies may cause. For you these bodies are containers of diseases." Fadi's face relaxed, "Yes, in fact that is our main concern, our main concern is with the living," he answered. Given this lack of attention, one could say, the bodies did not enter the realm of forensics. They did not demand attention and engagement from society.

The lack of accountability for dead-bodies-at-the-border stands in stark contrast to the painstaking work that Western authorities put in identifying the bodies of Western citizens in cases of disasters. A clear example is the Dutch concern with the body parts of the passengers on Malaysia Airlines flight MH17, which was shot down near the Ukraine on July 17, 2014. However, there are numerous other cases, such as the identification of the victims of the September 11 terrorist attack in the United States (Toom 2016), or the identification of the victims of the Tsunami of 2004 in the Indian Ocean. As many commentators have observed with reference to the latter, there was a clear hierarchy seen in whose bodies were prioritized during the identification process, and it is perhaps of no surprise that the bodies of Western nationals were at the top of the list (e.g., Merli and Buck 2015). There are also examples from conflict situations, such as the identification of the remains of the estimated eight thousand men and boys killed in the Srebrenica massacre in Bosnia-Herzegovina in 1995. Whereas the identification of Western victims of the tsunami was mostly based on dental examinations, in the case of Srebrenica forensic DNA moved to center stage. In 2001, the International Committee of Missing Persons (ICMP), the organization that was responsible for carrying out the identification process, received full political support and ample resources to erect laboratories and started to use DNA profiling alongside dental examination in order to identify the victims of the Srebrenica massacre (see Wagner 2008).[6] The ICMP identified more than 80 percent of the victims.

It is important to note that these cases not only concerned Western nationals or politically fueled Western concerns such as the case of Srebrenica, but that, in contrast to the dead-bodies-at-the-border, in all cases there was a more or less clear idea about where the victims came from. Passenger lists were available (MH17), dental records and associated documents were available (the 2004 Tsunami), or evidence was given by family members who were looking for their relatives (Srebrenica). From a forensic perspective, this means that bodies or body parts could be compared to so-called reference data in order to conclude that a particular body belonged to a particular person. Such reference data is mostly missing in the case of deceased in the Mediterranean Sea.[7]

The above examples highlight the issue of forensic infrastructure: the kind of organization that needs to be in place to manage bodies and to arrive at identification. The work of the ICPM in Srebrenica provided such an infrastructure but one that was organized around DNA profiling. When it was introduced into the criminal justice systems of European countries and the United States, this technology was contested in terms of the reliability of DNA (does it really identify per se?). Questions were also asked about the soundness of the technology, that is, the infrastructural requirements and the enrollment of the different actors in such ways as to ensure their proper contribution to the production of a DNA profile (see M'charek 2000; Lynch et al. 2008; M'charek 2008; M'charek, Hagendijk, and de Vries 2012). When one thinks about a profile deemed legitimate in court, one has to consider the movement of biological traces from the crime scene to police stations where they are registered, on to forensic laboratories where they are to be analyzed, and then on again to the courtroom where they are reported on and used as evidence in trial. All of the links in this chain had to be trained and reconfigured in line with the infrastructural requirement of DNA profiling (M'charek 2008; 2016). To transform bodily substances into DNA and DNA into numbers and numbers into evidence that could help identify a suspect in court, the contributions of the different actors along the chain had to be standardized and routinized. It is these highly standardized procedures together with the mindboggling numerical substantiation of the evidence (so-called matching probability) that has contributed to the enormous success of forensic DNA in criminal justice systems. Meanwhile, more than two decades later, it has become the gold standard in criminal investigation. In addition, DNA profiling has gained a solid position elsewhere, such as in the context of family reunification (Heinemann and Lemke 2013; C. G. M. Robben and Francisco J. Ferrándiz, this volume) and disaster victim identification (Wagner 2008; Toom 2016).[8]

However, as indicated above, in order to use DNA to identify a person, one must compare the DNA of that person to a reference population or to family members. However, in the case of the bodies of migrants and refugees there is no reference population readily available. Moreover, the geographical origin of the body is unclear (country, region, etc.), and even if this was clear, people have migrated from countries where the DNA infrastructure is obscured because of a lack of data or a reference databank. Added to this, dead bodies at the shore pose new technical issues even when other forensic anthropological techniques are used. Indeed, they challenge established limits of forensic science. When I attended the Seventh International Meeting of the New Mediterranean Academy of Forensic Sciences (nMAFS) in 2016, the Italian forensic pathologist Cristina Cattaneo gave details about the problems of identification (Cattaneo 2016). She noted cases in which victims had been in saltwater for long periods as a particular challenge: the bodies tend to be disfigured; putrefaction and skeletonization further complicate the process. In cases where bodies have not been in the water for too long and if the process of skeletonization did not kick in, the epidermis tends to detach from the body leaving the skin unpigmented and rendering all cadavers whitish, even especially in dark-skinned people. In such cases, fingerprints are no longer available because of the detached skin. Odontology (forensic dentistry) is also unviable, because there is nothing against which to compare a dental profile. And the same fate seems to hold for DNA. "We have to reinvent forensics anew," Cattaneo stated. She gave the example of social media. Given the central role of the mobile phone and the use of social media such as Facebook and Instagram, mining these media might provide forensic means of equal importance to more conventional identification technologies. "People send pictures home. A label on their clothing or a hair-do might help identify them." If it would be possible to link a label on a trouser to a picture out there in the cloud this might be crucial for giving a name to a body, Cattaneo explained.

"Forensics has to be invented anew!" I wrote this statement down in my notebook during this meeting. It is of the greatest importance to open up the space of what we count as part of the forensic infrastructure and what we exclude, what we constitute as knowledge and whose knowledge we privilege in the process of reinventing forensics. In short, we must ask this question: what will the forensic infrastructure of identification of dead-bodies-at-the-border look like? Rather than answering this question in a conclusive way, the following will give some hints about this emerging infrastructure.

Emerging Forensic Infrastructures

It is surprising that the management of European borders is a concerted effort dealt with at the EU-level, whereas the identification of bodies is delegated to local authorities only. There is, however, an official process of identification used by EU countries around the Mediterranean Sea. It entails bodies receiving a unique identifying number that starts with the telephone country code (in accord with the Dublin Regulation to register migrants in the first country entered). Bodies are photographed (also paying attention to personal belongings such as clothing, shoes, bags, watches, cell phones, etc.) and examined by a coroner; identifying markers have to be recorded (tattoos, freckles, injuries or other bodily traumas) and DNA samples taken. In practice, however, the situation looks less ordered. In many countries, bodies are simply buried without registration, sometimes piled into one grave. It often happens that there is no coroner available to examine the body. During warm seasons there is typically a lack of morticians (to carry the bodies) or too little room in the hospital-morgue to store the bodies until registration is completed. For example, in the southern Tunisian town of Zarzis the hospital-morgue only has six places, yet there were several cases in which more than twenty bodies were found at the beach of Zarzis. In addition, hospital personnel are hesitant to use an ambulance to carry the bodies because of possible health risk for their patients. In general terms, a proper management system that runs from finding the bodies on the beach to registration, examination, and burial is still to be established, resulting in bodies simply being buried without any additional information except for the date on which they were found.[9] While the resources and procedures on the European side of the Mediterranean Sea are slightly better, Kovras and Robins (2016) describe a lack of properly delimited responsibilities:

> The coast guard maintained that their responsibility is limited to collecting the dead body and transporting it to the hospital, after which responsibility lies with the district attorney. . . . The district attorney in practice assumes only a marginal role, typically declining any substantive investigation on the assumption that death was not caused by criminal activity, and then signing the relevant documentation to permit burial. . . . The body remains at the local hospital with the coroner, whose duty is limited to the examination of the corpse to establish the cause of death and carry out the autopsy. . . . When asked about the next steps, the coroner had no answer; he only revealed that a swift burial was necessary, as the hospital has no facilities to store bodies for more than a few days. The director of social services at the hospital informed us there is no budget available for burying dead "illegal" migrants, only for treating living migrants. . . . There is no standardized procedure to deal with a migrant body, and this policy vacuum legitimizes local authorities in denying their legal and moral responsibility to address the issue of identification. Most often relevant data found on the body—documents, tattoos, other identifying marks—are not systematically collected, analyzed and stored to support identification. Similarly, only a limited effort is made to collect other information—such as testimony from survivors of a shipwreck—that could advance this goal. (Kovras and Robins 2016, 41)

This long extract about the EU protocol shows the various actors who are in place to attend to the bodies of deceased migrants. However some actors and the crucial knowledge they could contribute are not included in the forensic infrastructure. For example, the information that could be provided by fellow travelers who survived the shipwreck, or the knowledge of fisherman or search and rescue volunteers, who are often first responders, is not included in the process of registration and identification.

Furthermore, the lack of responsibility for identification as well as the absence of central coordination for the management of bodies have been an issue for years among the forensic community. In November 2013, the International Committee of the Red Cross (ICRC) organized a conference in Milan initiated in collaboration with forensic scientists in Milan and attended by participants from of European Mediterranean countries. The conference addressed the coordination of work in order to facilitate identification. One of the outcomes of the conference was the drafting of a number of recommendations that are slowly shaping the infrastructure for the management of dead bodies.[10] The recommendations appeared in the journal *Forensic Science International* and aimed to improve "forensic analysis, documentation and identification of dead migrants; for ensuring their dignified management and for bringing answers to the bereaved." The following are the key recommendations:

- increasing the necessary political and institutional awareness and support, at national, regional and international levels, required for preventing and resolving the tragedy of unidentified dead migrants recovered from the Mediterranean Sea;

- improving the communication, coordination and cooperation of forensic and investigative agencies involved in the recovery, analysis, documentation and management of decedent migrants;

- ensuring the use of standardized procedures for the forensic analysis and documentation of the dead by all forensic and investigative agencies and practitioners involved in the management of dead migrants;

- creating centralized databases with information on unidentified dead and the missing reported in the region. These databases should be searchable and accessible by various agencies, including humanitarian organizations, for servicing the humanitarian plight of bereaved families;

- involving Governments and institutions of countries of origin of migrants in the efforts to identify and repatriate their dead nationals.

(CATTANEO et al. 2015, e2)

In 2016, two initiatives have scaled up the process of identification. The first initiative was the initiation of a DNA database in Athens. Headed by the forensic geneticist Penelope Maniati, this lab is part of the Forensic Sciences Division (DEE) of the Greek Police and aims to help identify deceased persons and make it possible for relatives to find out about their beloved ones by having their own profiles matched to the databank. A second initiative, which I will give more detail on, has been taken in Italy as collaboration between the special commissioner for missing persons, Vittorio Piscitelli; Paolo Procaccianti, of the Institute of Legal Medicine Palermo; and Cristina Cattaneo, forensic pathologist of Labanof Lab Milano. They initiated a large pilot project to convince the national and European authorities that it is possible to identify victims of shipwrecks and to set up working procedures for registration, sampling, and storing of data in a conclusive manner. This pilot aims to identify the victims of a shipwreck in April 2015 in which a fishing boat packed with hundreds of people floundered 135 kilometers of the coast of Libya. Following a communication, the Italian Coast Guard radioed *King Jacob*, a 157-meter large merchant vessel nearby to provide assistance. However, upon seeing the vessel approaching, the migrants rushed to one side of the deck, causing their boat to capsize. The boat sank, and only twenty-eight persons could be rescued. Estimates suggest that eight hundred to nine hundred people went down with the boat. As part of this pilot project this very boat was boarded in July 2016 in the Sicilian port of Augusta by the Italian Marine force by sending a remote-controlled robot down, 370 meters below sea level down to tow the ship and the 169 cadavers that were scattered around the boat. The remains were recovered with the help of liquid nitrogen and kept in refrigerator containers. Also, while the boarding of the ship has cost some nine million euros, paid for by the Italian government, a large team of experts from different universities and labs have been working in their spare time, without any compensation, at the military site where the remains are stored. Eight hundred body bags, some probably containing remains from more than one person, have been secured.[11] Bodies and body parts have been subjected to autopsies and registrations, and the analysis of the remains will take place in various Italian laboratories. However, the forensic work will not stop here. At the end of 2016, possible families of victims who did carry identification papers with them were contacted so as to help in the process of identification. This process will probably open up the space for other actors to become part of the forensic infrastructure, such as legal experts working on international law and human rights, or other social actors in the countries of origin.

Conclusions

In the context of the "refugee crisis" and in the aftermath of Paris, *vulnerability* has been a recurrent theme. In fact, it figures prominently in European policy. It does not come as a surprise that it is not the vulnerability of the refugees or even that of European citizens that is central, but rather that of Europe's borders. However, the vulnerabilities of the European borders, I want to suggest, help to make Other, and make invisible (out of our way and not our responsibility) the thousands and thousands of bodies that we so often find on our beaches. Attending to these bodies produces evidence. Obviously it produces evidence about the identity of the missing person. But more intensely so, it produces evidence about Europe's border management regime and the costs thereof. To know these bodies is to know the humanitarian price of our territorial borders.

In this chapter, I have attended to the costs of the European border regime by proposing forensics not only as a set of logics (Andersson 2014) or a tool, but as a methodological approach, an *art of paying attention*, as to open up a field that is not neatly ordered, but rather messy and contingent.

Forensics as art of paying attention allows for two related interventions, which I have only begun to outline in this chapter. First, it helps us to attend to the management of bodies and processes of forensic identification beyond the objectifying rendering thereof in mainstream forensics. That is, it allows us to bring into view an emerging forensic infrastructure that is utterly creative because it needs to "make do" with the limited resources: limited knowledge about the subjects whose bodies are in need of identification; limited technologies that can be applied given the state of the bodies; limited monetary resources, technologies, and devices to work with. This results in a constant creative process, whereby the knowledge of fisherman about the wind and the currents of seawater becomes key in estimating where a body is drifting from and at what speed; or a film taken by some Syrian friends containing information about what they were wearing before sailing off from Libya to Lampedusa, can become crucial in determining whether it was the body of one of them that washed ashore in 2014 on a beach in Zarzis; or yet again a setting in which, given the lack of laboratory equipment, a take-out coffee cup becomes a container in which the teeth of a dead subject are bleached before the forensic anthropological examination. All these odd elements have become part of a forensic process and begin to coshape forensic infrastructures. In some cases, this emergent infrastructure and the elements that help to bring it about will be transient, whereas in other cases it might become more durable. Attending to this nitty-gritty process is not only important as a work of valuing and appreciating the identification work done against all odds, but it also allows for a critical evaluation of what knowledge comes to matter, that is, what knowledge and whose knowledge can become part of forensics and how we might do this otherwise.

The second intervention that is possible by taking forensics as art of paying attention is related to the main object of forensics, namely, material traces. The material traces that figure in forensic cases typically have a talent for joining desperate places and events and inviting scenarios around them as to produce a possible story about what could have happened. Both the insistence on materiality and the invitation to bring things together that we are in the habit of keeping apart (Stengers 2005) allow us to tell a different story about what we have come to know as the refugee crisis. I thus suggested waste and litter as material evidence to think with and to resist a reduction of the problem of dead-bodies-at-the-border to a straightforward matter of identification or not identification. Waste might help us to hold the refugee crisis in close relation to Europe's colonial past, or to bring into conversation the care for borders and the care of citizens for people who seek refuge in Europe, or to think together the price paid for a life jacket and that paid for a drone to survey the border. Keeping the messiness on board, staying with the trouble (Haraway 2016), may well help to produce a forensic infrastructure that is more apt for the kind of identification work at stake. In this way, mess, like waste, is a virtue and not a sin.

Notes

I would like to thank the editors of this volume, especially Ursula Rao and Mark Maguire, for feedback and guidance throughout the process. I thank the many respondents that I am encountering in my fieldwork in Tunisia and Italy. I want to mention Faysal Khnissi in particular for invaluable help during my fieldwork in Tunisia and for sharing his knowledge and network with me. Finally I would like to thank the European Research Council (ERC) for supporting my research through an ERC Consolidator Grant (FP7–617451-RaceFaceID-Race Matter: On the Absent Presence of Race in Forensic Identification).

1   Later in 2011, and to process the stream of refugees, the UNHCR established the

refugee camp Choucha, a few kilometers from the Libyan border, which came to house up to 300,000 refugees. This camp would be closed down in June 2013.

2   For example, the Agency does not have its own equipment, but it has guaranteed access to the equipment of EU countries in advent of specific operations.

3   See also Ian Hacking (2006, 32–33), who argues that the evidence provided by things was lacking in our modern thinking. "The evidence of things is not to be confused with the data of sense, which in much modern epistemology, has been regarded as the foundation of all evidence." And he continues: "The evidence of things is distinct from testimony, the evidence of witnesses and of authorities." It is important to note here that this view on material evidence and the delegation of agency to things is at the heart of much of work in science and technology studies and in particular in Actor Network Theory.

4   For this and more details on the human costs of border control, see http://www.borderdeaths.org.

5   While some work has been taking account of the numbers of the deceased, as Kovras and Robins (2016) convincingly argue, most of the work also in critical migration studies has been focusing on the surveillance of the flows of people and surveillance and biometric technology.

6   The ICMP was initiated in 1996 as part of the Dayton Peace Agreement, which ended the fighting in the former Yugoslavia.

7   See also Claudia Merli and Trudi Buck (2015) on the lack of reference data for non-Western victims of the tsunami.

8   In fact, before forensic DNA entered the criminal justice system, it was used for the first time in a family reunification case in the UK by Alec Jeffreys (see M'charek 2008).

9   To be clear, my research in Tunisia has just started, and I have only had the chance to do short site-visits and hold first conversations with various different actors involved.

10   Cattaneo, personal communication, September 17.

11   Cattaneo, personal communication, September 17.

References

Andersson, Ruben. 2014. *Illegality, Inc.: Clandestine Migration and the Business of Bordering Europe.* Oakland: University of California Press.

Campesi, Giuseppe. 2011. "The Arab Spring and the Crisis of the European Border Regime: Manufacturing Emergency in the Lampedusa Crisis." European University Institute Working Paper Series, No. 59, Robert Schuman Centre for Advanced Studies, EUI, Fiesole, Italy.

Carrera, Sergio, Leonhard den Hertog, and Janet Parkin. 2012. "EU Migration Policy in the Wake of the Arab Spring: What Prospects for EU-Southern Mediterranean Relations?" August. MEDPRO Technical Report No. 15. Centre for European Policy Studies. http://www.ceps.edu/publications/.

Catteneo, Cristina et al. 2015. "The Forgotten Tragedy of Unidentified Dead in the Mediterranean." *Forensic Science International* 250: e1–e2.

Cattaneo, Cristina. 2016. "The Role of Forensic Anthropology and Pathology." Paper presented at the 2016 Symposium of the International Academy of Legal Medicine (IALM), 7th nMAFS International Meeting, "Mediterranean Countries and the Refugee Crisis: Emerging Issues and Potential Solutions," June 23, Venice, Italy. [Including oral communication, "Challenges in the postmortem examination of the victims of the recent Mediterranean shipwreck of April 18, 2015."]

De León, Jason. 2015. *The Land of Open Graves: Living and Dying on the Migrant Trail*. Berkeley: University of California Press.

European Commission. n.d. "Securing Europe's External Borders: Systematic Checks at External Borders." Accessed November 15, 2017. http://ec.europa.eu /dgs/home-affairs/what-we-do/policies/securing-eu-borders/fact-sheets/docs /systematic_checks_at_external_borders_en.pdf.

European Commission. 2015. "A European Border and Coast Guard to protect Europes' External Borders." December 15. Archived at https://web.archive.org /web/20160129130512/http://europa.eu/rapid/press-release_IP-15-6327_en.htm.

FRONTEX. 2011. "Hermes 2011 Starts Tomorrow in Lampedusa." February 19. Accessed October 9, 2016. http://frontex.europa.eu/news/hermes-2011-starts -tomorrow-in-lampedusa-X4XZcr.

FRONTEX. 2012. "EUROSUR." April 11. Archived at https://web.archive.org/web /20120411144452/http://frontex.europa.eu:80/eurosur. [Originally published at http://frontex.europa.eu/eurosur.]

Hacking, Ian. 2006. *The Emergence of Probability: A Philosophical Study of Early Ideas about Probability Induction and Statistical Inference*. Cambridge: Cambridge University Press.

Haraway, Donna. 2016. *Staying with the Trouble: Making Kin in the Chthulucene*. Durham, NC: Duke University Press.

Hetherington, Kevin. 2004. "Second-Handedness: Consumption, Disposal and Absent Presence." *Environment and Planning D: Society and Space* 22(1): 57–73.

Heinemann, Torsten, and Thomas Lemke. 2013. "Suspect Families: DNA Kinship Testing in German Immigration Policy." *Sociology* 47(4): 810–27.

Keller, Ska. 2013. "European Border Surveillance (EUROSUR)." *The Greens, European Free Alliance*. October 10. https://www.greens-efa.eu/en/article/european -border-surveillance-eurosur-4777/.

Kovras, Iosif, and Simon Robins. 2015. "The Families of Missing Migrants and Refugees May Never Know Their Fates." *The Conversation*. October 1. http:// theconversation.com/the-families-of-missing-migrants-and-refugees-may -never-know-their-fates-48396.

Kovras, Iosif, and Simon Robins. 2016. "Death as the Border: Managing Missing

Migrants and Unidentified Bodies at the EU's Mediterranean Frontier." *Political Geography* 55: 40–49.

Last, Tamara, and Spijkerboer, Thomas. 2014. "Tracking Deaths in the Mediterranean." In *Fatal Journeys Tracking Lives Lost during Migration*, edited by T. Brian and F. Laczko, 85–108. Geneva: International Organization for Migration (IOM).

Lynch, Michael, Simon A. Cole, Ruth McNally, and Kathleen Jordan. 2008. *Truth Machine: The Contentious History of DNA Fingerprinting*. Chicago: University of Chicago Press.

M'charek, Amade. 2000. "Technologies of Population: Forensic DNA Testing Practices and the Making of Differences and Similarities." *Configurations* 8(1): 121–58.

M'charek, Amade. 2008. "Contrasts and Comparisons: Three Practices of Forensic Investigation." *Comparative Sociology* 7(3): 387–412.

M'charek, Amade. 2016. "Performative Circulations: On Flows and Stops in Forensic DNA Practices." *TECNOSCIENZA: Italian Journal of Science and Technology Studies* 7(2): 9–34.

M'charek, Amade, Rob Hagendijk, and Wiebe de Vries. 2012. "Equal before the Law: On the Machinery of Sameness in Forensic DNA Practice." *Science, Technology, and Human Values* 38(4): 542–65.

Médecins Sans Frontières (Doctors without Borders). 2016. "EU Migration Crisis Update." February 24. http://www.msf.org/en/article/eu-migration-crisis-update-february-2016.

Merli, Claudia, and Trudi Buck. 2015. "Forensic Identification and Identity Politics in 2004 Post-tsunami Thailand: Negotiating Dissolving Boundaries." *Human Remains and Violence* 1(1): 3–22.

Online Focus. 2015. "So will die EU ihre Außengrenzen kontrollieren." December 15. http://www.focus.de/politik/ausland/fluechtlings-krise-so-will-die-eu-ihre-aussengrenzen-kontrollieren_id_5156747.html.

Puig de la Bellacasa, Maria. 2011. "Matters of Care in Techno-science: Assembling Neglected Things." *Social Studies of Science* 41(1): 85–106.

Stengers, Isabelle. 2005. "Introductory Notes on an Ecology of Practices." *Cultural Studies Review* 11(1): 183–96.

Toom, Victor. 2016. "Whose Body Is It? Technolegal Materialization of Victims' Bodies and Remains after the World Trade Center Terrorist Attacks." *Science, Technology, and Human Values* 41(4): 686–708.

Wagner, Sarah. 2008. *To Know Where He Lies: DNA Technology and the Search for Srebrenica's Missing*. Berkeley: University of California Press.

Weber, Leanne. 2010. "Knowing-and-Yet-Not-Knowing about European Border Deaths." *Australian Journal of Human Rights* 15(2): 35–58.

Weizman Eyal, Tavares Paulo, and Schuppli Susan. 2010. "Forensic Architecture." *Architectural Design* 80(5): 58–63.

FIVE

———

The Transitional Lives of Crimes against Humanity

Forensic Evidence under Changing Political Circumstances

ANTONIUS C. G. M. ROBBEN AND FRANCISCO J. FERRÁNDIZ

The photograph *Death of a Loyalist Militiaman*, popularly known as *The Falling Soldier*, was taken by Robert Capa during the Spanish Civil War. The photo depicts a combatant with a rifle in the hand of his outstretched right arm, his head tilted slightly toward his left, as he falls backward on a dry grassy slope near the hamlet of Cerro Muriano on September 5, 1936. The mortally wounded militiaman was recognized by a cousin in 1995 as twenty-four-year-old Federico Borrell García. His final resting place is unknown. This iconic image of warfare and human sacrifice has become the subject of a several controversies in the last forty years that are indicative of the intricate process of detection, construction, and interpretation by which evidence is collected, and multiple traces of diverse nature are transformed into competing evidential narratives.

Doubts about the soldier's identity, the place of death, and the circumstances under which Capa took the photo have been raised through the decades. The suggestion was made in 1975 that the photograph had been staged by Capa during a pause in the fighting between Franco's rebel forces and the Republican government troops, not at Cerro Muriano but about fifty kilometers away near the town of Espejo. An alternative hypothesis was that the show maneuvers attracted hostile fire, and caused the tragic death of Borrell García (Knightley 1975, 212; Barca 2008).

In 2007, the documentary *The Shadow of the Iceberg* appeared in which, as the Spanish filmmakers called it, "an autopsy of the mythical photograph" was made (Doménech and Riebenbauer 2007). A geodesist inferred from the landscape that the picture was not taken at Cerro Muriano, and an astrophysicist concluded from the soldier's shadow that the photo was not taken at 5 PM, as Robert Capa had said in an interview, but at 9 AM. At this hour, however, there was no armed combat at Cerro Muriano. The forensic pathologist Fernando Verdú claimed that he could not ascertain a cause of death from the photo, and that the soldier's backward fall could only have been produced by a high-caliber weapon, but that then there would have been a visible impact on the impeccable white shirt. Finally, a comparison between the facial features of *The Falling Soldier* and a photo of Federico Borrell García showed, according to Verdú, that the fingers, earlobes, and teeth of the two men were different, and that therefore the militiaman on Capa's image was not Borrell García (Doménech and Riebenbauer 2007).

How credible is the documentary's evidence, and what does it say about its construction? The puzzle of *The Falling Soldier* begins already with the unsure conditions under which the photograph had been taken. Capa remained vague in interviews, but war correspondent John Hersey remembered an informal meeting with Capa in which he explained how he had been crouching in a trench during heavy charges by Republican militias against a Nationalist machine-gun nest in Andalusia. Retold in Hersey's words: "Finally as they charged, the photographer timidly raised his camera to the top of the parapet and, without looking, at the instant of the first machine gun burst, pressed the button" (Knightley 1975, 211).

There was also the suggestion that Capa's lover Gerda Taro (née: Gerta Pohorylle) had taken the rectangular picture with her Leica camera because

Robert Capa (née: Endre Ernö Friedmann) generally used a Rolleiflex with its typical square picture format. Furthermore, the two photographers often published their pictures under Capa's name, as both used pseudonyms. Unfortunately, the couple could not be consulted when the photo's authenticity was questioned. Taro had died in Spain in 1937 during a road accident involving a tank, and Capa was killed in Vietnam in 1954 when he stepped on a landmine. With the photo's origin story lost and the evidence dispersed among municipal archives in Spain, the file cabinets of Magnum Photos in New York, the unknown burial grounds of Federico Borrell García and the dead militiaman, and perhaps the confidential testimony of a deceased eyewitness to a son or daughter, we are left with a heterogeneous reservoir of material remnants and inconclusive clues. Maybe Robert Capa's brother Cornell and Richard Whelan, Capa's official biographer, could have provided answers. Whelan (1985, 97) could have reassessed his earlier dismissal of the posed photo hypothesis, and Cornell Capa could have given full access to the series of photos made at Cerro Muriano. However, they refused an interview with the documentary filmmakers, suspecting them of a neofascist attempt to discredit the iconic image. Whelan died in 2007 and was buried next to Robert Capa. Cornell Capa passed away in 2008.

The process of interpreting bodies as evidence is further complicated when not only the precise circumstances are unknown but when forensic traces have been erased deliberately. The World War II mass graves in Russia's Katyn Forest come to mind readily as an example of the manipulation and misrepresentation of material evidence. German troops invading the Soviet Union during Operation Barbarossa located a number of mass graves near the city of Smolensk that contained an estimated twenty thousand people, among whom four thousand were officers of the Polish Army. The German Army supervised in April 1943 an international team of medical and criminology experts to exhume the graves. The investigation established that the victims had all been shot at close range. The Soviet Union was held responsible for the massacre. Soviet troops retook the forest six months later, and a commission was set to work in January 1944 that accused the Germans of slaughtering the Polish officers and civilians. The commission's report entered the Nuremberg Trials as proof of Nazi atrocities on the Eastern Front. Documentary evidence of the Soviet responsibility for the Katyn massacre had to wait till the early 1990s when Russia's archives were finally opened (Paul 1991; Paperno 2001).

A second, much more recent, example concerns the massacre of around eight thousand Muslims in July 1995 near the town of Srebrenica in Bosnia-

Herzegovina. Serbian troops commanded by General Ratko Mladić had over-run a battalion of Dutch troops stationed in the UN enclave. The women and children were evacuated, and the men and boys were executed after the Dutch peacekeepers had left Srebrenica. The bodies were buried in mass graves that were opened several weeks later with heavy equipment to disturb the evidence of the massacre. The partially deteriorated bodies were disarticulated, and the remains commingled, before being buried at different sites for the second time. The first forensic exhumation was carried out under the auspices of the International Criminal Tribunal for the former Yugoslavia (ICTY) in July 1996, which was investigating war crimes and crimes against humanity in the Balkans. These exhumations revealed the difference between criminal evidence and forensic evidence, and showed that the interests of a court seeking the conviction of perpetrators may be at odds with the humanitarian aim to identify the victims for their religious reburial by the surviving family members (Crossland 2013; Wagner 2015).

This chapter analyzes the complexity of collecting and interpreting forensic evidence about the victims assassinated during Argentina's dictatorship from 1976 to 1983, Spain's Civil War from 1936 to 1939, and the decades of authoritarian rule in Spain until Franco's death in 1975. What makes the comparison of the Argentine and Spanish cases of exhumation presented here so interesting is how the transitional lives of the crimes against humanity developed in parallel or interactive ways, and how the combination of forensic exhumations, legal accountability, and political circumstances gave rise to different bodies of evidence. Political refugees fled Franco's dictatorship to Argentina after 1939, and Argentines escaped from their country to Spain after the military coup d'état of 1976. Both regimes made great efforts during authoritarian rule to destroy the evidence of their crimes against humanity, and the two countries have collaborated and inspired one another since the mid-1980s to find disappeared citizens; exhume mass graves; and pursue memory, truth, and accountability.

The concealment and destruction of evidence were common practice in the authoritarian regimes of Spain and Argentina, and only scattered traces remained in secret documents, personal testimonies, and circumstantial evidence that, when placed in the proper context, could establish the crime. The crimes against humanity of both dictatorial regimes had therefore transitional lives during the time span between the classification and destruction of evidence and the piecemeal historical and forensic reconstruction decades later. This chapter compares and contrasts the concealment and disclosure of the mass killings of Spanish and Argentine citizens, which share the systematic disappearance of the victims of repression and the tenacious attempts by relatives to find their missing loved ones. The assassinations were concealed and the identity of perpetrators blurred for complex strategic, legal, and cultural reasons. Anonymous burials instilled fear and uncertainty among the population, destroyed incriminating evidence, and denied the bereaved and the deceased culturally important funerary rites. Both cases reveal how evidence was accumulated during decades of intermittent examinations spurred by unexpected political, forensic, and judicial developments.

In March 1996 there were large street demonstrations in Argentina against the continued impunity of known perpetrators of the disappearances. Amnesty laws had been passed in the late-1980s, and convicted officers had been granted presidential pardons. The Spanish prosecutor Carlos Castresana was emotionally moved by when he saw the Argentine protests on television, and within days set a legal process in motion that eventually allowed Judge Baltasar Garzón to request in March 1997 the extradition of former Argentine dictator Leopoldo Galtieri in (Roht-Arriaza 2005, 2–3). The arrest of Chilean dictator Augusto Pinochet in October 1998 when he was visiting Great Britain for medical reasons became internationally Garzón's most celebrated case, but the sentencing of Argentine Navy captain Scilingo in 2005 for his participation in two death flights was his most significant achievement, and the start of a growing legal collaboration between Spain and Argentina in pursuit of accountability. Spain asked Argentina to help establish the fate of Spanish citizens who had been disappeared during the Argentine dictatorship. Conversely, a number of Spanish memory associations and victims—including the case of the Valley of the Fallen in Spain discussed below—filed in 2010 in Argentina a lawsuit against the crimes against humanity committed during the civil war and Francoism on the grounds of international law (known as Querella Argentina). This successful lawsuit has resulted in legal actions in Spain by Argentine judge María Servini de Cubría, involving testimonies by victims, requests for exhumations and identifications, and a demand for the detention and extradition of more than twenty Francoist torturers and public officers. In other words, the two countries were prosecuting each other's suspects who could not be indicted at home because of the reigning amnesty laws. The threat of extradition to Spain made the Argentine armed forces accept the derogation of the impunity laws in 2005 and, in effect, agree to their prosecution at home, while the extradition requests of Spanish suspects to Argentina helped at least raise the issue of impunity in Spain. So far, the

Spanish state has refused to extradite to Argentina the culprits identified by Servini de Cubría, alleging that their presumed crimes have expired under the 1977 Amnesty Law.

The detention of Pinochet and the legal attention of Spanish judges to Argentina's perpetrators in the late 1990s influenced Spanish journalist Emilio Silva in the year 2000 to search for his grandfather who had been executed in 1936. The remains were located in a mass grave near the hamlet Priaranza del Bierzo. Subsequently, Silva published an article entitled "My Grandfather Was Also a Disappeared" that showed the direct impact of Argentina's exhumation movement on Spain. Within years, mass graves throughout Spain were exhumed by a grassroots movement propelled by family members and activists. The prominent place of Argentine relatives in finding their disappeared, not just in the tireless search and protest but as well in the monitoring of the exhumations, was also inspirational for Spain. The Spanish children and especially grandchildren who searched for their relatives stood at the edge of opened mass graves as forensic team members interviewed them about the ante mortem characteristics of the exposed skeletons. This procedure had been developed by Argentine forensic anthropologists during the late 1980s and was now adopted in Spain: the trust of the searching relatives was cultivated, and they became active research participants amid close attention to the political and legal implications of the identification process and the exposure of crimes against humanity (Fondebrider 2015). Furthermore, Spanish and Argentine forensic anthropologists have collaborated in various exhumations and have exchanged information and expertise. In January 2016, the first exhumation in Spain ordered by Judge Servini de Cubría, oriented to find the body of Timoteo Mendieta, took place in the Cemetery of Guadalajara, a city close to Madrid, and the genetic samples were sent across the ocean to the Argentine Forensic Anthropology Team, or Equipo Argentino de Antropología Forense (EAAF), forensic anthropologists for identification. The DNA testing in Argentina was negative for Mr. Mendieta's presumed body and a new exhumation in the same cemetery has been requested from the Argentinean Judge in early 2017, to the indifference and even feet-dragging of Spanish authorities. Exhumations and identifications have become transnational practices that are intertwined with human rights discourse and processes of transitional justice (Ferrándiz and Robben 2015).

Finally, the exhumation movements in Spain and Argentina and the pursuit of evidence of human rights violations transformed in the 2010s because of a shared cosmopolitan preoccupation with memory and commemoration, where iconographies of human right violations travel back and forth. Starting around 2008, transnational imageries of the disappeared started to proliferate in public acts by the memorial movement in Spain. In 2010, Spanish activists and family members started to carry photos of the missing during weekly protests in the main square in Madrid (Ronda de la Dignidad de Sol) that are reminiscent of the weekly marches of the Mothers of the Plaza de Mayo in Buenos Aires; and echoes of the Holocaust are heard in the denunciation of the Argentine and Spanish disappearances as genocide (Baer and Sznaider 2015; Ferrándiz and Silva Barrera 2016). The meanings of the bodies of evidence have been changing under the ideological polarization in the two countries, and the growing globalization of memory and accountability have given rise to similar stakeholders, imageries, narratives, and discourses. Nevertheless, the relatives of disappeared citizens in Spain and Argentina have been struggling with the different political and legal consequences of the exhumations because of other historical circumstances, as will become clear in the ensuing analyses.

Death Flights in Argentina

The first reference to death flights in Argentina was made on March 24, 1977, in an open letter to the military junta by the journalist Rodolfo Walsh. Walsh was a prominent member of the Montoneros guerrilla organization, and he denounced the Argentine military on the first anniversary of the coup d'état of 1976, for "carpeting the bottom of the River Plate with dead bodies or throwing prisoners into the sea from cargo planes of the First Air Brigade" (Walsh 1995, 419). Walsh was killed the next day in an exchange of gun fire with a naval task group that tried to abduct him.

In hindsight, we know that Walsh was right, but what was the source of his information? Walsh was a Montonero intelligence officer, and probably received the information from Montoneros who did their military service at the Buenos Aires city airport Jorge Newbery or at the secret detention centers of the Campo de Mayo Army Base and the Navy Mechanics School, or Escuela de Mecánica de la Armada (ESMA). One of them was the conscript Sergio Tarnopolsky, who was stationed at the ESMA and was passing information to Walsh. He and four family members were abducted by ESMA officers in July 1976 and assassinated (CIDH 1984, 85; Baschetti 2001, 38).

Next to presenting the direct evidence of testimonies, Walsh referred to material evidence that we can now link to the death flights. Walsh described in his open letter how between March and October 1976 twenty-five mutilated bodies that he assumed had been thrown in the River Plate from Argentine naval vessels had washed ashore on the Uruguayan coast. He also mentioned that dozens of bodies had appeared on the Argentine shore (Walsh 1995, 419). The information came from local newspapers that reported on the gruesome discoveries and from how the unidentified bodies were buried in local cemeteries.

The first detailed public testimonies about death flights were given by three Montoneros who had been held captive at the ESMA for more than one year and were sent into exile to Europe. Their eyewitness accounts were presented at the French National Assembly in Paris on October 12, 1979. The three explained that inmates were transported on Wednesdays, and occasionally Thursdays. They were told by naval officers that they were going to other secret detention centers or to work camps near the Patagonian town of Rawson. All captives were placed under lockdown on these days, and they only heard the case numbers of the transferees being called out at 5 PM. The three exiled Montoneros described the atmosphere at the ESMA when a group of captives was destined for a death flight as follows: "A very tense climate reigned on the day of the transfers. We, the abducted, did not know whether or not it would be our turn that day. The guards took many more severe measures than usual. We couldn't go to the bathroom. Every one of us had to remain strictly in his place, hooded and shackled, without making any attempt to see what was going on" (Martí, Pirles, and Osatinsky 1995, 40). Placed in a single file, the selected inmates were ordered to walk down the stairs to the building's basement.

Where were the captives taken? The three Montonero witnesses discovered their fate in February 1977, when Emilio Carlos Assales Bonazzola reappeared in the ESMA after having been put on transport earlier that day. He slept through the night and the following day, and then told them how he and twenty other captives had been taken to the infirmary in the basement and were supposedly vaccinated to prevent any contamination at their place of destination. Within minutes he was unable to move his limbs. Others began to vomit or fell unconscious. The group was loaded onto a truck and driven to Jorge Newbery Airport. When he was boarded into a Fokker aircraft, the guard asked for his name. Assales Bonazzola responded with his nickname: Tincho. "You have saved your life, kid," the guard responded as he was taken from the plane and driven back to the ESMA (Martí, Pirles, and Osatinsky

1995, 42). Apparently, a secret detention center in Mendoza had requested to interrogate him, and he was taken there in March 1977. The testimony of 1977 was confirmed in 1982 and 1988 by other ESMA captives (Daleo and Castillo 1982, 33–34; Gasparini 1988, 106; Anguita and Caparrós 1998, 384; Robben 2005, 267–69). The three ex-disappeared could now explain the rubber marks on the basement floor the day after a transport. The streaks had been made by the shoes of sedated captives hauled to the trucks waiting outside. When Coast Guard officer Gonzalo Sánchez commented once that the transferees would be thrown from planes flying above the ocean, they suddenly understood why the clothes of transported captives were found in the storage room (Martí, Pirles, and Osatinsky 1995, 41–43).

How reliable were the testimonies of former disappeared captives who told about lengthy torture sessions, constant humiliation, and prolonged incarceration in small cells—including cubicles of only 2 × 0.7 × 0.7 meters—while being handcuffed, shackled, and hooded? Were they not too traumatized to give reliable accounts of their experiences? Traumatic experiences create a mental overload that impedes a comprehensive cognitive encoding (McNally 2003, 190). As Ana Douglass and Thomas Vogler (2003, 2) have explained, "it is by definition in the nature of a mental trauma to exceed and violate our normal mental processing ability and frames of reference. The more massive the traumatic impact, the more it will affect our ability to register it."

The epistemological issue of testimony, truth, and trauma has been analyzed by Ruth Leys (2000, 298–307) in terms of a mimetic and an antimimetic position. The mimetic position maintains that people cannot describe traumatic experiences, because these never enter ordinary memory but are impressed straight on the brain. The experiences exist in sense memory as smells and sounds, or in dreams and flashbacks, but were not mediated cognitively. Echoing Charlotte Delbo about her experience in Auschwitz, Lawrence Langer (1991, 6) distinguishes between mimetic deep memory and antimimetic common memory: "Deep memory tries to recall the Auschwitz self as it was then; common memory has a dual function: it restores the self to its normal pre- and postcamp routines but also offers detached portraits, from the vantage point of today, of what it must have been like then. Deep memory thus suspects *and* depends on common memory, knowing what common memory cannot know but tries nonetheless to express." The antimimetic position claims that traumatic events do not restructure the psyche, and can therefore be expressed in a narrative account after enough emotional distance has been taken (Agger and Jensen 1996, 90–93). The ex-disappeared could provide thus both sensorial and verifiable evidence, but, in the political circumstances of 1979 when the Argentine military were still in power, they focused on a detailed documentation of the spatial layout of the ESMA building, the chain of command of the naval task force, the repressive operations, and the maternity ward where pregnant disappeared women were held. The personal experiences of the three eyewitnesses were downplayed. Verifiable knowledge was more important to convince foreign governments to take action against the Argentine junta than emotional displays of sensorial evidence.

The military regime fell quickly from power after losing a war with a British expeditionary force over the Falklands/Malvinas Islands in June 1982. Elections were held in October 1983, and Raúl Alfonsín became Argentina's new president in December 1983. He installed the National Commission on the Disappeared, or Comisión Nacional sobre la Desaparición de Personas (CONADEP). The commission gathered thousands of depositions, including some about death flights, but doubted their veracity. "This is scarcely credible, but is mentioned by many witnesses: some because they had heard about it, others because of direct references made by their captors. Then there were the bodies washed up by currents on the shore. It is indeed difficult to believe, but in the general context of this savage repression one can imagine that for those who practiced it" (CONADEP 1986, 221). The CONADEP report of 1984 included the testimony of the three ESMA survivors from 1979 quoted above, as well as two depositions. One witness said about the ESMA: "As far as we know from the comments of some Task Force officers, the 'transfer' prisoners were given an injection of pentothal, loaded asleep into the plane and thrown into the sea" (CONADEP 1986, 222).

Did the depositions provide reliable evidence? The truth commission created a trusting environment for witnesses to acknowledge their suffering, allowing them to share the harrowing experiences in their own way. The commission pursued testimonial evidence through personal depositions, and forensic evidence through exhumations. The poor quality of the forensic evidence gave therefore precedence to emotional narratives that were persuasive because people empathized with the stories of enforced disappearance and were moved by the accounts of torture.

The death flights were also examined during the trial in April–December 1985 against the nine junta commanders who had ruled Argentina between March 1976 and June 1982. The former captive Carlos Muñoz testified that ESMA officers had explained that transferees were injected with a sedative and thrown from helicopters at sea (Muñoz 1985, 455). Others survivors gave similar testimonies, aware that they could be subjected to cross-examination by the defense lawyers. The public truth finding in Argentina's inquisitional criminal law system was therefore fundamentally different from making a confidential deposition at the CONADEP. The judges questioned the witnesses, and would then allow prosecutors and defense lawyers to continue the oral examination. The difficulty with substantiating the allegations with documents, signed orders, confessions by officers, and forensic evidence explains why the testimonies about death flights were not pursued in the trial against the junta commanders.

The Argentine military maintained silence about the nature and extent of their repressive practices, let alone confessing to such an unforgiving crime as throwing people alive from planes and helicopters. Nevertheless, the retired police-inspector Rodolfo Peregrino Fernández told a human rights commission in March 1983 that planes of the Argentine Coast Guard were employed to launch abducted political prisoners into the sea. One officer told him that one time, "a prisoner had dragged the NCO entrusted with his elimination in his fall into the sky" (Fernández 1983, 71). Somehow, this circumstantial evidence did not receive much attention, other than confirming what former ESMA captives had been saying since 1979. The self-incriminatory account of retired Navy captain Adolfo Francisco Scilingo in March 1995, made at a time when the Argentine military were immune from prosecution because of sweeping amnesty laws, did finally call the death flights to national attention.

Captain Scilingo approached the prominent journalist Horacio Verbitsky in late 1994 to express his chagrin about the treatment of veterans of the so-called war against subversion. He himself had been refused promotion and had resigned in 1986. Scilingo told Verbitsky that he had flown two missions in June and July 1977 with thirteen and seventeen ESMA captives, respectively (Verbitsky 1995, 180). He explained that the sedated captives were put on the plane, given an additional tranquilizer, and then prepared for their fall to death by multiple injuries or drowning:

> They were undressed while being unconscious and when the flight commander gave the order, dependent on the location of the plane, the hatch was opened and they were thrown out naked, one by one. This is the story. A macabre but real story that no one can deny. They did it with Skyvan planes of the Coast Guard and Electra planes from the Navy. In the Skyvan through the rear hatch that opens from top to bottom. It's a large hatch

without intermediate positions. It's closed or open, and therefore maintained in open position. The NCO stepped on the hatch, a sort of swivel hatch, so that there would be an opening of forty centimeters towards the void. Next, we began lowering the subversives that way. (Verbitsky 1995, 58)

Eighteen years after Rodolfo Walsh first mentioned the death flights, Scilingo's confession finally completed a picture of the entire procedure from taking captives from their cells to their fall to death. The detailed account provided many new leads, and corroborated the veracity of testimonies that had been doubted, such as Police-Inspector Fernández's hearsay about an officer almost falling to death. This officer was Captain Scilingo, and it happened on his first flight after the captives had been undressed: "Next, we began lowering the subversives that way. As I was quite nervous about the situation, I almost fell and tumbled into the abyss. . . . I slipped and they grabbed me" (Verbitsky 1995, 58). Luis Moreno Ocampo, the assistant prosecutor at the trial of the commanders in 1985, remembered hearing a different version from Scilingo, namely that Scilingo did not slip but that he was almost dragged into the sky by an awakening captive: "Despite the injection, this prisoner woke up, and half-conscious resisted being thrown out and almost dragged him into the abyss" (Verbitsky 1995, 149). These different versions show that even self-incriminating evidence must be treated with suspicion because it may serve ulterior motives. Captain Scilingo turned himself into a victim who was ordered to carry out a gruesome task, almost died in the duty, and ended up being traumatized and expelled from the navy.

Scilingo was protected from prosecution by Argentina's amnesty laws, but he was not safe from revenge by his former comrades. They abducted him, and carved the initials of three journalists with whom he had spoken into his face. He fled to Spain to testify in a trial, and was accused himself. He was convicted in 2007 to 1,084 years in prison for crimes against humanity, which translated into an effective term of twenty-five years. Furthermore, Scilingo's impunity strengthened the resolve of the human rights movement to pursue the derogation of the amnesty laws.

Scilingo's testimony about the death flights had convinced the Spanish judges and the Argentine human rights movement, but there was no documentary or forensic proof. An important break came in 2005. The Argentine Forensic Anthropology Team, or Equipo Argentina de Antropología Forense (EAAF), had gained access to the Judicial Archive in Buenos Aires, and discovered that around sixty bodies had washed ashore on the beach of Mar del Plata between 1976 and 1978. Some bodies were fingerprinted and buried anonymously at General Lavalle Cemetery (Río Negro 2005). A number of sets of fingerprints matched with the records of the National Identity Document, or Documento Nacional de Identidad (DNI), and the EAAF requested that the judge exhume the anonymous bodies at the cemetery. There were no bullet impacts that could explain the cause of death. The autopsy reports made by the police at the time listed polytraumatism as the cause of death (interview with Luis Fondebrider on July 3, 2015). Positive identifications were made in 2005 of five persons who had been disappeared in December 1977 and were seen alive at the ESMA (CONADEP 1986, 343). They were members of the Mothers of the Plaza de Mayo, including its founder, Azucena Villaflor de De Vicenti, and the French nun Léonie Duquet, who had been assisting the human rights organization.

The forensic examination of the five skeletons reached the following conclusion: "During the laboratory study the team established that the fractures on the bodies were consistent with those of people who had fallen from a great height onto a hard surface (even though water is not a 'hard' surface, when a body falls from a great height, it acts as a hard surface). This case is important because it is the first forensic investigation providing evidence indicating that kidnapped people who had been seen alive in ESMA and remained disappeared were actually dropped into the ocean" (EAAF 2006, 18). The skeletal fractures resembled those of suicide victims who had jumped from high bridges (Abel and Ramsey 2013). The forensic evidence of death flights served multiple purposes: searching relatives whose disappeared loved ones were seen at the ESMA of Campo de Mayo military base realized that they would probably never find any remains; testimonies that had been doubted acquired truth-value; the history of the military regime could be rewritten; and when perpetrators and victims could be tied to particular flights, convictions could follow. The total number of dead from death flights has been estimated at 2,000–3,500 captives (Somigiliana and Olmo 2002, 27).

The derogation of the amnesty laws in 2005 resulted in the resumption of the criminal trials against the Argentine military in 2006, but the forensic evidence about disappeared captives who had fallen to their death did not provide enough ground for legal action because the perpetrators could not be identified. Important new evidence arose in September 2009, when a witness declared that navy helicopter pilot Emir Sisul Hess had told him about his participation in the death flights at which captives had begged for their lives and fallen like ants into the sky (Martínez 2009). In November 2012, the coast guard pilots Mario Arru, Alejandro D'Agostino, and Enrique De Saint Georges, the navy pilots Emir Hess and Julio Poch, and the naval mechanic Rubén Ormello were accused of their roles in the flights. Their identification allowed the prosecution to find documentary evidence in the flight records at Buenos Aires city airport Jorge Newbery. The logbooks from 1976 to 1978 were analyzed in terms of four variables:

1. duration (flights of more than 2.5 hours)
2. destination (flights that departed from or arrived at Jorge Newbery Airport)
3. nocturnal flights (flights between 6 PM and 6 AM)
4. purpose (e.g., training mission or transporting personnel)

Eleven flights were marked as suspicious, including one flight in which a Skyvan PA-51 aircraft departed at 9:30 PM on Wednesday December 14, 1977. The flight was operated by the coast guard pilots Arru, D'Agostino, and De Saint Georges, with the ESMA captives Azucena Villaflor de De Vicenti and Léonie Duquet probably on board—the two captives whose bodies washed ashore about one week later and were identified in 2005. The three pilots denied having carried any passengers on this particular flight and stated that it had been a nocturnal training mission (Martínez 2011). The verdict was passed on November 29, 2017. Poch and Hess were found not guilty. Arru and D'Agostino were handed life sentences, and De Saint Georges died in February 2017.

The crimes against humanity in Argentina were of such complexity that the repressive structure became visible only gradually through the different types and instruments of evidential regimes employed during thirty years of democracy. The case of Argentina's death flights demonstrates how a processual intertwinement of different types of evidence produced under changing political and technical circumstances forged complex personal, political, legal, and historical truths. The following case from Spain shows a different manifestation of this processual intertwinement of accountability, politics, and truth through an analysis of the politicization of the skeletal remains of Valerico Canales, a socialist militant executed and buried in a mass grave in 1936 and then exhumed thirty years later and reburied anonymously in a labyrinth of crypts.

Impenetrable Ossuaries:
Vanishing Evidence in the Valley of the Fallen

On October 11, 2003, a team of archaeologists located a lost mass grave in Aldeaseca, a municipality in the province of Ávila, Spain. There, seven civilians from the neighboring village of Pajares de Adaja reportedly had been buried after having been executed by Franco's paramilitary on August, 20, 1936, in the midst of the early, "hot terror" phase of the Spanish Civil War (1936–39), when a furious stream of blood crossed the country. This initial burst of violence gave way to what historians have labeled the phase of "legal terror," in which killings of civilians continued at a slower pace and were preceded by administrative and legal procedures. While the Republican government tried to inhibit extrajudicial killings in the areas under their control, in the rebel (Nationalist) areas military justice took over, and mock war tribunals (*consejos de guerra*) became responsible for the systematic repression of civilians (Casanova 1999). According to current historiography, around 55,000 civilians were executed in the Republican rearguard during the war, and at least 150,000 by militias working in parallel to the rebel, or "Nationalist," army, including some 20,000 after the war (Rodrigo 2008; Preston 2012).

The end of the war and the advent of Franco's thirty-six-year-long dictatorship brought about the emergence of two radically dissimilar "spaces of death" (Taussig 1987), resulting in what Emilio Silva has called a long-lasting "funerary apartheid" (personal communication), one space of death constituted by the bodies of the winners and another containing the bodies of those considered loyal to the Republic and declared traitors to the country, despite their fidelity to a democratically elected government. The latter bodies were mostly erased from public memory and administrative or legal inscription, but were opened right after the war. Specific funerary legislation was passed to protect them, and instructions were distributed by the central government to organize the unburials and reburials, as well as the gathering of evidence of the so-called "red terror" committed by "Marxist hordes." A large countrywide judicial case was opened, known as Causa General, where all rearguard crimes attributed to Republicans and their alleged perpetrators were listed. Many of them were executed or sent to jail. Forensic physicians were recruited to participate in the exhumations of Nationalists and help with building evidence of crimes and identifying the corpses. The emerging politicoreligious ideology of the new regime, National Catholicism, rooted its legitimacy in the sacrifice and martyrdom of those "fallen for God and Spain" that were being exhumed. Most villages in the country listed the names of the fallen in preferential locations on the church's outside walls for everyone to see, presided over by the name of the "martyr of martyrs," José Antonio Primo de Rivera. Primo de Rivera was the founder in 1933 of the Spanish fascist party, Falange, executed in jail in the early months of the war, and reburied in 1939 in the basilica right above the Royal Pantheon in the Monastery of El Escorial, Spain's ultimate imperial monument (Ferrándiz 2014, 145–74). By doing so, the dictatorial state symbolized its connection with Spain's "most glorious times."

The mass graves of the defeated were radically excluded from this unburial and reburial process that marked a high-profile celebration of the birth of the New Spain (Box 2010). By contrast, as a crucial ingredient of Franco's National security policy—based on widespread repression of the defeated (jails, concentration camps, fines, mistreatment of women) in the frame of an admonitory *blood pedagogy*—they continued to multiply in the early postwar years in order to consolidate a topography of terror affecting almost every village: a safety network activated to inhibit any potential political dissidence. As places of exemplary memory, or *fear memorials*, the presence of the mass graves of defeat on the national landscape contributed not only physically, but also politically, symbolically, and socially, to the shoring up of the postwar dictatorial regime under the rule of General Francisco Franco. The investment in terror expressed in thousands of mass graves across the country undoubtedly bore fruit in the dictatorship (Rodrigo 2008), though its bitter legacy evolved and transformed with the Francoist regime, their original efficacy declining as the broad, heterogeneous social body of the defeated absorbed the impact. Even so, the unexpected twenty-first-century reappearance of these graves in the national and international debate on the civil war, Francoism, and political repression shows that the wounds left in the social and political fabric by Franco's military rebellion (1936–39) and dictatorship (1939–75) were very deep and affected several generations.

The year 2000 marked a major turning point in Spain's funerary apartheid, when a mass grave containing the remains of thirteen people killed by Nationalists was opened in Priaranza del Bierzo (province of León) under the initiative of sociologist and journalist Emilio Silva, the grandson of one of the slain. The principal Spanish memorial association, Asociación para la Recuperación de la Memoria Histórica (ARMH), over which Silva has since presided, was soon created. A wave of exhumations followed. In 2017, this process has reached at least 450 mass graves, including the recovery of more the 8,500 bodies (Ferrándiz 2013, 2014). These contemporary unburials of Republican civilians have three main characteristics:

1. They take place in a globalized information society that guarantees high media exposure. (Castells 1996)

2. Although initially advanced by civil society—the grandchildren of the defeated—they eventually attracted some institutional involvement, notably a Historical Memory Law (2007) passed by the Socialist government and around twenty million euros in public funding from 2005–2012.

3. The unburials are carried out through technical archaeological and forensic protocols allowing for a scientific evidentiary reinscription of the executions and the bodies. (Etxeberria 2012)

This production of knowledge about human rights violations is based on a rigorous methodology, evidentiary logic—scientific, but not legal because of a statute of limitations and Spain's refusal to honor international human rights laws—forms of technical and digital imaging, scientific custody, electronic archive building, and the growing yet intermittent use of DNA identification and its associated rationale of genetic kinship and statistical certainty (Baeta et al. 2015). Beyond these technical considerations, the scientific approach to opening and interpreting mass graves has gained considerable social prestige, within the broader impact of what some researchers call the CSI effect, namely the contemporary popularity of forensic serials in the mainstream media (Kruse 2010; Ferrándiz 2013). Many memory activists and victims' relatives started to consider that next to the exhumations, the largest price of the political agreements leading to democracy in Spain was the impunity of the crimes of Francoism for the sake of reconciliation—the Amnesty Law and the failure to reverse the institutional abandonment of the tens of thousands of Republicans executed and improperly buried in mass graves. Through this scientific evidentiary inscription (Crossland 2013), the penumbra which these dead bodies had inhabited for decades, defying oblivion not only during the dictatorship but also in the interstices of democracy and modernization, has given way to a regime of public presence and visibility unthinkable a few years ago. A transition has occurred from fugitive ghosts (Steedly 1993; Gordon 1997) into openly visible civil war skeletons widely circulating in the public space and challenging solid legal and political pacts, such as the Amnesty Law of 1977 or the formerly exemplary Spanish transition to democracy.

The exhumation in 2003 in Aldeaseca was an early case in this high-profile wave of unburials of Republican civilians mostly led by the generation of the grandchildren of defeat, though many sons and daughters, and later great-grandchildren, also joined in as the diggings picked up momentum. The Aldeaseca exhumation was promoted by Fausto Canales—a retired engineer whose murdered father was a leader of the Socialist trade union (UGT) in Pajares de Adaja—with the support of archaeologists from a local memory association. While the excavation was largely unsuccessful, it provided one major evidentiary surprise that was to transform Spain's perception of its most controversial monument: the Valley of the Fallen, built by Franco as the main memorial place of his victory in 1939. To the technical team's astonishment, only a few small, left-behind human bones were found during the digging, as well as pieces of a broken skull. Enough evidence to prove that the mass grave had been there but . . . where had the bones gone? Who had visited the abandoned grave before the relatives and why? Fausto and his collaborators were at a loss to explain this unexpected development. The families made the joint decision to bury these remains together on August 28, 2004, in a monument-grave erected in the Pajares de Adaja Cemetery. Since then, an annual tribute is paid there to mark the date. Fausto and the other relatives placed the scattered remains in a small urn to represent all those who were in the grave, in a fragmentary reproduction of the community of death—if they died together, they should be reburied together—and initially renounced any identification process of individual remains, including DNA tests.

The archival investigations undertaken by Fausto Canales after the exhumation fiasco indicated that the bodies had been moved to the Valley of the Fallen in 1959, without the families' knowledge. He found diverse documentation about the tasks of locating, excavating, and transferring the remains found in the grave. The documents included definitive proof that their suspicions were correct: the exhumations had been carried out by an expedition organized by the Avila Office of the Civil Governor, signed March 6, 1959. The report indicated that on March 1 of the same year, the Aldeaseca Grave had been dug for about two hours and that the grave was not easy to find because the people who knew of the existence of the remains had disappeared owing to the time elapsed. Further research on the case also permitted the localization in the valley memorial of a box (Columbarium No. 198) containing six unknown corpses from Aldeaseca and six others from another grave in the same area. These discoveries turned Fausto Canales into one of the key figures in bringing the monument into the spotlight in the search for people who were disappeared during the civil war and Franco's subsequent rule. The fact that an unknown number of Republican dead had been surreptitiously transported to the memorial during late Francoism came as a shock to many. Canales's story perfectly reflects the astonishment experienced by relatives of Franco's victims, who gradually discovered the fate of their next-of-kin, whom they now considered trapped in an exceptional and complex ossuary born of a religious, political, and symbolic delirium and offensively riveted to the graves of Falange founder Primo de Rivera and Franco himself, buried there in 1975. Since the evidence of the reburial of the corpses from Aldeaseca in the Valley of the Fallen became public, Canales has sought every possible legal means to retrieve his father's body from what he considered a "cavern of horror," including appeals to different Spanish judicial entities and even to the Strasbourg European Human Rights Court, so far to no avail (Ferrándiz 2014). In what follows, I will briefly outline some crucial facts in the history of the monument and the mounting evidence that many Republican bodies were transferred to a place soaked in Francoist iconography and symbolism as part of a dubious reconciliatiatory gesture in the late dictatorship, and explore the difficulties in unmaking Francoism's last stronghold.

It took Franco twenty years to build this huge mausoleum, barely thirteen kilometers away from the Monastery of El Escorial, where the Royal Pantheon is located. To do so, a mountain was drilled to build Christianity's second largest basilica after Saint Peter's, topped by a conspicuous 150-meter-high cross. In 1958, a few months before its inauguration on the twentieth anniversary of the civil war "victory" (April 1, 1959), there was a nationwide call for the bodies of *Caídos por Dios y por España* (Those fallen for God and Spain), including Republicans as long as they were proven Catholics. According to the register kept by the Benedictines in charge of the monument, 33,833 bodies entered the crypts, mostly between 1959 and 1971. A total of 12,410 are "unknown," though at the current stage of research it is impossible to trace how many of them are Republicans. The Spanish people were unaware of this transfer of bodies, and the scale and details of the crypts until the Canales case erupted in the media.

The fact that twenty years had passed since the war had finished, with many Fallen for God and for Spain consolidated in family or municipal pantheons, conditioned this massive body-transfer operation. Resistance in Nationalist quarters to the pressure from the central government to produce bodies promoted the semiclandestine, yet official, digging of Republican mass graves. The remains of Fascist leader Primo de Rivera were moved from El

Escorial to the Valley of the Fallen to preside over the altar at the inauguration in 1959. In 1975, a major state funeral took place in the valley when Franco was buried behind the altar. With this latest burial, an unmistakably Francoist funerary hierarchy was consolidated in the monument. During the transition to democracy and the subsequent decades, the valley was beyond dispute and remained a major tourist attraction. Until the passing of the Law of Historical Memory in 2007, every November 20, the date of both Primo de Rivera's and Franco's death in 1936 and 1975, neofascist political ceremonies took place there with official acquiescence. With the most recent wave of exhumations starting in 2000, all of this changed, as claims for the recovery, identification and dignification of the Republican bodies reached its subterranean crypts, threatening for the first time the integrity of the monument.

The Historical Memory Law passed in Parliament in 2007 put an end to any political display at the monument but did not include any special provision to rescue the bodies and only established an outsourcing model for other mass graves (Ferrándiz 2013). Relatives of the Republicans buried in the valley then filed complaints before the Spanish High Court (Audiencia Nacional) and thus were part of a short-lived attempt in 2008 by internationally known judge Baltasar Garzón to apply International Human Rights Law to the crimes of Francoism using the penal concept of forced disappearances. The initiative was derailed by the Spanish Supreme Court. Its ruling acquitted Garzón but foreclosed every possibility of prosecuting the crimes of Francoism. On the legislative front, a major development took place in 2010 regarding the scientific study of the crypts. The Socialist vice-president Teresa Fernández de la Vega asked the Ministry of Justice to assess the state of the crypts and the human remains and to evaluate the feasibility of exhumations and identifications. Forensic physician José Luis Bedate produced a very significant but discouraging report. Bodies had been distributed in twenty-eight different burial levels, behind eight chapels. The lateral chapels in the central nave had three levels of burials each, while the chapels on both sides of the transept had five burial levels each, the most complex of them containing more than ten thousand bodies. Due to technical limitations and legal uncertainties about the status of the cemetery, Bedate could only open one hole in each chapel and superficially explore the state of the burials. His team took some pictures, though these were not included in the official report. His assessment was that exhumations posed a "high technical risk" and that the individual identifications were of "extreme complexity" due to the collapse of the different stories and the consequent intermingling of bones (Bedate 2011).

Associations of Republicans buried in the valley, some of which were allowed to be present during the forensic study, were shocked. At this point, DNA technology had become a more widespread practice in the identification of bodies exhumed in mass graves throughout the country, and the official forensic report all but shattered the associations' hopes of legally authorized operations to rescue their relatives from the cemetery's depths. For their part, the Benedictine custodians were struggling to keep the ossuary intact and retain full control over it. In the midst of heated public debate, the then abbot, Anselmo Álvarez, drafted a double strategy to prove the intractability of the crypts: one numerical, the other both physical and symbolic. First, he cast doubt on the number of people buried there, suggesting that the total may be double the number of those formally registered by his own religious order: a numerical mess. Second, as a sort of mystical counterevidence, sources close to him publicly disseminated the idea that many of the bones had actually dissolved into the bedrock, melting into the very monument for eternity. The tens of thousands of skeletal remains had become an integral part of the structural foundations of the valley—a physical impossibility. Supporting the Benedictines' evidentiary lockout are the Neo-Francoist associations for the defense of the valley, with yet another shot in the barrel: legal complaints against tomb profanation in the name of those families that agreed to the reburial were any forensic action to take place in the valley.

In 2011, I was appointed by the Socialist government as a member of a Commission of Experts to democratize and resignify the valley. My task was mostly oriented toward providing solutions for funerary aspects. The main proposal, which created a public outcry, was to undo the dictatorship's funerary hierarchy by removing the bodies of Franco and Primo de Rivera from priority burial on both sides of the altar. Furthermore, any attempt at transforming the meaning of the monument demanded that the dictator Francisco Franco abandon its premises. What was more difficult was to provide solutions for the Republicans unexpectedly surfacing in the crypts in the last decade. In coordination with memorial associations, we proposed a thorough re-evaluation of the ossuaries by bringing in an internationally recognized forensic committee, including the International Red Cross. The proposal was turned down but, as a trade-off, three forensic physicians, including leading expert Francisco Etxeberria, were called to a commission meeting to reassess Bedate's report in the light of the photographs taken during the exploration. A senior Ministry of Justice official brought the pictures on a memory stick, allowed us to see and discuss them for a few minutes and then left with the memory stick in her pocket. The panorama was certainly grim, and at that moment we realized why these pictures had become a state secret and were not displayed in the forensic report. Were they to be made public, an outcry was certainly guaranteed, even among those families of Franco supporters who had allowed the reburial of their relatives in El Valle a few decades ago. The Commission of Experts report also reflected the "extreme difficulty" of exhumations. Yet, the possibilities of a more thorough forensic assessment, and of advanced DNA identification techniques, can still offer a minimal hope that keeps many relatives fighting, despite the odds.

All of Fausto Canales's judicial appeals in Spain have been turned down in the last decade, as if he were hitting an indestructible impunity wall blocking any access to evidence. His claim was also dismissed in the European Court of Human Rights in Strasbourg. A claimant in the Querella Argentina since 2010, he was able legally to testify in 2014 to the Argentinean judge Servini de Cubría by videoconference from the Argentinean Consulate in Madrid—after being twice blocked by the Spanish government—to no avail so far. Yet on March 10, 2016, a judge in El Escorial ordered the exhumation of two Republicans executed during the war in the town of Calatayud (Zaragoza Province), opening a new judicial channel for other valley exhumation claims. The State Heritage Department, which owns the monument, responded to the judicial order imposing conditions unacceptable to the relatives. After their lawyer filed a new lawsuit for noncompliance in late July 2016, the case appeared before the Supreme Court, where, in turn, it was sent back to the local judge. Meanwhile, both the Benedictines and the central right-wing government are actively prohibiting any new entry into the crypts, despite the legal mandate. All attempts to unbury Franco from the valley and turn him in to his family have been systematically blocked, as the monument increasingly armors itself against what its supporters—Benedictines, Franco nostalgics, and the very political party in power in Spain—consider vengeful assaults from those who lost the war and now want to win it by other means.

Conclusion

The Spanish and Argentine cases demonstrate that crimes against humanity committed in the framework of military coups and dictatorships were concealed for reasons of state security and authoritarian domination, and that the complex processes of gathering evidence and managing forensic investigations are more often elucidated and driven by family protests, media exposure, and the political arena than by courts and tribunals. In one case, evidence of crimes appears to be dissolving into the bedrock, and even minimal access is being blocked powerful reactionary forces, to the desperation of relatives. In the other, some bodies washed ashore on the beach provide proof attesting to a daunting criminal practice and may serve to incriminate perpetrators. In both cases, evidence is hard to reach and comes in discontinuous, multiple, interlocking, and competing narratives and truth regimes.

The fate of corpses resulting from human rights violations provides an extraordinary roadmap to understand the inner workings of repressive apparatuses. That concealment and denial are an integral part in the establishment of regimes of fear goes without saying. Yet, the multiple evidential regimes emerging around such dead bodies after dictatorial control of history, memory, and criminal evidence start to diagram the depth of the damage that was intended, express the regimes of visibility and invisibility underlying structures of terror, and are tragically inscribed by traces of exclusionary nationhood and belonging.

Since the mid-1980s, with the identification of Mengele's skull in Brazil by Clyde Snow and his forensic team, and the foundation of the Argentine Forensic Anthropology Team (EAAF), the exhumation of corpses from episodes of mass violence and genocide has become a major tool in the search for "truth, justice and reparation" of victims in transitional processes around the world. The consolidation of increasingly prestigious technologies established around wounded bodies implies the emergence of a novel and transformative necropolitical regime associated with the management of human rights violations—part of a broader forensic turn in the understanding of human experience and suffering (Anstett and Dreyfus 2015). Mass graves and unburials become a ground zero, where mass assassinations, disappearances, and tortures can be deciphered in different degrees of elaboration.

This regime of knowledge and reparation of the violent past is both promising and contradictory. For one thing, the amount and quality of information and evidence that a dead body can provide is enormous, from visible fractures to minuscule traces of torture and killing, as in the case of the death flights in Argentina. In parallel, a new corporeal epistemology is emerging, where, as Klinenberg states, dead bodies become "the site and surface of essential but otherwise obscured social truths" (2002, 121). Also, the forensic and archaeological protocols leading the search, unburial, interpretation, and identifications of such bodies produce different kinds of evidence: judicial, scientific or genetic (Crossland 2013). The increasing availability and constant technical improvement of these new modalities of evidence building are deeply transforming the nature of the relationship with the violent past and, very importantly, cast a threatening shadow on present and future would-be perpetrators, who are forced to develop new and more sophisticated techniques for concealing evidence.

But, as in Spain and Argentina, political, social and cultural contexts are diverse, and the limitations are plenty. Despite their prestige as the silver bullet of international criminal justice and the fight against impunity—partially an aftereffect of the infallible CSI effect—the new human rights technologies of evidence building can also prove very problematic as they create false, even imaginary, expectations for victims. This is the case of the Valley of the Fallen, where the possibility of DNA identification, if almost impossible technically, keeps alive the flame of hope in relatives but may create long-term frustration as evidence melts into the bedrock and gets lost in political, judicial, and religious labyrinths.

Also, as these evidence-based technologies for deciphering the violent past become hegemonic and naturalized, they have the potential to displace or even contradict alternative forms of historical, political, and emotional connections with both kin and the violent past. Both in Argentina and Spain, sections of the associative movement are resisting these increasingly hegemonic, almost commonsensical, technologies for truth and justice and their associated evidentiary regimes. In Argentina, because exhumations and identifications may provide a false closure and short-circuit deeply embedded political ideals rooted in claims for the disappeared to return: "vivos los llevaron, vivos los queremos" (they took them alive, we want them back alive). In Spain, because the lack of a legal umbrella for the exhumations amounts—for some associations—to an erasure of genocide, where media, spectacle, flashy forensic evidence, and bogus mourning reign, gravely disturbing the political continuity between those assassinated in the civil war and its aftermath and contemporary social struggle. Also in this context, the availability of genetic identification is interpreted as fostering a neoliberal individualization of memory of what is interpreted as a mass, collective crime. In both cases, these resistances coincide in a deep fear that the new empire of technical and scientific evidence bulldozes alternative forms of mourning, memory politics, and truth making.

References

Abel, Suzanne M., and Scott Ramsey. 2013. "Patterns of Skeletal Trauma in Suicide Bridge Jumpers: A Retrospective Study from the Southeastern United States." *Forensic Science International* 231: 399.e1–e5.

Agger, Inger, and Søren Buss Jensen. 1996. *Trauma and Healing under State Terrorism*. London: Zed Books.

Anguita, Eduardo, and Martín Caparrós. 1998. *La voluntad: Una historia de la militancia revolucionaria en la Argentina*. Vol. 3. Buenos Aires: Editorial Norma: 1966–78.

Anstett, Élisabeth, and Jean-Marc Dreyfus, eds. 2015. *Human Remains and Identification: Mass Violence, Genocide and the "Forensic Turn."* Manchester, UK: Manchester University Press.

Baer, Alejando, and Natan Sznaider. 2015. "Ghosts of the Holocaust in Spanish Mass Graves: Cosmopolitan Memories and the Politics of 'Never Again.'" *Memory Studies* 8(3): 328–44.

Baeta, Miriam, Carolina Núñez, Sergio Cardoso, Leire Palencia-Madrid, Lourdes Herrasti, Francisco Etxeberria, and Miriam M. de Pancorbo. 2015. "Digging Up the Recent Spanish Memory: Genetic Identification of Human Remains from Mass Graves of the Spanish Civil War and Posterior Dictatorship." *Forensic Science International: Genetics* 19: 272–79.

Barca, Antonio Jiménez. 2008. "El soldado, el fotógrafo y la muerte." *El País*. 5 October.

Baschetti, Roberto. 2001. *Documentos 1976–1977, vol. 1, Golpe militar y resistencia popular*. La Plata, Argentina: de La Campana.

Bedate, Andrés. 2011. *Viabilidad de identificación en el enterramiento del Valle de los caídos*. Madrid: Ministerio de Justicia.

Box, Zira. 2010. *España, año cero*. Madrid: Alianza.

Casanova, Julián. 1999. "Rebelión y revolución." In *Víctimas de la Guerra Civil*, edited by Santos Juliá, 57–177. Madrid: Temas de Hoy.

Castells, Manuel. 1996. *The Information Age: Economy, Society and Culture, vol. 1, The Rise of the Network Society*. Malden, MA: Blackwell.

CIDH (Comisión Interamericana de Derechos Humanos). [1980] 1984. *El informe prohibido: Informe sobre la situación de los derechos humanos en Argentina*. Buenos Aires: OSEA and CELS.

CONADEP. [1984] 1986. *Nunca Más: The Report of the Argentine National Commission on the Disappeared*. New York: Farrar Straus Giroux.

Crossland, Zoe. 2013. "Evidentiary Regimes of Forensic Archaeology." *Annual Review of Anthropology* 42: 121–37.

Daleo, Graciela, and Andrés Ramón Castillo. 1982. *Informe*. Madrid: CADHU.

Doménech, Hugo, and Raúl M. Riebenbauer. 2007. *La sombra del iceberg: Una au-*

topsia de la mítica fotografía de Robert Capa *"El miliciano muerto."* Documentary film. Valencia: DACSA Producciones.

Douglass, Ana, and Thomas A. Vogler. 2003. Introduction to *Witness and Memory: The Discourse of Trauma*, edited by Ana Douglass and Thomas A. Vogler, 1–53. New York: Routledge.

EAAF (Equipo Argentino de Antropología Forense). 2006. *2006 Mini Annual Report: Covering the Period January to December 2005*. Buenos Aires: EAAF.

Etxeberria, Francisco. 2012. "Exhumaciones contemporáneas en España: Las fosas comunes de la Guerra Civil." *Boletín Galego de Medicina Legal e Forense* 18(January): 13–28.

Fernández, Rodolfo Peregrino. 1983. *Autocrítica policial*. Buenos Aires: El Cid Editor.

Ferrándiz, Francisco. 2013. "Exhuming the Defeated: Civil War Mass Graves in 21st-Century Spain." *American Ethnologist* 40(1): 38–54.

Ferrándiz, Francisco. 2014. *El pasado bajo tierra: Exhumaciones contemporáneas de la Guerra Civil*. Barcelona: Anthropos.

Ferrándiz, Francisco, and Antonius C. G. M. Robben. 2015. "Introduction: The Ethnography of Exhumations." In *Necropolitics: Mass Graves and Exhumations in the Age of Human Rights*, edited by Francisco Ferrándiz and Antonius C. G. M Robben, 1–38. Philadelphia: University of Pennsylvania Press.

Ferrándiz, Francisco, and Emilio Silva Barrera. 2016. "From Mass Graves to Human Rights: The Discovery of Forced Disappearances in Contemporary Spain." In *Missing Persons: Multidisciplinary Perspectives on the Disappeared*, edited by Derek Congram, 74–101. Toronto: Canadian Scholars' Press.

Fondebrider, Luis. 2015. "Forensic Anthropology and the Investigation of Political Violence: Lessons Learned from Latin America and the Balkans." In *Necropolitics: Mass Graves and Exhumations in the Age of Human Rights*, edited by Francisco Ferrándiz and Antonius C. G. M Robben, 41–52. Philadelphia: University of Pennsylvania Press.

Gasparini, Juan. 1988. *Montoneros: Final de cuentas*. Buenos Aires: Puntosur.

Gordon, Avery. 1997. *Ghostly Matters: Haunting and the Sociological Imagination*. Minneapolis: University of Minnesota Press.

Klinenberg, Eric. 2002. "Bodies That Don't Matter: Death and Dereliction in Chicago." In *Commodifying Bodies*, edited by Nancy Scheper-Hughes and Loïc Wacquant, 121–32. London: Sage.

Knightley, Phillip. 1975. *The First Casualty: From the Crimea to Vietnam: The War Correspondent as Hero, Propagandist, and Myth Maker*. New York: Harcourt Brace Jovanovich.

Kruse, Corinna. 2010. "Producing Absolute Truth: CSI Effect as Wishful Thinking." *American Anthropologist* 112(1): 79–91.

Langer, Lawrence L. 1991. *Holocaust Testimonies: The Ruins of Memory*. New Haven, CT: Yale University Press.

Leys, Ruth. 2000. *Trauma: A Genealogy*. Chicago: University of Chicago Press.

Martí, Ana María, María Alicia Milia de Pirles, and Sara Solarz de Osatinsky. [1979] 1995. *"Trasladados": Testimonio de tres liberadas*. Buenos Aires: Abuelas de Plaza de Mayo.

Martínez, Diego. 2009. "Las hormiguitas del capitán Hess." *Página/12*. September 7. https://www.pagina12.com.ar/diario/elpais/1-131334-2009-09-07.html.

Martínez, Diego. 2011. "Navegación nocturna." *Página/12*. April 12. http://www .pagina12.com.ar/diario/elpais/1-166061-2011-04-12.html.

McNally, Richard J. 2003. *Remembering Trauma*. Cambridge, MA: Harvard University Press.

Muñoz, Carlos. 1985. "Testimonio del señor Carlos Muñoz." *El Diario del Juicio* 24: 452–64.

Paperno, Irina. 2001. "Exhuming the Bodies of Soviet Terror." *Representations* 75(1): 89–118.

Paul, Allen. 1991. *Katyn: Stalin's Massacre and the Seeds of Polish Resurrection*. Annapolis, MD: Scribner.

Preston, Paul. 2012. *The Spanish Holocaust: Inquisition and Extermination in Twentieth-Century Spain*. London: Harper Press.

Río Negro. 2005. "Por primera vez hallan cuerpos de 'vuelos de la muerte.'" *Diario Río Negro*. July 9. http://www1.rionegro.com.ar/arch200507/09/n09a01.php.

Robben, Antonius C. G. M. 2005. *Political Violence and Trauma in Argentina*. Philadelphia: University of Pennsylvania Press.

Rodrigo, Javier. 2008. *Hasta la raíz: Violencia durante la Guerra Civil y la dictadura franquista*. Madrid: Alianza.

Roht-Arriaza, Naomi. 2005. *The Pinochet Effect: Transnational Justice in the Age of Human Rights*. Philadelphia: University of Pennsylvania Press.

Somigiliana, Maco, and Darío Olmo. 2002. "La huella del genocidio." *Encrucijadas* 2(January): 22–35.

Steedly, Mary. 1993. *Hanging without a Rope: Narrative Experience in Colonial and Postcolonial Karoland*. Princeton, NJ: Princeton University Press.

Taussig, Michael. 1987. *Shamanism, Colonialism, and the Wild Man: A Study in Terror and Healing*. Chicago: University of Chicago Press.

Verbitsky, Horacio. 1995. *El Vuelo*. Buenos Aires: Planeta.

Wagner, Sarah. 2015. "The Quandaries of Partial and Commingled Remains: Srebrenica's Missing and Korean War Casualties Compared." In *Necropolitics: Mass Graves and Exhumations in the Age of Human Rights*, edited by Francisco Ferrándiz and Antonius C. G. M. Robben, 119–39. Philadelphia: University of Pennsylvania Press.

Walsh, Rodolfo. 1995. *El violento oficio de escribir: Obra periodística (1953–1977)*. Buenos Aires: Planeta.

Whelan, Richard. 1985. *Robert Capa: A Biography*. Lincoln: University of Nebraska Press.

SIX

Policing Future Crimes

MARK MAGUIRE

The computer then cranks and heaves and gives an answer, and there is some temptation to obey the computer. After all, if you follow the computer you are a little *less responsible* than if you made up your own mind.
—GREGORY BATESON, *Steps to an Ecology of Mind*

After Ferguson

Just before noon on August 9, 2014 Officer Darren Wilson responded to a robbery in the Market and Liquor convenience store in Ferguson, Missouri. Wilson scoured the rundown streets in search of two "Black males" and quickly encountered Michael Brown and Dorian Johnson on Canfield Drive. Minutes later, Michael Brown lay dead in the street. Residents and relatives gathered at the scene, and several recorded what they saw on their smartphones. Videos spread quickly and virally through social media, especially one in which a narrator declares, "The police killed him, yeah. Say he had his hand up and everything; they still shot him" (CNN 2014).[1] The spot where Brown died became the focus of a spontaneous and peaceful gathering. However, Ferguson police assembled in force, and violence soon erupted.

A SWAT team armed with tear gas, rubber bullets, flash grenades, and smoke bombs confronted protesters a few days after Brown's death. The protesters started out decrying the militarization of police and ended up watching as weaponized law enforcement failed before their eyes. The Missouri governor, Jay Nixon, declared a state of emergency, implemented nightly curfews, and eventually called out the National Guard. In November, following the decision by the grand jury not to indict Officer Wilson, a state of emergency was again declared in Ferguson. On this occasion, several international demonstrations accompanied local protests.

The events in Ferguson are the subject of many thousands of international newspaper articles and many more social media posts and exchanges, together with investigations and reports, books and films.[2] Fundamentally, the events centered on the body of a Black youth with two discursive afterlives. The U.S. Department of Justice issued two reports in March 2015. The "Investigation of the Ferguson Police Department" documented how police undermined community trust, noting a "pattern of stops without reasonable suspicion and arrests without probable cause" coupled with a fixation on "revenue generation" (DOJ 2015a, 2). Activists read this as a vindication of their claim that a racialized state violence is unjustly targeting Black bodies. However, the second Department of Justice report (DOJ 2015b) presented evidence from the three autopsies conducted on Brown's body, together with eyewitness statements, DNA, ballistic and crime-scene analysis. The report concluded that there was no prosecutive merit in charging Wilson. Apparently, several eyewitnesses lied: Michael Brown was not shot while attempting to surrender. Juridical evidence collided with the sociological reality of activists in a battle over facts. As if to highlight the impossibility of neutrality, activist and journalist, Jonathan Capeheart (2015) changed sides, reflecting on the "uncomfortable truth" that this youth was perhaps "someone who would otherwise offend our sense of right and wrong."

At first glance, then, the shooting in Ferguson seems to illuminate an entire world of law enforcement in one kinetic moment. Here, however, I propose that by focusing on specific encounters we miss broader transformations of great importance. Indeed, one of the most significant transformations internationally is the move toward policing future crimes. Today's intelligence-led and predictive policing efforts are targeting near-future encounters between crime and law enforcement such that, the assumption is, some encounters will never occur in the first place. Today in the neighborhoods surrounding Ferguson, the St. Louis County Police Department is experimenting with predictive policing. This is not simply crime mapping or neighborhood profiling; rather, it is a particular way of conceptualizing the behavior of human beings and their near-future actions.[3] Thus, the social-scientific question is: What if the robbery in the Ferguson Market and Liquor never happened? This chapter addresses this question.

It may be possible to discuss predictive policing by exploring it ethnographically from the perspective of a specific law enforcement institution. Here, however, I wish to avoid framing a world of stable cultural institutions that resist or accommodate change from the outside (change theorized as an unambiguous process of militarization, for example). Instead, I wish to tell a broader and more elusive story that takes us from the nineteenth century to the present day and from Los Angeles to cities in the UK. It is a story about specific efforts to think about human life itself using statistics, software, and anthropology.

Anthropological ideas and trained anthropologists are certainly in great demand these days. Indeed, several disciplinary leaders have made important statements on the ethical and other challenges presented by the anthropological "moment" in a variety of military and counterinsurgency contexts (e.g., Price 2011). However, two points of clarification are worthwhile here. First, associations between academic knowledge and application in law enforcement are not especially controversial in many branches of anthropology, especially those influenced by evolutionary theory (e.g., Durrant and Ward 2015). Second, discussions about what makes us human, what is universal, and how we know the meaning of action are alive in the contemporary. This is certainly the case in security contexts where "the human" is a body of knowledge and evidence and a target for intervention. Indeed, French philosopher Frédéric Gros (Gros, Castillo, and Garapon 2008), among others, identifies a "new philosophical anthropology" in the realm of security. In this chapter, I explore the ongoing experiments by anthropologists and others that aim to police the future.

This chapter begins with a brief overview of the anthropology of policing, which highlights the important role of governmental reasoning. My concern, drawing from the work of Michel Foucault, is to show that pioneering statisticians, operating within what one might term apparatuses of security, brought together data and visualizations to the point of noting anthropological patterns and phenomena. Thereafter, I explore contemporary predictive policing by focusing on its evidential underpinnings in anthropology, namely, the use of evolutionary theories about human behavior, before turning to a specific example in the UK. The conclusion I offer is this: ethnographic treatments of policing and security institutions must be augmented by multi-sited studies that track the discourses and practices—bodies as evidence—that move along the fault lines of societies. Anthropological concepts are crucial to police restructuring in the contemporary moment, and here I open a new body of evidence for analysis.

Anthropology of Policing as Security

We must situate the unrest in Ferguson, Missouri, alongside numerous international protests over policing, from the violence in France in 2005 to the UK riots in 2011, and from the 2013 Gezi Park revolts in Turkey to recent protests by lawyers in Lahore. Of course, one should hardly be surprised to find the so-called thin blue line running along global fault lines of race, gender, class and inequality, or find that new media forms and video records are disturbing older ways of weighing evidence. It does seem surprising, however, that the anthropology of policing remains a small, recent, and somewhat narrow field to this day. A cursory review of early anthropological studies that mention policing indicates some of the reasons for this narrowness. It is difficult to find many early discussions of police as a distinct societal institution; but it is easy to locate discussions of "customary" law or "traditional" justice (e.g., Lowie 1912). This suggests that what we now call the anthropology of policing is, in fact, the particular intersection between a "modern" but culturally sensitive institutional form and the varieties and alternatives available in people's efforts to maintain and enforce social order.

John Comaroff (2013) also notes the relatively few theoretical touchstones used in the anthropology of policing. Of course, several scholars have unsettled the Weber-inspired perspective that police embody legitimate state force by drawing on fieldwork in contexts where policing is paramilitary, private, or even absent (e.g., Goldstein 2016). Other anthropologists probe the spectral law-making and law-preserving violence beyond the state (e.g., Jauregui 2013). Recently, anthropologists inspired by the work of Michel Foucault are attending to governmentality, normalization, surveillance, and resistance. However, most of these ethnographic studies are attempts to contextualize and understand the everyday encounters between the police and the policed.

But what if international transformations now involve efforts to change the nature of everyday law enforcement, such that many encounters will be cancelled out before they even occur? According to *Moving toward the Future of Policing*, an influential RAND Corporation report, momentous changes are sweeping through law enforcement, and these changes manifest themselves in intelligence-led and predictive policing (Treverton, Wollman, and Wilke 2011). So, how might we discuss the shifting international law enforcement landscape without falling for the seductive power of technology or being persuaded by what is in part a corporate push for new markets? Indeed, some might suggest that predictive policing is really little more than an entrepreneurial fad, a species of the contemporary endowed with more significance than it deserves by neoliberalism or biopolitics. Here, instead, I situate the rise and spread of predictive policing within the broader history of the present.

In his lectures in 1978 at the Collège de France, Michel Foucault recognizes the illusion of permanence staged by modern policing institutions. He excavates the broad understanding of order and force that characterized seventeenth and early eighteenth-century European uses of "police," which encompassed inequalities, medicine and hygiene, charity, urbanization, and circulation, though not necessarily justice.

> Generally speaking, what police has to govern, its fundamental object, is all the forms of, let's say, men's coexistence with each other. It is the fact that they live together, reproduce, and that each of them needs a certain amount of food and air to live, to subsist; it is the fact that they work alongside each other at different or similar professions, and also that they exist in a space of circulation; to use a word that is anachronistic in relation to the speculations of the time, police must take responsibility for all of this kind of sociality (*socialité*). (Foucault 2007, 422)

There is a striking family resemblance here between "police" and the term "policy" as it is used today. Indeed, Gregory Feldman reads Foucault as commenting on the historical flourishing of "indefinite regulation, of permanent, continually renewed, and increasingly detailed regulation . . . —policy and administration in a biopolitical society" (Feldman 2014, 76). But here I wish to point to other insights that are of help when exploring contemporary predictive policing.

Foucault's analysis of policing history is predicated by discussion of Ireland as a colonial laboratory. As is well known, before Sir Robert Peel established the world-leading London Metropolitan Police in 1829, experiments had already taken place on John Bull's other island. Ireland offered "favorable" conditions in which to test technologies of rule such as the modern governmental statistics as developed by William Petty ([1691] 1970) and others. On the back of many years spent surveying and producing extraordinarily detailed maps (all while carpetbagging aggressively), Petty's political arithmetic unleashed the power of statistics to quantify people's value or "worth." Indeed, statistics provided the "technical knowledge that describes the reality of the state itself" (Foucault 2007, 354). Following Petty, technical reality could be conceived, perceived, and acted upon, and actions could occur with reference to how reality might change in the near future.

William Petty's nascent efforts to produce crime data were later improved upon in nineteenth-century France, especially the capacity to visualize such data. From the 1820s onward, statisticians represented crimes, suicides, and even school instruction levels using choropleth maps. Later, more technically precise efforts followed from Adolphe Quetelet's social physics of the average man (*l'homme moyen*) to Henry Mayhew's statistical and ethnographic portraits of British poverty and criminality.[4] According to historian Mary Poovey (1991), early debates among statisticians show a concern for objectivity and reluctance to enter into discussions of causation. Yet, many were struck by the power of data qua data to not only count the *worth* of people but also to capture the always-emergent *sociality* of people. William Cooke Taylor's reflections on French crime data are illustrative in this regard:

> There is no better attested, nor more astonishing, record in history, than the sudden appearance of a disposition to commit some certain crime in a definite manner spreading like a contagious disease, reaching a fearful height in defiance of every effort to repress it, and then gradually sinking into oblivion. The madness of witch-finding in our country and in New England, the crime of poisoning in France when the *Chambres Ardentes* were established, the rick-burning in England within our own memory, are familiar examples. Does not this seem to prove that we might reckon a certain sympathy or principle of imitation among the leading incentives to crime? (Taylor 1835, 213)

Taylor's protoanthropology may seem to be a long way from software-based policing in the neighborhoods surrounding Ferguson, but the distance is closed by a simple set of observations. First in colonial laboratories such as Ireland and thereafter in the metropolitan heartlands of empire we find the coeval development of social data gathering, mapping, and statistical reasoning. This process occurs prior to the emergence of modern policing institutions and, in fact, provides key conditions for the possibility of those institutions. Of course, this is not to suggest a Whig history of our inevitable progress toward enlightenment and reason. Rather, my aim is to situate policing within the expansion of governmental statistical reasoning and thus note the power of data qua data in the history of efforts to secure populations. Nineteenth-century scholars recognized that data had emergent qualities and might reveal patters in human behavior, and thus data, statistical reasoning, and visualization could establish a near-future milieu in which to act. Foucault describes such milieus as being fundamental to apparatuses of security that operate by "standing back sufficiently so that one can grasp the point at which things are taking place, whether or not they are desirable. This means trying to grasp them at the level of their nature . . . grasping them at the level of their effective reality. The mechanism of security works on the basis of this reality, [*responding*] to a reality in such a way that this response cancels out the reality to which it responds—nullifies it, or limits, checks, or regulates it" (Foucault 2007, 46–47). Efforts in data gathering, crime mapping, and criminological theory certainly expanded throughout the twentieth century. However, ongoing experiments in predictive policing, such as in St. Louis County, have implications far beyond the modern police institutions and crime-busting efforts. Predictive policing is a specific assemblage within broader apparatuses of security that targets life itself with anthropology.

The Anthropologist as (Police) Hero

In order to tell the story of contemporary predictive policing, one must attend to the central role of Jeffrey Brantingham, UCLA anthropologist and expert on the environmental adaptations of hunter-gatherers in Northern Tibet. Brantingham's anthropological fieldwork convinced him that the behavioral patterns of humans are less elaborate and more predictable than one might assume. If hunter-gatherer behaviors are based on established patterns, then why not attempt to predict the behavior of an urban forager hunting a Mercedes Benz?

Brantingham explored the LA crime data and developed a strong relationship with the city's police. He drew together expert collaborators such as mathematicians George Mohler and Andrea Bertozzi, and criminologist and former RAND analyst George Tita. Their work suggested that neighborhoods were at greater risk of crime in the wake of a crime. In nineteenth-century terms, they uncovered a principle of sympathy or imitation. But, in quantitative terms, the crime patterns seemed more approachable as earthquakes and aftershocks, so they repurposed mathematical earthquake models. The key concept deployed was self-excitation: in data, the existence of a crime self-excites the possibility of a future crime, which can be represented in time and space, in 500 × 500 square-foot digital boxes to be precise. This is *not* merely an effort to use historical data to model the future; this is an experiment in emergence (cf. González 2015).

The LAPD were quick to begin experimenting with predictive policing, and cops soon found themselves patrolling the near future. Early results seemed remarkable, and so was the press coverage. Brantingham and his colleagues launched PredPol, a cloud-based software company, which made *Time Magazine's* list of the fifty top inventions of 2011. Today, numerous international law enforcement agencies use PredPol services, and there are a great number of other predictive systems in operation. Most, however, share certain assumptions about human behavior rooted in evolutionary anthropology.

In order to understand predictive policing, it is useful to consider Brantingham's evolutionary approach to crime. In a recent and illustrative paper on "prey selection" among LA's car thieves, Brantingham (2013) proposes that contemporary crime shows similar patterns to age-old foraging behaviors. These patterns do not arise from rational choices but, rather, from an evolutionary disposition to learn the long-term costs and benefits involved in selecting, encountering, and processing or handling prey. In other words, when an array of choices is presented, humans make suboptimal choices due to a long evolutionary history of necessity.[5] If this sounds like an effort to equate human behavior with algorithms, then one will not be surprised when Brantingham (2013, 2) speaks of "cognitive scripts" that allow one to make decisions on the suitability of prey. When all of this reasoning is translated into data on car theft, one finds that foragers do seem to make suboptimal choices and respond "primarily to environmental abundance" (10). In short, a Mercedes Benz may be more desirable, but it is the Nissan or the Honda that is most likely to vanish from a driveway. Car theft, burglary, and other forms of petty crime can be modeled using this style of reasoning, and advanced models that consider "self-exciting points" can potentially predict gang behavior, or even the casualties of terrorist attacks (Brantingham and Short 2011; see also González 2015).

Today, predictive policing is used around the world, but PredPol remains most closely associated with U.S. cities, from Memphis to Minneapolis and

Miami. The early adopters were the city of Santa Cruz and LA's Foothill Division. There, one morning in LA, someone switched the computer on, and officers were suddenly less responsible for their patrols. Instead, during morning briefings patrol officers received a map indicating the concentration areas. Officers were expected to spend as much time as possible on patrol in their box. According to all sound analysis, the crime rate dropped since the rollout of predictive policing. For Jeffrey Brantingham, the core issues at stake are clear. Speaking at a UCLA panel in 2014 on contemporary crime and criminality, he had this to say:

> The challenge that I set out a number of years ago with collaborators in mathematics was really to say . . . to the police, "Listen we understand why the crime pattern is evolving, and if you use that information you can get out ahead of the crime, and do something to prevent it!" So, I'm a strong believer in the idea that prevention is much better than waiting for the crime to happen, trying to find out who did it, and incarcerating them. We know the limits of incarceration. . . .
>
> But, what's driving the behavior, what's driving the crime? Here again I would say that I have a slightly different perspective. It's not ethnographic. It's more thinking about . . . the commonalities that describe all burglaries, regardless of whether you're looking at them in Los Angeles or Chicago, or London or Tel Aviv. . . . You would be surprised how similar criminals are regardless of where you are looking. . . . A great example of this is . . . most offenders commit the crime in the immediate vicinity of where they live, where they work or play. . . .
>
> Los Angeles Police Department has been doing what you'd call predictive policing for the past two and a half years. . . . You have a little box, a 500 × 500 sq. ft. box that basically says this is where the risk of crime today is highest. . . . It's often not recognized that 80–90 percent of the crime that police respond to comes from public reporting. The number of crimes that police actually discover on their own is very, very small. Policing is really a public-police partnership. (Brantingham 2014)

There is certainly much of interest in this statement, but, before unpacking the contents, it is worth observing the gulf between Brantingham's remarks and the portraits painted in recent ethnographies of policing.

As noted earlier, the whole world of policing sometimes appears to be available in kinetic encounters and critical moments. In Alice Goffman's (2014) controversial study of fugitives in Philadelphia, policing is rendered as structurally violent occupation characterized by constant stop-and-search, circling helicopters, and CCTV cameras. Although it is a complex work, Didier Fassin's *Enforcing Order* (2013) opens with similar images drawn from his work on policing Parisian banlieux. For Fassin, police stop-and-search tactics are mundane but structurally violent in that they target—through embodiment and internalization—the bodies of racialized youths, such that "the individual is ashamed of the violence to which he has been subjected, and feels guilty of a sin that he has not committed" (2013, 8). When racialized and marginalized youths encounter police, then, they are confronted by culturally coded and embodied behaviors. Police actions "depend very largely on their personal history, the training they have undergone, the supervision they receive, the conditions of work imposed on them, the tasks conferred by government policies, and the representations of the social world that society produces" (Fassin 2013, 24). But what happens, to paraphrase Eric Wolf, if we take cognizance of the processes that transcend separate cases, moving through and beyond them and transforming them as they proceed? Here we are looking at processes that aim to cancel out difficult cases before they arise.

Looking at contemporary policing—especially in the Western world, but elsewhere also—Jeffrey Brantingham's cognitive map of law enforcement is rather different from the one that circulates among urban ethnographers. When looking at today's Los Angeles, he sees a city with a reduced serious crime rate that is facing decisions about the efficient deployment of law enforcement resources. Responding to Brantingham at the UCLA panel in 2014, criminologist Daniel Fessler exemplified the new intelligence-led approach to policing:

> There's substantial debate in criminology as to what has led to the drop in crime, but I think that a case can be made that policing practices are in part responsible: . . . redeployment of resources, community-based policing; as you know here in Los Angeles we've had a radical shift following civil unrest in the way that the LAPD tried to connect to communities. So one of the reasons that [*predictive policing*] is so effective is because the potential offender is making calculations about probability of getting caught, and if you see police officers in your community at about the time that you were thinking about offending then that really does deter crime. (Fessler 2014)

Doubtless in response, and with events such as Ferguson in mind, commentators will note the "disappearance" of young marginalized and racialized youths from city streets, those taken into the arms of the criminal justice systems across many Western-world countries. But questions might also be posed about the displacement of crime from heavily policed neighborhoods or the displacement from street crime to more "sophisticated" criminality. During 2013 and 2014, I set out to ask these questions of senior police in the United States and UK in a series of interviews. Those semiformal interviews led to invitations to examine predictive policing systems in operation in several cities. I became interested not in PredPol the company but, rather, in alternative approaches to intelligence-led community policing, especially in law enforcement institutions where those approaches were largely bottom up and even suspicious new technology fixes. As one might expect, during the past decade law enforcement agencies participated in countless discussions about the "power" of so-called Big Data and the insights that algorithmic governance will surely deliver. It quickly became apparent that most senior police managers and technical analysts understand that Big Data often means medium data at best, and algorithms depend entirely on the cultural coding that give them their rules. Analysts worked on crime data before the current conversation about data analytics. What is of interest to me is the style of reasoning, constraints, gaps, and tensions that characterize contemporary police efforts to engage with new technology and forms of evidence. Below, I briefly discuss research conducted with a police force in a large northern UK city. I propose using this case example to tease out ways to study predictive policing as a specific technosocial assemblage—and a body of evidence—rather than as an empirical example in itself.

Criminal Anthropology in Action

The numbers are there to see, especially for burglary and car theft—it works. But . . . it's weird, like science fiction. I mean, one day you turn on the computer and, well, now it's the computer running things.
—Interview (informal) with police technician (2013)

It took Dave a while to adjust to there being an anthropologist in his office.[6] He blinked rapidly in what seemed to be an effort to wish me away. That day police headquarters was a tense place. The borough was being evaluated as part of a national quality initiative. Dave was plainly hoping that the Analysis Unit he directed would escape the attention of senior officers conducting a site visit. He was quite literally attempting to keep his head down when his manager entered his office unannounced and introduced me as a visiting researcher intending to study crime mapping. Dave's manager disappeared with "Top brass wants you to give him what he needs, ok?" The top brass in question was Sir Peter, a senior figure who blessed my short project on alternative approaches to predictive policing. At first, I was surprised by the access that I had been given, but it soon became clear that there were plenty of opportunities for me to bump into the evaluators, and predictive crime mapping was the borough's "stand-out initiative." Although the technical work of the Analysis Unit was regarded as somewhat mysterious by seasoned officers, headquarters staff described it as a "miracle factory"—certain types of crime had been driven down, by 38 percent in the case of burglaries, and, after all, "the numbers don't lie."

Well before my first visit, I interviewed several police officers by phone or over Skype to become familiar with current operations and policing history. I learned about the nineteenth-century slum gangs—mostly Irish migrants—the conflicts between Black British and West Indian youths, football hooliganism, and the drug-related crime wave that swept the city during the 1990s. But Dave seemed vague on the historical context in which he worked. He had graduated a few years previously from a local university where he specialized in criminology and completed advanced training in Geographical Information Systems. He joined the borough police force as a civilian employee, sensing in the role of analyst the opportunity to strengthen his research network and gain experience as a "practitioner" before hunting for an academic post.[7] Until 2010, the Analysis Unit was dedicated to crime mapping, mostly efforts to identify "hot spots" based on historical cases in a borough with a quarter of a million residents spread over forty square miles. Dave began working with a few seasoned police officers who were seeking to develop their skills, together with two young graduates. I felt sure that he would have interesting stories about the early days, especially efforts to implement predictive techniques shoulder to shoulder with policemen trained to walk the beat, cultivate street-level contacts, and follow hunches. However, he seemed vague about those early moments. "So," I eventually asked, "how exactly does the system work, and how does it differ from the American approach?" Dave's demeanor changed. The turned his chair to the two large monitors on his desk with, "Watch this!" He pulled up a real-time map of the borough and talked me through the image of city, explaining with great intensity how the different neighborhoods yielded data and interacted with one another.

The policing borough has four distinct spaces that dominated its cardinal points. To the north, the district abuts a large public housing area, a "sink-hole estate" with a very high general crime rate and several gun crime incidents each year. Nearly 90 percent of residents in the policing borough identified as "white" in official statistics, but over half of the population in the public housing area identified as "Black" or "South Asian." To the east, a large football stadium dominates the urban landscape, while to the west an enormous shopping mall and retail park extends on both sides of the main road. The stadium and shopping mall are areas with few crimes as they are saturated with CCTVs and have significant private security in place. Private security personnel in the mall did not feel free to speak to researchers formally, though one individual did grab my elbow and confide, "We keep the crime out by not letting certain people in!" (informal conversation 2013). Crime, as Dave explained, is generally concentrated to the north, in the center of the borough, and occasionally in the south of the district. To the south, one finds a large area composed of several affluent neighborhoods. These are gated communities—"footballers' wives," according to Dave. The crime rate is low in those neighborhoods, though in recent years police recorded several violent home invasions. From the analyst's perspective, these broad spatial features can be understood as exercising real-time force that manifests in data— and the data is itself emergent.

Starting in 2010, the Analysis Unit began working to normalize historical data and make crime reporting more efficient. Relatively quickly, Dave and his colleagues were able to produce detailed daily maps that indicated the likely locations of future crimes. The maps are provided to patrols during morning briefings and indicate risk (referred to as "heat") by means of colored circles—red indicates high risk. The intensity of the color indicates the likelihood of crime in a particular area based on spatiotemporal relationships to recent crimes and historical data. The theoretical underpinning for this approach is found in this often-cited recommendation by UK criminologists:

> In domestic burglary, for example, the danger of a further crime is greatest at the home of the original victim and spreads out some 400 meters, but disappears over six weeks to two months. . . . Instead of mapping past events in the conventional way we should map the risk they generate for nearby homes, with the map being dynamic to reflect how the risk declines

over time. . . . Forecasts can be displayed using a Geographical Informa-tion System (GIS) and overlain on a map of the relevant area, allowing patrolling and other resources to be deployed to the areas of highest pre-dicted risk.

While it is an unhappy comparison, the logic mirrors that used in the culling of farm animals in epidemics of foot and mouth disease. Cull-ing only animals on farms where there is an outbreak ignores the way in which disease spreads. (Ross and Pease 2008, 314)

Patrols are given copies of the map—each marked with the Crown copyright of the Official Secrets Act, 1911—that will determine where they should spend the majority of their time. And the maps are of course "smart" in that specific details of recent crimes and near-future risks appear in dialogue boxes when one interfaces with the maps live in the system. Moreover, to assist in this process of making the maps "real," officers' radios and cars are GPS locatable, and they are expected to be where the system suggests they be. It is important that patrols are not expected to simply cruise about in their designated circles.

Again following Ross and Pease (2008), borough resources are assigned on a variation on the so-called Pareto Principle, which holds that a small num-ber of things are responsible for a large number of outcomes. A few criminals commit a large number of crimes, and the spatial distribution of crime will be limited by our suboptimal foragers. Moreover, a small number of victims also account for the majority of cases of victimization. In other words, we have the phenomena of repeat victimization. Thus, the borough's crime maps repre-sent future crimes and future victims. The style of reasoning here has led the force to "cocoon" neighborhoods, where, say, a burglary occurred. Police pa-trol the streets visibly; contact with the community intensifies; public service workers are encouraged to wear high-visibility clothing; and advice on "target hardening" is given to victims, potential victims, and nearby residents.

Over the past several years, extraordinary successes have been attributed to the approach taken in this borough. In the United States, cities that have experimented with PredPol have shown decreases in some crimes of up to 25 percent. In this UK borough, burglary is down by 38 percent and car theft is down by 29 percent, and all at zero cost. With some justification, a senior officer claimed that the results are attributable to organizational change, and targeted patrols spurred by new technology implementation: "Future polic-ing is about effective management, knowing your organization and how to implement change across it, across the different skill sets, while ensuring buy-in. It's about service and evaluating that service, asking the tough questions" (interview 2013). With some justification, outside commentators question the "displacement" of crime to other boroughs—though there is no substantive evidence to support this theory—or to other forms of crime. Car theft does seem to be declining internationally as technology changes, and thefts from cars are increasing, but the borough seems to counter such displacement by targeting the patterns of criminal foragers. However, the most accurate critical evaluations seem to be implicit in the muted comments of police on patrol. I spoke to several officers in this borough and in other cities in the UK and United States. During a conversation in 2013, one officer synthesized the on-the-ground perspective in one question, "Isn't this just community policing?" (interview 2013).

There is a new body of evidence here, one that exceeds the evidence (*videre*) of the sociologically visible and even the relations of cause and effect in intelligence-led and predictive policing. We must also attend to evidence in more Foucauldian terms, "those *évidences* on which our knowledges, our agreements, our practices, rest," and thus attend to evidence of events unseen (Foucault in Perrot 1980, 44). Contemporary approaches such as predictive policing constitute their own milieu and evidential regimes, but they are also nested in broader institutional configurations and taken-for-granted ways of perceiving and acting in the world. On the one hand, then, as I carried out my research, I watched as a law enforcement organization shifted toward predictive policing, a catalyst for changes in reasoning, management, resource allocation, and actual patrols. On the ground, police seemed to be driving down crime by "doing nothing," as one veteran officer put it. Another reflected, "These days we get calls about barkin' dogs. Why don't you go around to your neighbor, knock on the door, and speak to them? Somethin's up there. And, what's that got to do with us?" (interview 2013). But for all the successes represented in management charts and reports, crime did not go away, especially violent and organized crimes that are not connected with so-called optimal foragers. In the gated communities to the south of the borough, residents (at least those few I could find to speak to) lived in fear of the rare but terrifying home invasions by professional gangs that bring the threat of violence along with metal cutters and automatic weapons. Those residents call for tougher laws and better armed response. Residents in the poor and racialized north of the borough felt that they were under "surveillance." They feared local drug dealers and disliked the heavy-handed police who occasionally screeched into their estate. And, what of the perspective of those police who deal with non-foragers? The extracts below are from ethnographic notes taken during November 2013 and show the predictive system in operation from the perspective of an elite tactical response unit.

11.13   *I've just left the chief's office and am waited in an anteroom. I'm thinking that I'll never get to see things from the side of patrols unless I talk to police in other boroughs and cities. The GIS guys attributed 79 percent of all burglaries to "optimal foragers." They say that they have driven down burglaries by 61 percent in recent months! We all have the same questions. Is it true? Is this about changing patrols? Is it sustainable? Are crimes simply being displaced to other districts? What do the patrol guys think? Will I be given permission to work with them?*

The chief's secretary appears. . . . I'm informed that I will be allocated specific times to interview patrols, but I'm also given permission to "hang out" with the guys in tactical. . . .

15.13   *The tactical unit are "suiting up." One group will be training while the others circle around where the predictive maps indicate the risks are greatest. The men and women in tactical quietly go about their roles. Their no-nonsense offices and equipment rooms are in good order, and their dark uniforms and visible weapons give them the appearance of soldiers. The unit commander is curious to know exactly what I'm observing. We talk for some time about my previous experiences studying counterterrorist operations. He doesn't blink. I mention my lengthy discussions with Dave. "Yeah," he says, "the Analysis, right? Dave . . ." He places the daily predictive heat map on the table, and as if on cue three other officers gather around. "Our radios are tagged," one says, "and they know if you're not in the circle at the correct time." "I haven't noticed a decrease in crime, to be honest," volunteered another. "It's just that now you can't nip home." We laugh for a moment or two. "But I suppose they're right—I mean the numbers are there," says the unit commander. Everyone stares at the map silently. One officer points at a time and heat-sensitive circle. He hesitates before asking, "What do the colors mean exactly?" Everyone knew what to do, but nobody seemed to know what they knew.*

"So, the maps tell you what to do now? But what was it like before?"
I asked. "We used to go looking for trouble," an older officer said.
"We knew the people and where to look, and what to look for, you
know, before something kicked off." "What about now?" I asked.
"We stay in our little colored circle." "Maybe it's working." "What
about you?" I asked the unit commander, "If it's so restrictive, why
do you still do this job?" "Ah," he said, "they left us with the good
bit: we just love kicking down doors!"

But why is a tactical unit thriving alongside software-mediated policing and alongside community policing in the form of target hardening, the co-opting of local public service workers and the "cocooning" of neighborhoods? If Foucault (2007) is right in suggesting that to police is to take responsibility for various forms of sociality (*socialité*), then one may simply observe that this responsibility is unevenly distributed and received. Some are gently cocooned against the near future, while darker forces circle around and occasionally produce kinetic encounters. It may well be the case that this new criminal anthropology is front and center in a redistribution of societal security.

Concluding Remarks

As protests against racialized and violent policing continue around the world, many of which cite the shooting of Michael Brown in Missouri, it is all too easy to fold contemporary predictive policing initiatives into a preexisting image of the world, an image that is confirmed by the very nature of how the social sciences study policing. Ethnographers, especially urban ethnographers, show their hard-to-acquire skills by getting close to hard-to-study communities, from marginalized populations to those who police them. Indeed, in recent years several ethnographers illuminated the interactions between security forces and poor communities, from Didier Fassin's (2013) study of policing in Paris to Alice Goffman's controversial analysis of structural violence—policing as "a battering ram knocking [*your*] door at three in the morning' (2014, 59). But such studies offer only one form of evidence (*videre*), that which can be seen directly. Such evidence can be misleadingly vivid and thus distract from broader transformations. This chapter is a call attention to another body of evidence shaping policing, one conveyed predictive policing systems.

As I have shown, predictive systems such as PredPol are not old wine in a new bottle, contemporary software licenses for long-standing efforts to profile the poor.[8] Here I have attended to the new criminal anthropology encoded in such systems as indexing broader transformations in how societal security is distributed. Of course, the effects of redistribution will be felt unevenly. Just as software will not fix institutional racism, even if implemented well technological solutions may simply result in more stops, more arrests, and more racialized youths in prison. And I do not wish to elide the danger that, as one research participant put it, one "day you turn on the computer and, well, now it's the computer running things" (interview 2013). There is certainly a danger of so-called surveillance creep together with intrusions into privacy and civil liberties. However, perhaps the most widely discussed danger arises when one considers the range of functions that can be added to polyfunctional predictive systems. Most predictive systems target the spatiotemporal dimensions of human behavioral patterns, not the persons themselves. Recently, and mainly in the United States, systems have begun to include personal information gained from data mining in order to forewarn possible future offenders of the consequences of their current actions. According to a *New York Times* report, analysts are now looking at the predictive qualities of social networks that include "previous arrests; unemployment; an unstable home life; friends and relatives who have been killed, are in prison or have gang ties; and problems with drugs or alcohol" (Eligon and Williams 2015).[9]

Having said this, if the critical social sciences simply engage with new policing and security technologies in terms of their possible nefarious uses, we will lose the possibility of genuine critique, by which I mean an understanding of the core assumptions from which those technologies emerged and the possible alternatives available at root. It may be possible that the current obsession with policing encounters in urban ethnography is limiting our capacity to engage in genuine critique, because we are not attending to the transformations that are occurring more broadly.

Even if we distrust technological governance and despise the advocates of predictive solutions, we must ask ourselves this: what if the robbery in the Ferguson Market and Liquor had never occurred? This essay opened with an epigraph from Gregory Bateson, one of the earliest anthropologists to engage openly with the positive and negative potential of new technology. Bateson saw in social computing the potential hope for humanity, but he worried that its style of reasoning would supersede our own and that we would be "a little *less responsible*." He concluded thus, "If you do what the computer advises, you assert by that move that you support the *rules of the game* which you fed into the computer. You have affirmed the rules of that game. The problem is to *change* the rules" (Bateson 1972, 481–82).

Notes

Mark Maguire's research is supported by the Global Foresight Project in Stockholm University, funded by the Riksbankens Jubileumsfond, the Swedish Foundation for Humanities and Social Sciences.

1   In extended footage, other residents audibly dispute this version of events.

2   One could easily describe the shooting of Michael Brown as a "critical event" that opened the world to evaluation and inaugurated new modalities of action that obtain to this day, but this chapter is in part a critique of anthropological obsessions with "events" and "encounters" as the really real stuff of ethnographic research. The critique here is that what counts as ethnographic evidence may not be sufficient for understanding all policing transformations.

3   Several prominent and widely circulated papers on predictive policing have served up confusion rather than clarity. Most notably, "Predictive Policing" by Sarah Brayne, Alex Rosenblat, and Danah Boyd (2015) confuses crime mapping and predictive policing and discusses opportunity theory rather than suboptimal foraging theory. Sociocultural anthropologists, in contrast, have been quick to appreciate the significance of these experiments in the context of shifts in global policing and governance. Roberto González criticizes predictive policing as academic entrepreneurialism lending "dubious" theories to potentially oppressive systems that are only a short step from counterinsurgency (e.g., González 2015). This is a useful critique, but this chapter discusses the rise and spread of predictive policing in ways that show its flexibility and adaptability as a mode of engaging with intractable problems of crime in the contemporary moment. Much will be learned by attending to actually existing efforts to police future crimes before deploying a hermeneutics of suspicion or disposing of them under the rubric of faddish "Big Data" solutions.

4   Here one should underscore the fact that governmental innovations in knowledge and rule occurred in contexts of empire and moved back and forth along the route ways carved by colonization. Michel Foucault (2003) recognized this as the "boomerang effect" of colonial governance.

5   (Sub-)Optimal Foraging Theory has been criticized on a number of grounds—aside from the potential downsides of applying unmodified a behavioral ecology to human beings—with many critics pointing to one rather obvious issue: for all its neatness and suitability for modeling, foraging theory does not admit to falsification. Specific predictions may be more or less accurate, but it is dif-

ficult to test the underlying assumptions, the "rules of the game," so to speak (see Johnson 2014).

6   All names hereafter are pseudonyms.

7   Today, police officers face fast-changing and complex threats not from the perspective of coherent institutions but, rather, as the front line of service provision assemblages. Technologies such as public video-surveillance are often outsourced, and even the back office is now potentially differentiated. For example, in 2012 the private security company G4S was contracted to build and staff many functions within a police station by the Lincolnshire Police Authority. The Police Authority claimed that the move would result in "the leanest police force in Britain," capable of delivering "services" at an even lower "cost per head of population" (see Plimmer and Warrell 2012, 4; see also Treverton, Wollman, and Wilke 2011, 34).

8   If one were tempted to propose that the entire process is simply a glossy version of "profiling" poor neighborhoods, then one would entirely miss the evidence being represented. In short, criminals such as car thieves will respond to environmental abundance; the real-time crime maps show where crimes will occur, not where criminals reside, for now at least.

9   Indeed, one might situate such approaches alongside broader efforts to look for risky personality types using neurological evidence, the "new diagram" in criminal justice identified by Nikolas Rose (2010) as "risky brains."

References

Bateson, Gregory. 1972. *Steps to an Ecology of Mind: Collected Essays in Anthropology, Psychiatry, Evolution, and Epistemology.* Chicago: University of Chicago Press.

Brantingham, Jeffrey P. 2013. "Prey Selection among Los Angeles Car Thieves." *Crime Science* 2(3): 1–11.

Brantingham, Jeffrey P. 2014. "Comments during the Crime and Criminality in the 21st Century Panel." April 30, featuring Jeffrey Brantingham, Daniel Fessler, and Jorja Leap, UCLA Department of Anthropology.

Brantingham, Jeffrey P., and M. B. Short. 2011. "Crime Emergence." In *When Crime Appears: The Role of Emergence*, edited by J. M. McGloin, C. Sullivan, and L. W. Kennedy, 73–95. New York: Routledge.

Brayne, Sarah, Alex Rosenblat, and Danah Boyd. 2015. "Predictive Policing: Data and Civil Rights." Workshop Primer for Data and Civil Rights: A New Era of Policing and Justice, October 27, Washington, DC.

Capeheart, Jonathan. 2015. "'Hands up Don't Shoot' Was Built on a Lie." *Washington Post.* March 16.

Comaroff, John. 2013. Foreword to *Policing and Contemporary Governance: The Anthropology of Police in Practice*, edited by William Garriott, xi–xxiii. London: Palgrave Macmillan.

CNN. 2014. "Warning: Startling Cell Phone Video from Michael Brown Shooting Scene." *YouTube*. Accessed June 24, 2016. https://www.youtube.com/watch?v=nvE-1qAs1W4.

DOJ (United States Department of Justice). 2015a. "Investigation of the Ferguson Police Department." *United States Department of Justice Civil Rights Division*. March 4. https://assets.documentcloud.org/documents/1681213/ferguson-police-department-report.pdf.

DOJ (United States Department of Justice). 2015b. Department of Justice Report Regarding the Criminal Investigation into the Shooting Death of Michael Brown by Ferguson, Missouri, Police Office Daren Wilson. Accessed June 24, 2016. https://www.justice.gov/sites/default/files/opa/press-releases/attachments/2015/03/04/doj_report_on_shooting_of_michael_brown_1.pdf.

Durrant, Russil, and Tony Ward. 2015. *Evolutionary Criminology: Towards a Comprehensive Explanation of Crime*. London: Elsevier.

Eligon, John, and Timothy Williams. 2015. "Police Program Aims to Pinpoint Those Most Likely to Commit Crimes." *New York Times*. September 24.

Fassin, Didier. 2013. *Enforcing Order: An Ethnography of Urban Policing*. London: Polity Press.

Feldman, Gregory, 2014. "Location, Isolation, and Disempowerment: The Swift Proliferation of Security Discourse among Policy Professionals." In *The Anthropology of Security: Perspectives from the Frontline of Policing, Counter-Terrorism and Border Control*, edited by Mark Maguire, Catarina Frois, and Nils Zurawski, 62–82. London: Pluto Press.

Fessler, Daniel. 2014. "Comments during the Crime and Criminality in the 21st Century Panel." April 30, featuring Jeffrey Brantingham, Daniel Fessler, and Jorja Leap, UCLA Department of Anthropology.

Foucault, Michel. 2003. *Society Must Be Defended: Lectures at the Collège de France, 1975–1976*. London: Allen Lane.

Foucault, Michel. 2007. *Security, Territory, Population: Lectures at the Collège de France, 1977–1978*. Houndsmill, UK: Palgrave MacMillan.

Goffman, Alice. 2014. *On the Run: Fugitive Life in an American City*. Chicago: University of Chicago Press.

Goldstein, Daniel, M. 2016. *Owners of the Sidewalk: Security and Survival in the Informal City*. Durham: Duke University Press.

González, Roberto J. 2015. "Seeing into Hearts and Minds (Part 2): Big Data, Algorithms, and Computational Counterinsurgency." *Anthropology Today* 31(4): 13–18.

Gros, Frédéric, Monique Castillo, and Antoine Garapon. 2008. "De la sécurité nationale à la sécurité humaine." *Raisons politiques* 4(32): 5–7.

Johnson, Shane D. 2014. "How Do Offenders Choose Where to Offend?" *Legal and Criminal Psychology* 19(2): 193–210.

Jauregui, Beatrice. 2013. "Dirty Anthropology: Epistemologies of Violence and Ethical Entanglements in Police Ethnography." In *Policing and Contemporary Governance: The Anthropology of Police in Practice*, edited by William Garriott, 125–57. New York: Palgrave MacMillan.

Lowie, Robert H. 1912. "Some Problems in the Ethnology of the Crow and Village Indians." *American Anthropologist* 14(1): 60–71.

Perrot, Michelle, ed. 1980. *L'impossible prison: Recherches sur le système pénitentiaire au XIXe siècle*. Paris: Editions du Seuil.

Petty, William. [1691]1970. *The Political Anatomy of Ireland, with the Establishment for that Kingdom and Verbum Sapienti*. Shannon, Ireland: Irish University Press.

Plimmer, Gill, and Helen Warrell. 2012. "Cuts Prompt Police to Use More Contractors." *Financial Times*. March 7.

Poovey, Mary. 1991. "Figures of Arithmetic, Figures of Speech." In *Questions of Evidence: Proof, Practice, and Persuasion across the Disciplines*, edited by James Chandler, Arnold I. Davidson, and Harry D. Harootunian, 401–22. Chicago: University of Chicago Press.

Price, David. 2011. *Weaponizing Anthropology: Social Science in the Service of the Militarized State*. Oakland, CA: Counterpunch and AK Press.

Rose, Nikolas. 2010. "Screen and Intervene: Governing Risky Brains." *History of the Human Sciences* 23(1): 79–105.

Ross, Nick, and Ken Pease. 2008. "Community Policing and Prediction." In *The Handbook of Knowledge-Based Policing: Current Conceptions and Future Directions*, edited by Tom Williamson, 305–23. London: John Wiley and Son.

Taylor, William Cooke. 1835. "Objects and Advantages of Statistical Science." *Foreign Quarterly Review* 16(October): 103–16.

Treverton, Gregory F., Matt Wollman, and Elizabeth Wilke. 2011. *Moving toward the Future of Policing*. Santa Monica, CA: RAND Corporation.

SEVEN

"Intelligence" and "Evidence"

Sovereign Authority and the Differences
That Words Make

GREGORY FELDMAN

A man arrived on a Thursday evening by plane with a young woman and checked into a pension close to the city's downtown core.[1] An hour later, they exited the pension, walked through the historic district, and returned. The team set up surveillance again by 8 AM on Monday morning, but neither of the couple left the pension until 7 PM. The team divided into two shifts lest the monotony of sitting in a car and a café across the street wear down their concentration. Brian, a member of the team, also enlisted the support of the family owners of the pension, who also managed the establishment. Throughout the week, they would always call if either of the two individuals passed through the lobby. This happened rarely before 7 PM. This situation made it difficult to gather some information about the man's activities before they left. Since they stayed in a pension, rather than an apartment, the team surmised that they would not stay in the country for too long, especially if the man's base of operations was in Denmark. He did not appear to be meeting anyone and, so, the value of whatever information might be found in the pension room increased considerably.

Therefore, the team had to make a decision: either they request a judge's warrant authorizing them to search the room, or they simply search it without a warrant. The former option could not even be seriously considered given the tight frame they faced compared to the length of time it takes a judge to issue a warrant. They chose the latter option. David and Max approached the pension owners and asked for them to let them into the room. The owners obliged without hesitation, and even with some amount of giddiness and excitement. The young adult son even bragged that this was the second time a police team had requested his help in this regard.

In the small room, Max videorecorded with his smartphone items on an end table and in a handbag that included a credit card. He then flipped through a wallet. David carefully searched a suitcase that contained an iPad, but he left it alone. Max flipped through a daily planner, but saw nothing of interest. David then found an official letter from his government's immigration service and showed it to Max, who videorecorded it as well. Max then found an old cell phone that had been left on. He videorecorded all of the contact information in the incoming/outgoing calls menu. He was not able to access the phone's contact list. The manager and a cleaning lady assisted David and Max in whatever small way they could: they pointed to a bathroom, they helped put things back in their original place, they nodded in different directions to make sure David and Max checked everything possible. The work was done in fifteen minutes. All four double-checked to ensure everything was put back exactly where it was left. They casually exited the room and made their way down to the staircase to the lobby, chatting the whole time as if they were old friends. After we left, David explains that the manager was "happy to help. People help us all the time. People's lives are boring. He'll be able to brag to his girlfriend. They teach us about this stuff in the training courses."

Brian had been following the man and woman during the illegal search. His job was to phone David and Max if they were to *start walking back in the direction of the pension. When we all reconvene in the car across the street, Brian addresses my question about how the state prosecutor, who is responsible for the case, can possibly find useful information that they had just obtained illegally. He explains that they give useful information to the prosecutor, who does not always need to know how it was obtained and who does not always bother to ask. Crucial consequences hang on the two categories of information they obtain. "Evidence" is any information that is admissible in a court trial of an indicted suspect. In differs from "intelligence," which is information that police use to advance an investigation. Intelligence is not admissible in court for two reasons. First, it is often too vague to help make a case for or against a defendant. Second, more germane to this chapter, the methods by which it is obtained do not qualify it to be admitted in court. The legal protection of evidence is designed to protect defendants from cases fabricated against them. It also protects peoples' privacy and abusive police practices that can occur when police are looking for evidence. Thus, while most intelligence is gathered legally, some of it can only be acquired through quasi-legal means at best or illegal means at worst.*

This chapter is part of a larger four-year project that studies an undercover police investigative team. The project examines three particular aspects of their work. First, it addresses the modes and conditions in which the team makes ethical judgments while conducting their street work. Many of those judgments take place in the "gray zone," or that space in the margins of the law and beyond. Second, it compares the form of sovereign action they undertake in that gray zone against the form of action taken in the context of traditional nation-state sovereignty. Third, it examines the interface between transnational criminal networks and the security state to better conceptualize the way in which state sovereignty is effected in the contemporary moment.

This chapter examines the technical conditions of the team's undercover investigative work to identify the circumstances in which they can enter the gray zone. The point of this exercise is to describe the spaces in a wider security apparatus in which its officials—undercover investigators in this case—can and do deviate from policy and legal mandates. Such deviations do not depend upon the random whims of police officers themselves. Even the roguest of cops need an opening or an opportunity in which they can disregard law. Yet, we must be careful not to sensationalize the fact because the law depends upon the gray zone, even if the most horrendous of violations also transpire in the same place. This chapter, then, outlines the bureaucratic context in which an undercover police investigative team works. It then explains the means through which the team enters the gray zone. This means is the team's control over the narrative of the street side of an investigation, which features almost no oversight from higher authorities. Primarily, it is their freedom to classify retrieved information as either "intelligence" or "evidence" that protects team members in the gray zone. Ironically, the judicial system itself also protects the team in that space should a gumptious lawyer push too hard on the question of how the team obtained their information.

The understanding of the gray zone used in this chapter draws on Giorgio Agamben's (1998) work on the basis of sovereign power. He argues that the sovereign is the entity that can suspend law, thus creating a "state of exception" in which it can act with impunity against those individuals whom the law no longer protects. Those individuals become *homo sacer*, whose vulnerability conceivably knows no ends. Lacking legal protection, homo sacer cannot politically assert himself and so can only be acted upon or neglected. Homo sacer is not even worthy of a ritual sacrifice because nothing about him is worth offering to a higher principle or deity. Therefore his murder comes with no penalty for the murderer because the loss of his life has no effect on the order that the principle or deity upholds. This chapter will address how the team enters the gray zone in the course of its own work and assumes sovereign authority over those tied to their investigations, if only in limited circumstances. As a side note, much research examines how great atrocities occur in the gray zone as actors endowed with sovereign authority abuse homo sacer. However, this is not an inevitable outcome, and elsewhere I have discussed how the particular situation in which the team works minimizes the likelihood of abuse of their sovereign authority (Feldman 2016).

An Immigration Service as a Blueprint and as a Process

The country in which the team works features a wide range of police forces, each with different mandates and competencies. These national-level forces are located under a variety of government ministries. The investigative team itself is housed in the Ministry of the Interior's immigration service, which is further subdivided into departments such as border control, document control, administrative analysis, and criminal investigations among others. The Criminal Investigations Department focuses on transnational organized crimes that carry at least eight-year sentences for the convicted. This department is subdivided into five separate groups, four of which focus on criminal rings originating in specific geographic regions of the world. These four groups work at headquarters, mostly at desktop computers. They conduct record searches and data analyses and have instant access to EU databases such as the Schengen Information System (SIS), Visa Information System (VIS), and EURODAC (the biometric fingerprint database for asylum applicants), which store information on all travelers who enter national/EU spaces. They also have access, by request or by warrant, to a number of national databases involving phone records, banking records, and vital statistics. A chief leads each of those groups and by extension will manage the case investigation on a daily basis for a state prosecutor. As the fifth group in the Criminal Investigation Department, the investigative team is not defined by geographic specialty, but rather by all the street-level investigative work such as surveillance, searches, and arrests. They perform these tasks at the request of the deskbound investigative groups. Sometimes responsibilities bleed across the lines between the team and the other groups. The latter will occasionally do surveillance themselves. The team does some data analysis itself, particularly the creation of cluster diagrams mapping social connections based on information downloaded from suspects' mobile phones.

A distinguishing feature between the team and the deskbound investigative groups is the indifference that the team holds toward their own official ranks. Their ranks, along with all other employees in the immigration service, are based on the year they that they completed their rookie training. Those in the same year ascend through the same pay grades. Those in relatively higher positions will be held responsible for problems that emerge in an investigation, but they will also be favored for any new opportunities that arise such as trips to other European cities to attend conferences and workshops in other EU cities. However, Frank has cultivated the team to work in a much more egalitarian manner. He explains, "My group, instead of the others, has no hierarchy. That means I don't interfere. There is a formal hierarchy, yes, but we don't care about that. If Max understands the Chinese case best, then it is best that he calls the shots on that one. I won't interfere." David jumped in immediately: "He listens to our ideas and opinions. He'll tell us if it is stupid or good. He'll let us go for it if it is good." His praise of Frank was hardly an empty platitude. David is the farthest thing from an ass-kisser I have ever met who still managed to keep his job.

Standard cases officially begin in a state prosecutor's office. The prosecutor coordinates an investigation with the chief of a deskbound investigative group and with a judge. The chief will manage the case on a daily basis by assigning people to conduct record checks, liaising with other governmental offices for information, and communicating with the team about the necessary street work. The judge ensures the legality of the investigation and must approve (and periodically reapprove) such measures as home searches, wiretapping, and deep-cover operations. The team conducts these types of operations, but, when following procedure, they ask the prosecutor to obtain a warrant from a judge. If the prosecutor relies on evidence brought in from another member state, such a judge would decide if the methods of its retrieval meet their own national legal standards. The need for this decision occurs fairly often, as organized crime moves across national borders within the union. If only one country is conducting the investigation, then cooperation among member states is usually done informally. Investigators regularly contact counterparts in other member states, often via email, for any helpful information that they might have on an investigation. In some cases, they may even ask those counterparts to conduct surveillance for them in their own countries. To be sure, investigators generally value informal cooperation. They share a unique sense of camaraderie in which they wish their counterparts in other member states to see the quality of their work. The relations across national lines tend to be much more collegial than adversarial. However, different police forces *within* member states compete against each other to accumulate contacts and co-operative arrangements with counterparts in other EU countries. They even conceal those contacts to protect their advantage over rival groups inside the department and beyond and beyond the immigration service itself. Intra-EU cooperation carries a high political premium in the senior levels of admin-istration. Some investigations are conducted jointly between member states requiring them to calibrate their legal standards in advance of opening the joint investigation. The EU agency EUROJUST facilitates this process so that evidence and investigative procedures in one participating country can be admissible in the court of another. The EUROPOL might also be involved as a clearinghouse of criminal records, legal information, and contact informa-tion for investigative personnel so that member states may better coordinate transnational investigation.

Of course, the overall process flowing across groups, units, agencies, and ministries faces plenty of obstacles, to say nothing of high officials placing politically sensitive cases on hold. Put differently, an organizational blueprint and an actual process conducted by situated actors do not squarely map onto each other. Conflicts, ambiguities over responsibilities, political interests, and personal interests cloud what might otherwise be a smoothly functioning investigation. For example, the team is occasionally asked, by implication, to do favors for the odd senior official and parliamentarian. Personal favors for information might be passed along discretely to Frank from higher-ranked officials, often those who owe their positions to top figures in their political parties. (As government appoints the senior strata of the ministries, obligations are owed to those who got them appointed to those positions.) Sometimes these requests pertain entirely to personal concerns, such as developing a profile on a daughter's new lover. Other times they pertain to political infighting, or internal cases in which it is hard to determine if the motivation is political or legal. Moreover, it always remains unclear as to what Frank himself understands about the request and how much he shares it to the team. Nevertheless, the team will do the job. I asked John if he felt awkward about these situations. He replied: "No, we know the rules of the game. We need equilibrium of the system. For example, we need them to support us when we go to in the gray zone. We might buy software that is illegal to use, but we need them to approve the purchase by identifying it as another cost. 'We scratch their backs and they scratch ours.' These requests are rare, only a couple of times per year." But, as Max reckons, "They last forever. They are golden. They are like stocks. Today they are worth y for an MP, but if he becomes a minister, then they are worth x. If he leaves parliament, then they are worth zero." The team, however, reaps little benefit beyond less bureaucratic hassle and more protection when they operate in the gray zone. Max adds, "We don't get that much, really. It is like nuclear deterrence. We would never use this information on our own. We wouldn't be offensive with it. Then, we would really lose. Ultimately, we just want to work and keep our lifestyle. We are low-ranking and low-paid. We just want to work without being troubled by politics."

As another example, tensions arise between the team and the other investigative groups in the Criminal Investigation Department. Part of the tension amounts to envy. The team enjoys certain freedoms that the deskbound investigators lack. They can set their own hours according to the needs of the street investigation. If they know that they do not need to start a surveillance until 1 PM, then they will not arrive at headquarters until noon. They must be prepared, however, to work that surveillance until their targets have returned home, which can be well after 11 PM. They keep street props in the office, such as a skateboard and a soccer ball, which are fun to play with during downtime. They also can dress according to the needs of the surveillance. Usually, this means informal attire, which contrasts with the professional dress code of the other investigative groups. The allure of operating clandestinely on the street makes for more interesting experiences than what is found in an office. The team enjoys tackling the challenges they encounter on the street as a form of self-expression. The topic always leads to lively conversation. Brian notes that "we can be our individual selves. This is different from other units. That's an asset for us but it would be a liability in other units. This is needed for the job." In addition to the deskbound investigators, the team regularly contrast these experiences of *being* to those of officers who stamp passports for the immigration service's Border Control Department. This task signifies to them the most monotonous and degrading type of work that can be assigned to someone in their profession. In the summer months, they are often seconded to border control to help process the heavy loads of tourists circulating through the city's airport. David commented,

> There's gotta be some point to what you're doing. If I stamp thirty passports, there are no consequences whether I do it or not. The job itself was just the most mind-numbing thing to do. At first, you try to be positive and do the best you can. Then, you try to do as little as you can. Have you seen the guys working all their lives at an egg processing plant? The eggs keep coming past them on a conveyer belt and they say, "good egg, good egg, good egg, good egg . . . rotten egg . . . good egg, good egg, good egg."
>
> I caught an African man with a passport that wasn't his own. The guy had a French passport, but he goes to the non-EU passport control line. The only similarity he had with the picture was that he was Black. The guy in the picture had a slightly swollen and droopy eyelid. You could see that the man with the passport poked himself in his eyelid to match the picture, but he poked himself in the wrong eye! I sent him to biometrics for a comparative analysis. He failed and was sent back. That was the most exciting part of the month.

Another source of tension is the deskbound investigators' accusations that the team relentlessly pushes its own agenda. Frank is not shy about championing the team's successes up the chain of command while strategically highlighting those investigators' mistakes. To stress their incompetence, he once rhetorically asked them if they needed him to "wipe their asses with baby lotion." They filed an official complaint of harassment in retaliation with the ministry's legal office. Yet, simple arrogance does not fully explain Frank's tone and persistence. Rather, shifts in the ministry's bureaucratic terrain and changes in senior personnel come with promises of starting the organization anew and finding ways to cut down on costs. Frank's promotion of his team aims at protecting them from any possible restructuring, most of which is only intended to give new senior figures an air of action. These potential changes not only threaten the team's thrill of working together, but also the quality of evidence procured for investigations.

For example, several senior officials would be quite comfortable having each of the desk investigative groups conduct their own street work. The team abhors this idea and not only because it puts their own role at risk. (They would likely not be laid off in an organizational restructuring, but they could be reassigned to positions that they would find much more boring and isolating.) In their opinion, the other groups are incompetent on the street. They underestimate the skill it takes and the personal disposition that one must have to appear inconspicuous during surveillance operations. They have neither the team ethos that street work requires nor the knowledge of the city's contours and how people move through it. They do not thrive on the uncertainty that appearing in public space brings. Conduct on the street where one must consciously act "normal" takes a considerable amount of self-confidence. David reasons that "they [desk investigators] would go out and think, 'I must act normal.' This is the beginning of a job gone bad. You really just need to be comfortable in your own skin when you are somewhere that you don't normally hang out." From the team's standpoint, street-level investigation could not differ more from the analytic tasks conducted in the office.

In a telltale example, one deskbound investigative group jeopardized the larger investigation and potentially placed the team in danger. As Brian not so delicately puts it: "When they do their own street work, they fuck it up and the target knows that he has been under surveillance. Then they ask us to do it, but don't tell us that the target already knows. This is dangerous. They [the targets] can trap us in an operation and ambush us. [This trick had recently happened to uniformed police in the city.] We need to know if the targets knows he is being followed. They should tell us. They are supposed to have us do it." The particular target in question, a Nigerian national suspecting of participating in a trafficking ring, knew how to conduct his own counter-surveillance maneuvers. Moreover, he was alerted to the fact that the police had been following him because of the sloppy street tactics of the deskbound investigators. They had decided to do their own surveillance because the team had been too busy with other assignments, but never mentioned to the team that they had done so and that the target had spotted them. Had the team been made aware, they would then have designed their own surveillance operation differently, Brian continues:

> The neighborhood this guy lives in is a rough neighborhood, all Black immigrants. He goes to the café when we see him. [Brian, Frank, and David were already in the café.] Then, he goes out and starts to pretend to go to a car to see if he could provoke us to move. We didn't move. He then walked across an open field so that he could expose us in an open space. That way he could confirm that we were the same people in café [i.e., by dragging the team along to an open space, the target could then spot them in two different places, on the safe assumption that the only likely reason to see them in those two different places was the fact they were following him].
>
> The guy goes into a car with someone else, and they drive to see his lawyer in another part of town. The lawyer gets into the car with them, and they start making funny moves in the car like turning around in odd locations, changing speeds randomly to see if anyone in a different car does the same thing to keep up with them. They go to a café, and we park near it. The lawyer comes out and knocks on our window and shows his card. He says, "I want your ID. I am these guys' lawyer. I want your ID, and I will call the police. I said, "I am not giving you my ID. You can call the police. From the back seat, David yells out, "I don't believe you're a lawyer. You wouldn't dress like that! You look like you sell cars!" [David's strategy was to act in such a way that no police officer would in a situation like this one.]

The lawyer still called the police and motioned his clients to come over to where he was standing by the car. Brian got out, and the clients identified him to their lawyer. The lawyer asked why they were following them, to which Brian replied that he will wait for the police before he talks. Ultimately, Brian had to lie to the police when they arrived to extricate Frank, David, and himself from the situation.

> I then lean into the car and tell Frank to start the engine and go. I stayed behind and told the lawyer that there are a lot of crooks in the world. The

police came, and I talked to them in private. I told them that our target is a woman who met these guys in a café and that we followed them as some of her contacts to learn a bit more about them. Then I left, and the police explained everything to the lawyer. . . . Now, imagine if those guys were selling drugs and they thought that we were also sellers moving into their territory. That would be very dangerous.

In fairness to the desk investigators, the Criminal Investigations department is overworked and understaffed. Cases take longer to close than anyone desires, and for every case a state prosecutor can actually investigate, many more criminal acts occur without notice. The dual pressures of time and financial constraints prompt the desk investigators to do their own surveillances, which also lead them to making basic mistakes in the operation.

Control of the Narrative as the Stepping Stone into the Gray Zone

Yet, mere bureaucratic overlaps, infighting within departments, and rivalries across policy terrain do little to illuminate the mode of action when sovereign agents forego legal restrictions or policy mandates. These issues alone shed no light on the gray zone. At most, they highlight opportunities for the ambitious to pursue their personal agendas, but the advancement of competing interests is not the question in this analysis. The questions here are how the investigative team enters the gray zone and how they conduct themselves while there. There is no singular path to the gray zone. Much depends on the political climate, the historical moment, and the state agent's position in the formal bureaucracy.

The contrast with overseas intelligence work best spotlights the delicate threshold into the gray zone. Operating in foreign countries, spies are not beholden to those countries' laws at all. Spies are not limited by legal considerations, but rather political ones. If spies get caught, then their fate rests in the hands of diplomatic negotiations. Their safe return home is a matter of bargaining between their own government and the government upon whom they spied. In contrast, undercover investigation is subject to legal restraint. Lawyers can examine investigative procedures before a judge. If summoned as witnesses in court, they will spend hours reviewing their surveillance reports so that they can answer a lawyer's questions in cross-examination.

Hence, even though the investigative team works under far less oversight than the desk investigators, lawyers, senior officials, and occasionally parliamentarians will still want to know, as David so characteristically puts it, "what the fuck we are doing?"

For these reasons, the team cannot enter the gray zone through fiat, holding a cavalier attitude either toward the law or the possible political fallout if things awry. Vincent explained, "It's like basketball, the ball is already over the line. If the player has his feet just inside the line, then he can reach over and try to bring the back to the court. You still have to respect the rules." Again, in contrast to the deskbound investigators, John explained that "in their work, they can get proof through the legal way. The person working in surveillance has to be very careful because everything will be written. This is different because we are on the street." The graceful and artful transgression into the gray zone occurs through their control of the storyline of what happened on the street during an investigation. They alone supply that narrative as no one else can corroborate events, signifying David Graeber's (2015, 80) point that bureaucratic structures of domination allow for those in positions of authority to provide the explanation of what happened. However, that control also gives them cover when they act on their own ethical judgments outside of legal and policy constraints.

Two examples are particularly relevant to understanding how the team shifts over from scripted legal and policy terrain to the nebulous gray zone. Illustrating the first example, Max invoked a metaphor while we sat at a sidewalk café watching a door across the street from which a suspect would eventually exit.

> This is a white cup. Everyone can see that this is a white cup. But a judge will not see that it is a white cup if the evidence that it is a white cup is not obtained the right way. He will ask, "Where are the warrants?" Everybody knows what it is, but if you don't follow the rules, then it is not part of the investigation. It frustrates me a lot. We have to give rights to everyone *for* justice, but what about *doing* justice. If we don't do it by the book, then there are disciplinary actions. A lawyer will always find a flaw. They will interrupt justice.

To preclude this potential problem with the judge, the team makes a crucial distinction between "evidence" and "intelligence," giving the team the power over the script and the necessary protection for entering the gray zone. Intelligence is any information used to investigate suspected criminal activity. It does not appear in court. Evidence is information directly tying a suspect to a crime that must appear in court. The team would never present intelligence in court lest the methods of retrieval be exposed: "If you don't follow the rules, then it is not [officially] part of the investigation." Evidence, of course, will appear in a surveillance report, while intelligence is never recorded in any official document, testifying to the fact that documents are not passive instruments of clear bureaucratic procedures. Rather, they are strategically crafted so that policy makers instrumentalize them for their own purposes (Hull 2012, 252). In this vein, the team will find a legal way to present intelligence as evidence. For example, the team needed to know if a Chinese owner of business suites in a downtown building was running a brothel. However, paying for sex with a prostitute managed by a pimp is illegal, and so no team member could patronize the establishment to obtain direct evidence. Yet, they could not determine if it served as a brothel without going inside (and furthermore Chinese brothels in the city only cater to Chinese clients). They provided a Chinese informant with €150 to solicit the establishment's services and to ultimately confirm it as a brothel. This information will be used only as "intelligence" because of the team's illegal involvement in its procurement, that is, soliciting sex from someone controlled by a pimp. With this intelligence, however, they can justify the time and money for an operation to legally obtain evidence: most likely including the sounds of people having sex; condoms found in the trash cans outside the building; and confessions from people patronizing its services when the bust occurs. If a judge, prompted by a defense attorney, were to ask how intelligence was obtained—that is, how they knew the actual use of those suites ahead of the bust—then the team would argue that they cannot reveal their sources lest it jeopardize their informant's safety. No judge would push further, thus tacitly approving the team's right to invoke a state of exception.

Frank described the second example as he stood in the door frame of the team's office at headquarters. Between drags on his cigarette, he explained, "For us, we always seek the truth. For us, the truth is the right thing, even if we have to lie." The lie to which he refers is not a falsehood, but rather an inference for which there is no direct evidence. They maintain that they know the truth based on experience rather than direct observation, which could never be obtained under any imaginable scenario. As a hypothetical example, if the issue in court is whether one suspect retrieved a bag left in a closet by another suspect, then it would normally stand to reason that if the latter was seen entering the closet with the bag and exiting it without the bag and the former entered the closet without the bag but exited with it, then the latter left it for the former even if the team never witnessed a direct exchange. Hence, the "truth" is not a specific object that the investigators must "see." Rather, the truth is that which a judge recognizes as sufficiently compelling reasoning, based upon some amount of sensory evidence, to reach a conviction. Thus, "lying" only means to obscure how information was obtained. Other forms of manipulation also occur. If warrants are needed to tap phones or enter houses, then they have learned how to present the argument to the prosecutor, who will then have a greater chance of obtaining the warrant from the judge. They could stress such urgencies as an underage prostitute in danger or suspicions that human trafficking is occurring. These situations are more likely to prompt a quick and favorable reply from a judge given the political importance of EU states being seen as committed to combatting these problems.

Indeed, the team has plenty of opportunity to blatantly lie and baldly fabricate reports. Brian rhetorically asked, "Do you know how easy it is for cops to frame people? We could do it very easily if we want to." A primary reason that they do not, and this can be argued without naiveté, is a sense of justice. Brian continued: "The underlying thing in our work is justice. Sometimes our work is dirty. But we don't harm anyone we don't need to. There is an honor among what we do: don't forge surveillance reports. Can you imagine how easy it would be to put someone in jail? Still, think if we were caught. The image of the unit would be tarnished. We would lose credibility. The judges would not trust us." Honor, as well as justice, are at play here. I replied to Brian, "Is honor important in other jobs like taxi driving or financial analysis?" He answered, "No, honor only matters when there is credibility on the line."

Conclusion

We should well know that truth is not a matter of some independent and objective reality against which the messy, subjectivity of human affairs should be compared. Truth, then, functions as a tacit agreement on the rules that enable what can and cannot be said. The structure of that agreement sustains and is sustained by the power arrangement of national security-cum-state sovereignty. The work of Michel Foucault (1990) well conceptualizes the practices through which power and knowledge become inseparable and constitutive of social order.[2] This much of the dynamics of modern power is well understood. The present case study, however, provides a subtle illustration of how situated actors work these rules in ways that can yield two different effects. The first effect is a mere reproduction of the current form of state sovereignty. The creativity that state security actors deploy in the course of their work does not inherently suggest a break from traditional forms of sovereign power. Neoliberal society, in particular, well appropriates the creativity and agency of its experts and technocrats (see Rose 1993). The second effect is to temporarily create a new form of sovereignty, if only operating within highly circumscribed space of action. While cases of well-documented abuse abound in the gray zone, abuse itself is not a foregone conclusion even if it is sadly all too common. Therefore, honor may seem like a naively optimistic way to end the chapter, but it is worth taking Brian's comments at face value. Although not the focus of this chapter, honorable action can be pursued by the team because the channel through which they can enter the gray zone is clear, but rather narrow. The intelligence/evidence distinction does not grant the team license to rewrite the law wholesale or simply abandon legal restraint. If they pushed too hard in the gray zone, then some sort of pushback would ensue and expose their illicit deeds. The thin distinction between the two key words of "evidence" and "intelligence" comes replete with significant opportunities and foreclosures within the power-knowledge grid of state sovereignty. While the latter are known well enough, the former remain quite mysterious to us, and so the opportunities may go untapped.

Notes

I would like to thank the members of the investigative team for their openness and accommodation. An Insight Grant from Canada's Social Science and Humanities Research Council funded this research.

1   The team works in the immigration and border service in an interior ministry of a southern, maritime EU member state. Their cases exclusively investigate transnational networks involved in burglary, prostitution, human smuggling, and human trafficking. They have granted me extensive ethnographic access on the condition that I do not identify the name of their country.

2   As the point specifically pertains to migration and security, see Didier Bigo (2006) and Gregory Feldman (2012).

References

Agamben, Giorgio. 1998: *Homo Sacer: Sovereign Power and Bare Life*. Stanford: Stanford University Press.

Bigo, Didier. 2006. "Globalized (In)security: The Field and the Ban-opticon." In *Illiberal Practices of Liberal Regimes: The (In)security Games*, edited by Didier Bigo et al., 5–50. Paris: Editions L'Harmattan.

Feldman, Gregory. 2012. *The Migration Apparatus: Security, Labor, and Policymaking in the European Union*. Stanford, CA: Stanford University Press.

Feldman, Gregory. 2016. "'With My Head on the Pillow': Sovereignty, Ethics, and Evil among an Undercover Police Investigators." *Comparative Studies in Society and History* 58(2): 491–518.

Foucault, Michel. 1990. *The History of Sexuality, vol. 1, An Introduction*. New York: Vintage Books.

Graeber, David. 2015. *The Utopia of Rules: On the Technology, Stupidity, and the Secret Joys of Bureaucracy*. Brooklyn, NY: Melville House.

Hull, Matthew. 2012. "Documents and Bureaucracy." *Annual Review of Anthropology* 41: 251–67.

Rose, Nikolas. 1993. "Government, Authority, and Expertise in Advanced Liberalism." *Economy and Society* 22(3): 283–300.

EIGHT

The Secrecy/Threat Matrix

JOSEPH P. MASCO

The constitution of a *national security* state transformed the United States into a new kind of secret society after World War II, one in which state power rests to an unprecedented degree precisely on the ability of officials to manage the public-secret divide through the mobilization of threat. This *secrecy/ threat matrix* marks all state secrets as equivalents of the atomic secret, making revelation a matter not just of politics but of the life or death of the nation-state. The Cold War arms race—founded on the minute-to-minute possibility of nuclear war—installed the secrecy/threat matrix as a conceptual infrastructure, enabling a new species of politics in the United States. Instead of enabling a system in which knowledge is power, the national security state's system of compartmentalized secrecy produces a world in which knowledge is increasingly rendered suspect. This is a profound shift in how secrecy functions socially. In such a nation-state, secrecy becomes an increasingly pathological administrative form, one that prevents confidence in knowledge, and where no one—citizen, solder, or official—is untainted by secrecy's distorting effects. As we shall see, the security state is increasingly structured not by the value of knowledge or by the power of withholding knowledge, but rather by the theatrical performance of secrecy as a means to power.

Instituting Secrecy

With the Atomic Energy Act of 1946 and the National Security Act of 1947, the United States effectively removed huge areas of governmental affairs from citizens' purview. These acts formally installed a new security state within the United States, constituting a rather fundamental change in the nature of American democracy. The Atomic Energy Act created the first kind of information—nuclear weapons data—that did not need to be formally classified: it was "born" that way. The National Security Act then created a wide range of new governmental institutions—most prominently, the Central Intelligence Agency (CIA), the first of what would become seventeen intelligence agencies in the United States—that *by charter* would not be publicly accountable to citizens. Created in peacetime, the new laws and agencies marked the establishment of a permanent wartime economy as well as a fundamental commitment to state secrecy in the United States. Rationalized as an effort to protect military secrets about the atomic bomb in an uncertain world and to prevent a "nuclear Pearl Harbor" (see Dower 2010, 27), these acts inaugurated a split between national security and state security in the United States, with citizens implicitly recognized as a potential barrier to state security policies. After 1945 the U.S. security state apparatus increasingly used nuclear fear as an affective means of reconstituting the line between the foreign and the domestic, and to mobilize citizens as Cold Warriors.

Although the concept of a state secret was not invented during the Manhattan Project, the state structures that were established to build the atomic bomb have subsequently evolved into an unprecedented and massive infrastructure in the United States—so massive, in fact, that its sheer scale is difficult to assess (see Burr, Blanton, and Schwartz 1998; and also Masco 2002 and 2006). Today there may well be more knowledge that is classified than is not, more knowledge that is produced and locked up in the military-industrial state than is offered by all nonmilitary academic literatures. Peter Galison has calculated the scale of secret versus public knowledge in the United States and offers this assessment (2004, 231):

> There are 500,000 college professors in the United States—including both two- and four-year institutions. Of course there are others—inventors, industrial scientists, computer programmers—responsible for generating and conveying knowledge, especially technical knowledge. But to fix ideas, four million people hold [security] clearances in the United States,

plus some vast reservoir who did in the past but no longer do. Bottom line? Whether one figures by acquisition rate, by holding size, or by contributors, the classified universe is, as best I can estimate, on the order of five to ten times larger than the open literature that finds its way into our libraries.

The classified archive is many times larger than the open library. Produced in the name of citizens who have no access to this knowledge except as employees of the security state, the classified universe is not simply a means of protecting the nation-state from the spread of dangerous military information; official secrecy is a social technology, a means of internally regulating and militarizing American society. The organizing principle for this system of secrecy is the atomic bomb, which is positioned within the universe of classification as the ideal type of state secret. Indeed, the system of secrecy that developed after World War II was premised on the idea that everything marked as *classified* had the potential to produce catastrophic results if made public. An important part of the cultural work accomplished by the state's recitation of nuclear danger in the first decades of the Cold War was to establish this linkage between the classified and the apocalyptic—merging a bureaucratic system for managing the military-industrial economy with images of imminent destruction of the nation-state at the slightest slippage or revelation. By discursively positioning every classified file as potentially an "atomic secret," the state transformed a provisional system of wartime secrecy into a fully nationalized system of perception management and control.

In essence, a new social contract was formed in the first decade of the Cold War, enabled and structured by the affective power of atomic weapons (Masco 2014). Simultaneously the ultimate weapon and the ultimate vulnerability, nuclear weapons presented a new set of contradictory resources and challenges to the state. For example, although declaring that the United States possesses "the greatest military potential of any single nation in the world," National Security Council Directive 68 (NSC 1993, 50)—the top-secret policy document that articulated the Cold War policy of Soviet containment in 1950—is nonetheless ultimately a text about U.S. nuclear vulnerability. The directive depicts the Soviet Union as an existential enemy in anticipation of its future nuclear potential and argues not only for a fourfold military buildup but also for a mobilization of all institutions of American society to fight a long Cold War. This reengineering of American society for a new kind of warfare required a widespread recalibration of everyday life, including political, economic, and military institutions as well as the urban landscape and ideas about the future (see Galison 2001; Masco 2008). The early Cold War military planners—Major General Walter E. Todd, commanding general of the Western Air Defense Force for the United Kingdom; Lieutenant General Willard S. Paul, an expert on economic mobilization in the U.S. Office of Defense Mobilization; and Val Peterson, head of the Federal Civil Defense Administration—all called in the same *Scientific Monthly* article (titled "National Defense against Atomic Attack"), for the construction of a "perfect air defense" involving the full accoutrements of now iconic "closed world" military technologies (see Edwards 1996), a dispersion of industrial sites away from urban centers, a relocation of housing stock to the periphery of cities, a constant war-gaming of potential Soviet attack scenarios along with domestic civil defense exercises, a massive program to stockpile critical materials to feed and care for the entire national population, new building standards for all construction designed to resist the effects of a nuclear blast's effects, and a significant military expansion of the U.S. capability to fight a nuclear war. Todd, Paul, and Peterson concluded (1955, 246):

> Mobilization is no longer to be undertaken upon declaration of war or after war starts. Either we stay ready at all times to absorb and survive the worst blow an enemy can strike, or we do not. If we do not, there probably will be no chance to mobilize afterward. If we do, there is a good chance that the blow will never be attempted, for we will have substituted many targets for a few. The enemy will no longer be able to destroy effectively the capacity to operate and, thus, to break the national spirit by a massive attack on major metropolitan areas.

We stay ready at all times. The immediate goal of the countercommunist state was to reengineer American society around and through the atomic bomb. Not only was nuclear fear integrated into military planning, but it also transformed the very nature of the nation-state.[1] Indeed, all the projects proposed by Todd, Paul, and Peterson were actually pursued, fusing the Cold War military project with a new kind of domestic military economic strategy. But what was the actual nature of the nuclear threat? In 1950, the Soviet Union had no more than 5 nuclear devices, while the United States had more than 350; by 1961, these arsenals had grown substantially: the Soviet Union had amassed more than 2,400 weapons, while the United States had more than 24,000 warheads and bombs (Norris and Kristensen 2006). Few Americans at the time, or today, understand that the United States maintained at least a ten-to-one nuclear advantage throughout the first decades of the Cold War, the period of the most intense nuclear paranoia in the United States. So how do we reconcile the clear nuclear advantage the United States maintained through the early decades of the Cold War with the domestic nuclear discourse of absolute vulnerability and imminent surprise nuclear attack?

Nuclear fear was the central concept within a larger project of emotional management campaign project designed and conducted by both the Truman and Eisenhower administrations to mobilize citizens for a new kind of war (see Oakes 1994). By concentrating public attention on specific images of nuclear threat and by classifying all other aspects of the nuclear economy, the early Cold War state sought to calibrate the image of *crisis* to enable the Cold War project. The primary goal of what was publicly called "civil defense" in the first decades of the nuclear age was not to protect citizens from the exploding bomb but rather to psychologically reprogram them as Cold Warriors. The calculated campaign of images—produced by the nuclear test program and delivered under the rubric of domestic civil defense—was an effort to access the emotions of U.S. citizens and thereby transform an emerging nuclear threat into a means of consolidating the power and importance of the security state. As a top-secret report to President Dwight Eisenhower put it in 1956 (Panel on the Human Effects 1956, 5), "Just as the Industrial Revolution of the early nineteenth century, with its far-reaching effects on war and peace, required vast social and psychological adjustments, so the present period faces extremely complex social and psychological changes." *Vast social and psychological adjustments are needed.*

Calling for a new state project to install "psychological defenses" in citizens, and challenging each individual to engage in an "emotional adaptation" to the thought and reality of nuclear warfare, the report concludes (Panel on the Human Effects 1956, 11; see also Vandercook 1986): "The keystone of the program is knowledge—not merely information made available but information, both frightening and hopeful, so successfully conveyed as to become useful knowledge translated into plans, procedures, and the capability for constructive action. . . . In order to prepare the people, we believe that it will be necessary to involve them, and to involve them at deeper levels than mere factual information." *A deeper level than facts.* Involving citizens meant teaching them about the effects of nuclear explosions—providing specific images of the bomb and censoring all others—while publicizing the emerging Soviet nuclear threat. Civil Defense was an explicit program to teach citizens to fear the bomb, fuse that fear with anticommunism, and modulate its intensity so that a potentially terrified public did not become unwilling to support the larger Cold War program. The ultimate goal of civil defense was the creation of a citizen who was permanently mobilized as a Cold Warrior, restructured internally for constant readiness and psychologically hardened by nuclear fear. One of the most powerful attributes of the atomic bomb, in other words, is that it offered new access to the emotional life of the nation, producing a new kind of public constituted and militarized through a highly tailored vision of totalizing threat.

But if publicizing a specific concept and image of nuclear danger was the key to mobilizing citizens—to establishing an everyday life infused with the minute-to-minute possibility of nuclear war—the corollary project was an expanding use of state secrecy to manage the production of threat and control its public image. In the early Cold War period, the atomic bomb was the ultimate key to achieving global "superpower" status, as well as to installing a concept of danger that was the exclusive domain of the security state. For the nuclear state, this secrecy/threat matrix became a concentrated means of managing domestic populations as well as pursuing the broader geopolitics of communist containment. Secrecy was not just about protecting technological secrets in a global competition with the Soviet Union; it was also a means of converting American society into a countercommunist state at the level of institutions, economies, politics, and emotions. The War on Terror is a contemporary effort to reproduce the success of this early Cold War project in population management, affective governance, and military-industrial expansion, while at the same time expanding existential danger itself through the phantasmatic figure of the "terrorist with a WMD" (Masco 2014). The Obama administration ultimately committed also to a "modernization" of the U.S. nuclear complex, planning a set of new warheads, bombers, and missiles to be developed through mid-century at a foreseeable cost of at least one trillion dollars, thus extending the U.S. commitment to military nuclear power through the twenty-first century (Wolfsthal, Lewis, and Quint 2014).

The Counterterror State

Since 2001, secrecy has become a core tool in transforming the United States from a countercommunist to a counterterrorist state, and its official use is an ever-expanding practice. In a variety of Executive Orders and formal directives in the aftermath of the 2001 terrorist attacks, the Bush administration required each federal agency of government to increase its control of information.[2] According to government audits, there were nine million formal classification decisions in 2001 but over sixteen million by 2004, a trajectory that continues well into the Obama administration. Moreover, the rate at which records that are over twenty-five years old were declassified fell by over 75 percent in the same period. Thus, the official past as well as the official present have become newly politicized as well as highly censored domains.[3] The cost of simply managing secret information in the United States grew to be over $7.2 billion a year, involving in one year alone over four thousand classification authorities and over 351,150 new classifications decisions.[4] However, these figures only deal only with explicit classification or declassification decisions, the making of which is a formal regulatory process. An expansive "Sensitive but Unclassified (SBU)" category of information is a potentially larger and more influential category of knowledge. Information that is SBU is not officially classified; it is information simply removed from public circulation and treated *as if* it were classified.

Officially justified as a means of protecting information about "critical infrastructures" following the terrorist attacks on New York and Washington in 2001, the SBU designation and its expanding use have radically changed the way information is handled within federal agencies. The Homeland Security Act of 2002 charged federal employees to "identify and safeguard homeland security information that is sensitive but unclassified."[5] However, the act defined none of its terms, leaving it up to each federal agency to draw the lines between public access and critical infrastructure protections. Concurrently, the Department of Justice advised all government agencies to limit the scope of Freedom of Information Acts (FOIA) requests wherever possible—forcing litigation and thus contradicting the law's intent—and while also pursuing an unprecedented application of the Espionage Act of 1917 to targeting whistleblowers within the government. These processes only accelerated during the Obama administration, including prosecutions of reporters writing about counterterror policies (Elsea 2013). In support of these new restrictions, the counterterror state has also embraced advocated a "mosaic theory" of information threat. This theory assumes that disparate items of information (particularly those that appear innocuous and of no obvious use to an adversary) can nonetheless be assembled to create a whole that is more powerful than the sum of its parts. According to this theory, any piece of information is potentially a national security threat, as it is the creative linking together bits of knowledge that are imagined to be dangerous. The extensive surveillance programs run by the National Security Agency after 2001—involving digital surveillance, archiving telecommunications across platforms, and data mining on a newly comprehensive global scale—also rely on this concept. David Pozen has consequently argued that an aggressive use of the mosaic theory of information synergy produces claims that are "unfalsifiable," leading inevitably to overclassification and threat proliferation (2005, 679).

The result of these new laws, practices, and interpretive strategies is obvious: information that flowed relatively freely a few years ago—for example, environmental impact studies of government projects—now fall into this SBU category and are often not available to citizens. A generalized state security concept trumps all other concerns (in this case, environmental protection) via the SBU approach. The images of prisoner abuse from Abu Ghraib prison fell within the SBU category and were released only after being leaked to *60 Minutes*, the *New Yorker*, and *Salon.com* and via litigation by the American Civil Liberties Union.[6] But less provocative information about government contracts, policy debates and initiatives, and anything that might have patentable potential—also falls within the SBU category. Thus, the overall strategy of the counterterrorist state has been to replace a presumption of transparency in nonmilitary matters with wide-ranging restrictions that emphasize noncirculation rather than, or in addition to, formal classification (see Roberts 2006, 36–41). It is via the SBU category that much of American society is being implicitly militarized—as keeping basic governmental information from citizens is increasingly normalized, equated with antiterrorism, and accepted as an administrative practice.

The most important aspect of the SBU category of information is that it has never been defined by federal law; it is a strategically vague concept that is used differently by each federal agency. The U.S. Government Accountability Office (2006) found fifty-six different definitions of SBU in use and could document few provisions to identify which (and how many) officials within an agency are authorized to designate information as SBU. The SBU designation is thus a largely unregulated category of information within the federal government. The first articulation of SBU as a category came from John Poindexter, while working as Ronald Reagan's national security advisor, before he gained notoriety for his role in the Iran-Contra scandal. At the start of the War on Terror, he also served as head of the Defense Advanced Research Projects Agency until public revelation of his proposed Total Information Awareness data-mining project (devoted to capturing all digital communication) forced him to step down in 2002. In 1986, Poindexter defined SBU information this way (quoted in Knezo 2003, 20):

> Sensitive, but unclassified information is information the disclosure, loss, misuse, alteration or destruction of which of which could adversely affect national security or other Federal Government interests. National Security interests are those unclassified matters that relate to the national defense or the foreign relations of the U.S. government. Other government interests are those related, but not limited to the wide range of government or government-derived economic, human, financial, industrial, agricultural, technological and law enforcement information, as well as privacy or confidentiality of personal or commercial proprietary information provided to the U.S. government by its citizens.

National security or "other" interests. The "related but not limited to" concept here expands the SBU category to include most of governmental work: today, perhaps as much as 75 percent of nonclassified government information could be designated as SBU. When fully deployed, the SBU category effectively expands national security to include any kind of information whose release might be inconvenient to the execution of state policy. When combined with the mosaic theory of information risk, there is literally no aspect of governmental work that could not be conceptualized as an essential part of U.S. national security and thus seen as a threat if made public. Increasingly, anticipatory defense trumps democratic process across governmental activities.

Indeed, the SBU category was aggressively mobilized by federal agencies as an antiterrorism provision in October 2001, as a means of protecting critical infrastructures (also a strategically vague term) from terrorist attack (Knezo 2003, 25). From the perspective of the counterterror state, the value of SBU as a category is not only its ambiguity—as literally anything in the government can be separated from the public sphere, according to its logics—but also because there is no formal review process that citizens can use to challenge the designation of information as SBU. There is no federal agency charged with regulating the use of SBU or hearing appeals. It is therefore up to each federal agency, branch, office, and official to decide where to draw the line between public accountability and security, which allows near-infinite flexibility in standards and logics. If having basic information about governmental practices can be constituted as a threat, then SBU functions to blur the distinction between the citizen and the enemy. It also allows any kind of federal information to be marked for noncirculation, creating an expansive new category of withheld information located between the explicitly classified and the public.

Following the declassification campaigns of the immediate post–Cold War era, and the enormous democratization of access to information access enabled by the Internet in the 1990s, the early twenty-first century has thus witnessed a fundamental shift in the idea and mechanisms of openness and transparency in the United States. Indeed, a central part of the conversion of the United States from a countercommunist to a counterterror state has been an information strategy of increased classification and noncirculation, and also of censoring of the existing public record. The U.S. National Archives have become an explicit front line in the counterterror project, as historical records relating to presidential authority, war authorizations, intelligence on WMD issues, and other military matters going back to the start of the Cold War have been removed, and designated as either designated as SBU or reclassified (ISOO 2006).[7] At least one million pages of previously declassified materials have been pulled from the National Archives since October 2001 (see Bass and Herschaft 2007). Thus, the historical formation, as well as the current projects, of the security state haves been subject to expanding forms of censorship. Official fear of the terrorist, and of the WMD, has enabled a formal reconstitution of the security state as secret entity generating a wide range of covert actions within the United States and around the world. Secrecy in all its forms is a political tool, with the art of redaction an additional method for withholding information while complying with federal law (see figure 8.1).

Agreeing with every major official study of state secrecy in the past thirty years, William Arkin (2005, 12) argues that this level of secrecy is not only excessive but also profoundly damaging to a democracy, because it confuses the domestic politics of secrecy with efforts to protect military operations. Arkin notes, for example, that U.S. military activities operations that are easily recognized as such in the Middle East (from special operations to drone strikes) are nonetheless classified by the United States government, a state of affairs that serves only to keep U.S. citizens—not foreign nationals, military leaders, or adversaries—in the dark (see also Sagan and Suri 2003, 150). Chalmers Johnson (2000), takes this insight a step further, by pointing out that the CIA term "blowback" addresses not only the retaliatory consequences produced by U.S. covert actions at home and abroad, but also the damaging crucial domestic effects of secrecy. Since U.S. covert operation actions are by definition unknown to U.S. citizens, then actions taken around the world in response to them are literally unintelligible to U.S. citizens. Secrecy works here in a dou-

8.1 "Endgame," redacted page from a CIA report on interrogation techniques (U.S. Central Intelligence Agency 2004).

bled fashion to enable state actions that might not be supported if they were subjected to public debate while at the same time denying citizens a means of understanding the long-term political effects of U.S. global activities. In a counterterror state, blowback has several additional perverse effects: since U.S. citizens have no insight into U.S. covert actions around the world, retaliatory acts appear to the American public as without context and thus irrational. And given that the premise of the War on Terror is that a "terrorist" is an irrational and inherently violent being who is dedicated to destroying the United States, blowback empowers yet another level of American misrecognition and fantasy: namely, that the United States is only a global military actor when provoked by irrationally violent attacks. As Joseba Zulaika (2009) has shown in great detail, terror produces terror, becoming a self-propagating circuit of fantasy, preemptive violence, and retaliation.

A similar observation was made by Daniel Moynihan (1998) in his post–Cold War review of official secrecy: he noted that the Cold War decision to keep the Venona intercepts of encrypted Soviet diplomatic communications classified to protect sources and methods in the 1950s actually worked primarily to keep U.S. citizens in the dark about the true scale of Soviet espionage in the United States, since the Soviets soon knew their code had been broken. Moynihan suggests that releasing the files before 1995 might have prevented or reduced the profound political divide in American society over the nature of Soviet infiltration—as the Venona intercepts documented that there were, in fact, Soviet spies in the United States but nowhere near the numbers imagined by Senator Joseph McCarthy (see also Shils 1996, 13). Thus, secrecy produces political fetishes that can fundamentally distort a democratic public sphere. For example, the CIA's increasing use of drones for targeted killings in Pakistan and Afghanistan has been the subject of widespread reporting (by nongovernmental agencies and mass media) and even confirmed by both President Obama and Secretary of Defense Leon Panetta, yet the CIA asserts in FOIA litigation that "the use (or non-use) of drones" is a "classified fact" and therefore not subject to any declassification claim.[8]

Jodi Dean (2002) argues that it is public recognition of state secrecy that enables a democracy to manage the split between what political life is supposed to be and what it is believed to be, between its ideal type and its lived experience. She argues that recognition of state secrecy—and the accompanying conspiratorial subtext to everyday life that it engenders—functions today to block political participation and curtail the possibility of truly democratic endeavors. Specifically, collective assumptions about the secret state (its capacities, interests, omnipotence) installs an ever-ready alibi for failed or stalled politics within the public sphere, allowing the fantasy of democracy to coexist within its distorted reality. In Dean's view, citizens now work more passionately to locate and reveal the secret than to enact structural change through direct political action. The democratic state form, which formally claims to be both transparent and accountable, has been reduced, via the logic of the secret, to a fight over the terms of the visible and nonvisible rather than social progress. For Dean, engaging the secret therefore becomes an act of misrecognition for citizens, who assume that revealing the hidden is the means of organizing democratic politics rather than mobilizing for collective action and is the way to organize democratic politics. She suggests that the evocation of the secret and the call to reveal it have therefore become surrogates for real politics in the United States—together constituting a fetish form that prevents the kind of collective mobilizations that enabled the social justice movements of past eras. Dean suggests, in short, that a belief in the secret constitutes the possibility of a democratic public—for *if only* citizens knew the state's secrets, they could correct the obvious failings of the current political system and create a more perfect society—but it also installs a public for which agency is therefore also endlessly deferred in the act of chasing greater transparency. But if an informed, democratically energized citizenry is the first victim of the elaborate system of secrecy in the United States, policy makers also suffer.

There is a remarkable moment in Daniel Ellsberg's autobiography in which he describes a conversation with Henry Kissinger, who was then on the verge of becoming Secretary of State. Ellsberg, the RAND analyst who eventually leaked the top-secret U.S. history of the Vietnam War known as the Pentagon Papers to the *New York Times* and the *Washington Post* (see Prados and Porter 2004), attempts to prepare Kissinger for the psychological effects of having access to above top-secret information. He informs Kissinger that, over the coming years, he will feel, in the following order: exhilarated (at the access), foolish (for what he once thought he knew), contempt (for those who do not have access), and increasing skepticism (about the quality of classified information). In the end, Ellsberg tells Kissinger (Ellsberg 2003, 237–38):

> It will become hard for you to learn from anybody who doesn't have these clearances. Because you'll be thinking as you listen to them "What would this man be telling me if he knew what I know? Would he be giving me the

same advice, or would it totally change his predictions and recommendations?" And that mental exercise is so torturous that after a while you give it up and just stop listening. I've seen this with my superiors, my colleagues . . . and with myself. . . . You will deal with a person who doesn't have those clearances only from the point of view of what you want him to believe and what impression you want him to go away with, since you'll have to lie carefully to him about what you know. In effect, you will have to manipulate him. You'll give up trying to assess what he has to say. The danger is, you'll become something like a moron. You'll become incapable of learning from most people in the world, no matter how much experience they may have in their particular areas that may be much greater than yours.

You become something like a moron. Ellsberg reveals here a rarely commented on aspect of compartmentalized secrecy: it relies not only on withholding information but also on lying. Individuals must lie in order to protect their own classification level in everyday interactions throughout the system, and thus, they distort their social relations to protect the system of secrecy. Knowledge itself thus becomes doubly corrupted: first, because of the effect of compartmentalization on perceptions of expert knowledge as described by Ellsberg, and second, because perception control becomes as important as information management. Deception via classification becomes the internal structure of the security state, which over time works not to underscore the value of information—often the assumed goal effect of a system of compartmentalized classification—but rather to corrode the very terms of knowledge and expertise, making individual motivations and judgments also suspect.

The role of deception is crucial in the transformation of a democratic state into a security state, as the public good becomes absorbed into that of a security apparatus that by definition seeks to extend its power and reproducibility. This logic is made visible by even a cursory look into the *state secrets privilege* in the United States—the tool whereby the security state blocks a legal proceeding to protect "national security interests."

The states secret privilege was formally established in 1953 in the Supreme Court case *United States v. Reynolds.*[9] After an Air Force B-29 aircraft crashed near Marion, Georgia, in 1948, family members of the dead and injured sued the government for negligence, and sought declassification of the accident report to support their claim. The families won in lower courts, but lost on federal appeal in the Supreme Court. The air force argued that the B-29 mission involved research on "secret electronic equipment" and that to release any information about the crash would damage national security. This case set the precedent for a "state secrets" privilege in the United States, which has become a now standard federal tool for nullifying legal challenges on national security grounds. The family members, however, continued to push for release of the accident report via the Freedom of Information Act, receiving several copies during the 1990s that were heavily redacted. Then, in 2000, they found an uncensored copy of the once-classified, and by then highly litigated, accident report on the Internet. It had been inadvertently released by the air force as part of a larger declassification of fifty-year-old records. The report made no mention of the "secret electronic equipment" that was the basis for the initial Supreme Court state secrets ruling, but it did document negligence in the maintenance of the aircraft and the training of the crew. Thus, the air force appears to have classified the report in 1948 not for national security reasons but rather to avoid liability for the accident. The families sued again to have the 1953 ruling overturned as fraud, and the Justice Department successfully deployed the mosaic theory of secrecy to stop the legal proceedings: in essence, federal lawyers argued that it is impossible to understand today what seemingly innocuous bits of information might collectively have had national security implications in 1948, regardless of the initial Air Force arguments (Fisher 2006, 203). It is crucial to recognize here that the foundational legal case for the state secrets privilege in the United States is grounded in deception rather than a principled theory of national security—illustrating how secrecy functions not only to protect information but to create new realities and new forms of bureaucratic agency and protection. Since 2001, the state secrets privilege has been evoked to nullify judicial hearings in an exceptional number of high-profile cases, including the extraordinary rendition of a German citizen by the CIA, retaliatory suits against whistle-blowers within the Federal Bureau of Investigation (FBI) and the air force, domestic data-mining operations in the United States, multiple cases involving the surveillance of U.S. citizens without a legal warrant, and accusations of targeted killing of foreign nationals and Americans abroad (Chesney 2007; Garvey and Liu 2011). The states secrets privilege is a central tool of the counterterrorist state in managing threat perception as well as legal standing. It reveals the extraordinary power of the secrecy/threat matrix, which promises catastrophic consequences for a revelation of the secret while simultaneously classifying the considerations, evidence, and precedents supporting such an assessment.

The Affects of Secrecy

The modern state form is, in many respects, founded on the assumption of secrecy. Michel Foucault (1995; 2003) has shown that the modern state maintains the right not only to keep secrets but also to subject its citizens to increasingly minute forms of surveillance. The eighteenth-century logic of the panopticon is of a sovereign who sees without being seen, a formulation built literally into the architectural infrastructure of the prison and ultimately the mind of the prisoner. A similar logic is today replicated across U.S. digital surveillance activities on an unprecedented scale—creating a counterterror state that attempts to be completely hidden while rendering citizens completely transparent. Similarly, the modern project of population management involves a fine mesh of institutions devoted to measuring individuals and creating statistical portraits of citizens across a wide range of subjects, from health, to education, to the economy. Foucault charts a steady progression in the forms of knowledge, as well as the psychosocial intimacy of these state projects, from the overthrow of monarchal authority to the early twentieth-century nation-state, as the tools of surveillance and technologies of population management steadily increase in both power and resolution. Thus, there has always been a profound separation between citizens and the state, and the practice of democratic politics has always been highly mediated by practices of secrecy. Yet, the kind of state produced in the aftermath of World War II in the United States—a nuclear-armed, global superpower—takes a core principle of the nation-state form, the use of secrecy in the name of collective security, and expands it into a totalizing structure that links all aspects of the state in a radical global counterformation. In this post–World War II system, secrecy becomes not just a technology of state power, a means of orchestrating policy and protecting state interests through the withholding of information, but also the basis for an entirely new kind of power: the ability to create new realities.

Specifically, in the nuclear age *the idea* of the secret knowledge becomes deployable on its own. Evoking the secret thus also becomes a means of claiming greater knowledge, expertise, and understanding than, in fact, is possible. How else do we explain the fantastic collective failure of the U.S. intelligence agencies to be attuned to the internal collapse of the Soviet Union in the late 1980s, even after generating nearly constant threat assessments of Soviet activities for four decades? How do we explain the constant tension within U.S. security culture over dissent in the United States and the frequent placing of nonviolent social activists into the category of the enemy? Secrecy has been enormously productive in terms of building and protecting a military-industrial economy, but it has also created new perceptions of state power that affect government officials as well as citizens. The linkage between the secret and the apocalyptic in the nuclear security state has transformed the citizen-state relationship both conceptually and in practice. The secrecy/threat matrix is, in this regard, ultimately a project of perception management, one that functions to create, protect, and project the idea of a "superpowered state." Thus, the atomic bomb inaugurates a new kind of social contract in the United States, one that separates national security as a public discourse from state security as an institutional practice. It ultimately grounds the power of the state in the perceived ability to destroy or be destroyed, rather than in the strength of its democratic institutions (see, for example, Armstrong 2002).

The WMD as a technological form has always promised apocalyptic consequences if used in combat, but the idea of the "WMD," its phantasmatic figuration, has been equally powerful in U.S. security culture. By defending all state secrets as the equivalent of the atomic secret, the U.S. security state has increasingly consolidated and defined its power via threat designation and inflation. The counterterror state's efforts to expand official secrecy alongside its amplification of the WMD as the single greatest threat to the United States (see U.S. White House 2002) reveals one long-term effect of the Cold War secrecy/threat matrix: an official desire to close off citizens' access to the state altogether, in the name of protecting the public. Official secrecy can now effectively restrict even the most banal forms of government information under the SBU category and mosaic theory concepts. These practices overturn the market logics of the information age, in which information made free was seen as a social good. The consequences of this information strategy are widespread in the United States, not only for systems of accountability but also for the sciences—in which self-censorship is increasingly sought for those working in fields of study that might have infrastructural, or military, or patent applications. Thus, the broader effect of these policies is to define the public sphere not as an inherent aspect of democratic order but as a fundamental risk to that very order, identifying rights that citizens should willingly surrender for their personal safety. The extensive data collection of the National Security Agency after 2001, for example, has rendered every detail of American citizens' digital lives a potential security concern in the name of counterterror. Indeed, what does it mean when the free flow of information is the exception rather than the rule in a global superpower that is also a self-proclaimed democracy?

Finally, and importantly, the secret society that is the state is ultimately headless, an effect of both the systematic distortion in the believability of knowledge as it moves up the levels of a compartmentalized infrastructure and the demands on individuals to protect perceptions. Thus the secret is transformed over time in such a system: indeed, the "idea" of secret knowledge itself becomes deployable, corrupting public understandings of what is possible and what is not, and giving those with executive authority the ability to seem more knowing then they actually are. Instead of limiting agency via protected knowledge, the secrecy/threat matrix empowers a new kind of agency, unrestrained by facts. In the lead-up to the invasion of Iraq in March 2003, the Bush administration systematically deployed *the idea* that there were WMDs in Iraq as well as an imminent threat to the United States, to enable war. Vice President Dick Cheney, for example, stated in a speech to the Veterans of Foreign Wars National Convention on August 26, 2002, that there was absolute certainty about the Iraqi threat (Cheney 2002): "Simply stated, there is no doubt that Saddam Hussein now has weapons of mass destruction. There is no doubt he is amassing them to use against our friends, against our allies, and against us. And there is no doubt that his aggressive regional ambitions will lead him into future confrontations with his neighbors—confrontations that will involve both the weapons he has today, and the ones he will continue to develop with his oil wealth." *There is no doubt.* Here is the secrecy/threat matrix in action, for Cheney implies that the intelligence community has documented with perfect clarity not only the technical terms of the Iraqi biological, chemical, and nuclear programs but also the intent of the regime to use them "against our friends, against our allies, and against us." This is not a deployment of actual knowledge, as the lack of any evidence of weapons of mass destruction in Iraqi after the invasion demonstrates, but it is a political deployment of a claim to secret knowledge.[10]

Secretary of State Colin Powell, in his historic presentation to the United Nations in February 2003, was even more exacting in his deployment of the secrecy/threat matrix.[11] He portrayed an Iraqi biological weapons program that was so advanced, it was already capable of threatening the continental United States. Claiming to have sources within the Iraqi government, he presented cartoon diagrams of mobile weapons labs (see figure 8.2) and satellite imagery of "WMD" production facilities (see figure 8.3). Powell stated conclusively (2003):

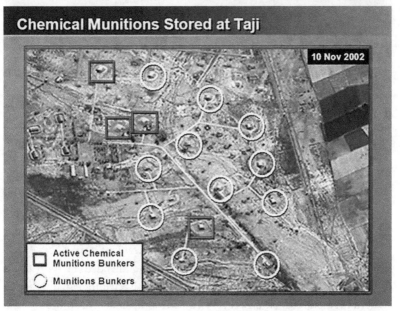

8.2 Iraqi mobile bioweapons laboratories, from Secretary of State Colin Powell's presentation to the United Nations, February 2003 (Powell 2003).

8.3 Iraqi WMD sites, from Secretary of State Colin Powell's presentation to the United Nations, February 2003 (Powell 2003).

We know that Iraq has at least seven of these mobile, biological agent factories. The truck-mounted ones have at least two or three trucks each.
That means that the mobile production facilities are very few—perhaps 18
trucks that we know of. There may be more. But perhaps 18 that we know
of. Just imagine trying to find 18 trucks among the thousands and thousands of trucks that travel the roads of Iraq every single day."

We know. This depiction of mobile "biological agent factories" effectively trans-
forms every truck in Iraq into a potential WMD laboratory, illustrating the
phantasmatic power of the concept of the WMD when used by officials deploying secret knowledge.

But the nature of the threat becomes increasingly specific in Powell's presentation, its very recitation of detail suggesting that even more exacting
knowledge existed in the classified domain:

We know from Iraq's past admissions that it has successfully weaponized
not only anthrax, but also other biological agents, including botulinum
toxin, aflatoxin, and ricin. But Iraq's research efforts did not stop there.
Saddam Hussein has investigated dozens of biological agents causing diseases such as gas-gangrene, plague, typhus, tetanus, cholera, camelpox, and
hemorrhagic fever. And he also has the wherewithal to develop smallpox.

We know. Powell claims that Iraq has the capability not only to weaponize biological weapons but also to deliver them via state-of-the-art technologies—
including unmanned aerial vehicles or drones:

The Iraqi regime has also developed ways to disperse lethal biological
agents widely, indiscriminately into the water supply, into the air. For example, Iraq had a program to modify aerial fuel tanks for Mirage jets. This
video of an Iraqi test flight obtained by UNSCOM [a United Nations Special
Commission] some years ago shows an Iraqi F-1 Mirage jet aircraft. Note
the spray coming from beneath the Mirage. That is 2,000 liters of simulated anthrax that a jet is spraying. In 1995, an Iraqi military officer, Muja-
hid Salleh Abdul Latif, told inspectors that Iraq intended the spray tanks
to be mounted onto a MIG-21 that had been converted into an unmanned
aerial vehicle, or UAV. UAVs outfitted with spray tanks constitute an ideal
method for launching a terrorist attack using biological weapons.

That is simulated anthrax. Iraqi jets as well as drones are presented here as a
means of threatening not only Middle Eastern states but also the home ter-

ritories of the United States and United Kingdom, a fantastic claim given the distances involved. After this expansive portrait of Iraqi military capabilities, Powell concludes that the weapons inspectors have failed to find the "WMDS" and that the threat from these weapons is immediate: "There can be no doubt that Saddam Hussein has biological weapons and the capability to rapidly produce more, many more. And he has the ability to dispense these lethal poisons and diseases in ways that can cause massive death and destruction." *There can be no doubt.* Powell's cartoons and fuzzy pictures of industrial sites appear today, years after the invasion, not simply as a fabrication of knowledge but rather as a tactical deployment of the idea of secret information, for his presentation was loaded with the promise that more detailed and exacting information existed, but that it could not be made public without putting U.S. interests at risk. Indeed, Powell began his presentation to the United Nations Security Council Assembly by stating: "I cannot tell you everything that we know, but what I can share with you, when combined with what all of us have learned over the years, is deeply troubling."

This deployment of "secret" knowledge relied on the mechanisms and techniques of government that were initially established after World War II to protect information about the atomic bomb—which linked existential threat and covert knowledge production in a new way. The campaign to invade Iraq also drew on culturally established forms of nuclear fear developed in the United States during the Cold War and cultivated for generations. We see here one result of a multigenerational system of state secrecy: a fundamental corruption in the terms of knowledge, where the *idea* of knowledge (imagined, projected, fantasized) replaces actual content as a means of engaging the world. The "will to believe" (in Iraqi WMDS and links between Saddam Hussein and al Qaeda) by the Bush administration remains a staggering achievement of the counterterror state, but it was only enabled as official policy by the structural effects of compartmentalized secrecy, which worked to limit debate, discount all alternative sources of information, and discredit and politicize any course of action short of war. It was not a lack of good intelligence that led to the invasion of Iraq in 2003; rather, it was the long-term corrosive effects of a compartmentalized and politicized worldview on the very possibility of governance. The secrecy/threat matrix is a core tool in the War on Terror, but it has also been revealed to be a highly overdetermined form, one that functions to fundamentally distort both expertise and knowledge.[12] And in a counterterror state where knowledge itself is rendered either suspect or irrelevant, only fear, desire, and ideology remain as the basis for action in a world constituted as full of emergent and proliferating existential dangers.

Notes

This chapter is excerpted and revised from an article first published in *Public Culture* (22:3) and later appearing in expanded form in *The Theater of Operations: National Security Affect from the Cold War to the War on Terror* (2014).

1   Indeed, the cultural, institutional, and environmental effects of the bomb have been installed very deeply in American society precisely because they are to a large degree constitutive of it after 1945 (Masco 2006; Masco 2014). See also Schwartz (1998), Wills (2010), and Priest and Arkin (2011).

2   President Bush signed Executive Order 13292 in 2003—which permitted classification of "scientific, technological, or economic matter related to the national security, which includes defense against transnational terrorism" (Bush 2003). For reviews of secrecy policy in the Bush administration, see Knezo 2003 and the detailed report prepared by Representative Henry Waxman (U.S. House 2004).

3   See OpenTheGovernment.org (2005a; 2005b) for a detailed assessment of the first George W. Bush administration's record on secrecy.

4   See U.S. Information Security Oversight Office (ISOO 2004a; 2004b). For an assessment of the Obama administration's record on secrecy of openness, see Aftergood (2013).

5   Homeland Security Act of 2002, Pub.L. 107-296, 116 Stat. 2135 (2002), sec. 896.

6   *American Civil Liberties Union et al. v. Department of Defense et al.*, U.S. District Court for Southern District of New York, 04 Civ. 4151 (AKH), 2005. See also Hersh (2004), Benjamin (2006), and Roberts (2006, 51–54).

7   For a detailed discussion and analysis of the reclassification program in the National Archives and Records Administration, see Aid (2006).

8   See *ALCU v. CIA*, No. 11-5320, 2013 WL 1003688 (DC Cir. 2013), Document #1377008, June 4, 2012, 6.

9   345 U.S. 1 (1953). For a detailed history of the case, as well as an analysis of the state secrets privilege in the United States, see Fisher (2006).

10 Cheney has long argued that a president should not be fully informed about covert actions, to enable plausible deniability in public statements. As vice president, he found various ways of restricting briefing information (including reducing the daily national intelligence estimate to a single page) for President Bush (Suskind 2006, 173–75; see also Gellman 2008).

11 For a transcript of his presentation to the United Nations, as well as images from his slide presentation, see Colin Powell (2003). For a detailed assessment of the biological weapons claims in Powell's presentation, see Kathleen Vogal (2008).

12   The categories "for official use only" and "sensitive but unclassified" have recently
      been replace by the term "controlled unclassified information," an official effort to
      reduce the number of information management markings in the federal govern-
      ment that does not change the core logic of the sbu designation (Obama 2010).

References

Aftergood, Steven. 2013. "An Inquiry into the Dynamics of Government Secrecy."
    Harvard Civil Rights–Civil Liberties Law Review 48(2): 511–30.
Arkin, William. 2005. *Code Names: Deciphering U.S. Military Plans, Programs, and
    Operations in the 9/11 World.* Hanover, NH: Steerforth Press.
Armstrong, David. 2002. "Dick Cheney's Song of America: Drafting a Plan for
    Global Dominance." *Harper's Magazine.* October, 76–83.
Bass, Frank, and Randy Herschaft. 2007. "1M Archived Pages Removed Post-9/11."
    Associated Press. March 13.
Benjamin, Mark. 2006. "The Abu Ghraib Files." *Salon.com.* February 16. https://
    www.salon.com/2006/02/16/abu_ghraib_10/.
Burr, William, Thomas S. Blanton, and Stephen I. Schwartz. 1998. "The Costs and
    Consequences of Nuclear Secrecy" In *Atomic Audit: The Costs and Conse-
    quences of U.S. Nuclear Weapons since 1940,* edited by Stephen I. Schwartz.
    Washington, DC: Brookings Institution Press.
Bush, George W. 2003. "Executive Order 13526." Classified National Security In-
    formation. *Federation of American Scientists.* Accessed March 18, 2014. http://
    www.fas.org/sgp/bush/eoamend.html.
Cheney, Richard. 2002. "Vice President's Remarks to the Veterans of Foreign Wars."
    The White House Office of the Press Secretary. August 26. https://georgewbush
    -whitehouse.archives.gov/news/releases/2002/08/20020826.html.
Chesney, Robert M. 2007. "State Secrets and the Limits of National Security Litiga-
    tion." *Wake Forest University Legal Studies Paper No. 946676.* Accessed March
    25, 2010. http://ssrn.com/abstract=946676.
Dean, Jodi. 2002. *Publicity's Secret: How Technoculture Capitalizes on Democracy.*
    Ithaca, NY: Cornell University Press.
Dower, John W. 2010. *Cultures of War: Pearl Harbor, Hiroshima, 9–11, Iraq.* New
    York: Norton.
Edwards, Paul. 1996. *The Closed World: Computers and the Politics of Discourse in
    Cold War America.* Cambridge, MA: MIT Press.
Ellsberg, Daniel. 2003. *Secrets: A Memoir of Vietnam and the Pentagon Papers.* New
    York: Penguin.
Elsea, Jennifer. 2013. *Criminal Prohibition on the Publication of Classified Defense
    Information.* Washington, DC: Congressional Research Service.

Fisher, Louis. 2006. *In the Name of National Security: Unchecked Presidential Power and the Reynolds Case*. Lawrence: University Press of Kansas.

Foucault, Michel. 1995. *Discipline and Punish: The Birth of the Prison*. New York: Vintage.

Foucault, Michel. 2003. *Society Must Be Defended: Lectures at the Collège de France, 1975–1976*. New York: Picador.

Galison, Peter. 2001. "War against the Center." *Grey Room* 4(Summer): 5–33.

Galison, Peter. 2004. "Removing Knowledge." *Critical Inquiry* 31(Autumn): 229–43.

Garvey, Todd, and Edward C. Liu. 2011. *The States Secrets Privilege: Preventing the Disclosure of Sensitive National Security Information during Civil Litigation*. Washington, DC: Congressional Research Service.

Gellman, Barton. 2008. *Angler: The Cheney Vice Presidency*. New York: Penguin.

Hersh, Seymour. 2004. "Torture at Abu Ghraib." *New Yorker*. May 10.

ISOO (U.S. Information Security Oversight Office). 2004a. "Report on Cost Estimates for Security Classification Activities for 2004." *National Archives and Records Administration (NARA)*. http://www.archives.gov/isoo/reports/.

ISOO (U.S. Information Security Oversight Office). 2004b. "2004 Report to the President." *NARA*. http://www.archives.gov/isoo/reports/.

ISOO (U.S. Information Security Oversight Office). 2006. "Audit Report: Withdrawal of Records from Public Access at the National Archives and Records Administration for Classification purposes." *NARA*. http://www.archives.gov/isoo/reports/.

Johnson, Chalmers. 2000. *Blowback: The Costs and Consequences of American Empire*. New York: Metropolitan Books.

Knezo, Geneviever J. 2003. *Sensitive but Unclassified and Other Federal Security Controls of Scientific and Technical Information: History and Current Controversy*. Washington, DC: Congressional Research Service.

Masco, Joseph. 2006. *The Nuclear Borderlands: The Manhattan Project in Post–Cold War New Mexico*. Princeton, NJ: Princeton University Press.

Masco, Joseph. 2008. "Survival Is Your Business: Engineering Ruins and Affect in Nuclear America." *Cultural Anthropology* 23(2): 361–98.

Masco, Joseph. 2014. *The Theater of Operations: National Security Affect from the Cold War to the War on Terror*. Durham, NC: Duke University Press.

Moynihan, Daniel Patrick. 1998. *Secrecy: The American Experience*. New Haven, CT: Yale University Press.

Norris, Robert S., and Han M. Kristensen. 2006. "Nuclear Notebook: Global Nuclear Stockpiles, 1945–2006." *Bulletin of the Atomic Scientists* 62(4): 64–67.

NSC (U.S. National Security Council). [1950] 1993. "National Security Council Directive 68." In *American Cold War Strategy: Interpreting NSC 68*, edited by Ernest R. May, 21–82. New York: Bedford.

Oakes, Guy. 1994. *The Imaginary War: Civil Defense and American Cold War Culture*. New York: Oxford University Press.

Obama, Barack. 2010. "Executive Order 13556 of November 4, 2010: Controlled Unclassified Information." *Federal Register* 75(2160): 68675–77.

OpenTheGovernment.org. 2005a. "Secrecy Report Card 2005." Accessed December
1, 2013. http://www.openthegovernment.org/sites/default/files/otg/SRC2005
.pdf.

OpenTheGovernment.org. 2005b. "Security Report Card 2005: An Update." Accessed March 18, 2014. http://www.openthegovernment.org/sites/default/files
/otg/OTG_RC_update.pdf.

Panel on The Human Effects of Nuclear Weapons Development. 1956. "The Human
Effects of Nuclear Weapons Development." *A Report to the President and the
National Security Council.* Washington, DC: Government Printing Office.

Powell, Colin. 2003. "Remarks to the United National Security Council." *Global
Security.org.* Accessed March 18, 2014. www.globalsecurity.org/wmd/library
/news/iraq/2003/iraq-030205-powell-un-1730opf.htm.

Pozen, David. 2005. "The Mosaic Theory, National Security, and the Freedom of
Information Act." *Yale Law Journal* 115(3): 628–79.

Prados, John, and Margaret Pratt Porter, eds. 2004. *Inside the Pentagon Papers.*
Lawrence: University Press of Kansas.

Priest, Dana, and William M. Arkin. 2011. *Top Secret America: The Rise of the New
American Security State.* New York: Little, Brown and Company.

Roberts, Alasdair. 2006. *Blacked Out: Government Secrecy in the Information Age.*
Cambridge: Cambridge University Press.

Sagan, Scott D., and Jeremi Suri. 2003. "The Madman Nuclear Alert: Secrecy, Sig-
naling, and Safety in October 1969." *International Security* 27(4): 150–83.

Schwartz, Stephen, ed. 1998. *Atomic Audit: The Costs and Consequences of U.S. Nuclear Weapons since 1940.* Washington, DC: Brookings Institution Press.

Shils, Edward. 1996. *The Torment of Secrecy: The Background and Consequences of
American Security Policies.* Chicago: Elephant Paperback.

Suskind, Ron. 2006. *The One Percent Doctrine: Deep Inside America's Pursuit of Its
Enemies since 9/11.* New York: Simon and Schuster.

Todd, Walter E., Willard S. Paul, and Val Peterson. 1955. "National Defense against
Atomic Attack." *The Scientific Monthly* 80(4): 240–49.

U.S. Central Intelligence Agency. 2004. "Office of Inspector General Special Review:
Counterterrorism Detention and Interrogation Activities" May 7. https://www
.cia.gov/library/readingroom/docs/0005856717.pdf.

U.S. House of Representatives, Committee on Government Reform, Minority Staff
Special Investigations Division. 2004. "Secrecy in the Bush Administration.
Prepared by Henry A. Waxman." *Federation of American Scientists.* https://
www.fas.org/sgp/library/waxman.pdf.

U.S. Government Accountability Office (GAO). 2006. *Information Sharing: The
Federal Government Needs to Establish Policies and Processes for Sharing
Terrorism-related and Sensitive but Unclassified Information.* Washington, DC:
U.S. Government Accountability Office.

U.S. White House. 2002. *National Strategy to Combat Weapons of Mass Destruction*. Washington, DC: Government Printing Office.

Vandercook, William. F. 1986. "Making the Very Best of the Very Worst: The 'Human Effects of Nuclear Weapons' Report of 1956." *International Security* 11(1): 184–95.

Vogal, Kathleen M. 2008. "'Iraqi Winnebagos of Death': Imagined and Realized Futures of US Bioweapons Threat Assessments." *Science and Public Policy* 35(8): 561–73.

Wills, Garry. 2010. *Bomb Power: The Modern Presidency and the National Security State*. New York: Penguin.

Wolfsthal, Jon B., Jeffrey Lewis, and Marc Quint. 2014. *The Trillion Dollar Nuclear Triad*. Monterey, CA: James Marting Center for Nonproliferation Studies.

Zulaika, Joseba. 2009. *Terrorism: The Self-Fulfilling Prophecy*. Chicago: University of Chicago Press.

NINE

___

What Do You Want?

Evidence and Fantasy in the War on Terror

JOSEBA ZULAIKA

"My colleagues, every statement I make today is backed up by sources, solid sources. These are not assertions. What we're giving you are facts and conclusions based on solid intelligence"—thus began Secretary of State Collin Powell his February 5, 2003, debriefing at the United Nations Security Council, with the tapestry reproduction of Picasso's *Guernica* behind him covered up with a blue curtain (Powell 2003). He was about to provide evidence of Saddam Hussein's possession of weapons of mass destruction before going to war with Iraq. At the outset Powell established the axiomatic nexus that should concern everyone; he had come, he said, "to share with you what the United States knows about Iraq's weapons of mass destruction as well as Iraq's involvement in terrorism." Then he immersed himself in enlisting a plethora of facts for what was, he insisted emphatically, irrefutable evidence. The information came from a variety of sources from various countries, including testimonies from various people, taped conversations among Iraqi officials detailing their deceptive practices, maps and photos showing the hiding of chemicals from inspectors in dozens of sites. A teaspoon of anthrax was all that it took to create panic in Washington the week after 9/11, Powell stated matter-of-factly while raising with his right hand a vial of simulated anthrax; Hussein was in possession of twenty-five thousand liters of anthrax, plus a stockpile of several hundreds of tons of chemical agents. Hussein's nuclear program included the development of ballistic missiles and drones. Previously, in his January 2003 State of the Union speech, President George W. Bush had left little doubt as to Hussein's nuclear ambitions: "The British government has learned that Saddam Hussein recently sought significant quantities of uranium from Africa." Powell's conclusion as to Hussein's possession of WMDs was definitive and undisputable. And there was more: "I cannot tell you everything that we know," Powell added.

But possession of WMDs by Hussein was not in itself the worst. "Our concern is not just about these illicit weapons," Powell went on to the heart of the matter. "It's the way that these illicit weapons can be connected to terrorists and terrorist organizations that have no compunction about using such devices against innocent people around the world." He linked Hussein to various terrorist organizations, including the "decades long experience with respect to ties between Iraq and Al Qaida," an organization that "continues to have a deep interest in acquiring weapons of mass destruction." The conclusion was unavoidable: "Leaving Saddam Hussein in possession of weapons of mass destruction for a few more months or years is not an option. Not in a post–September 11th world."

The Real, the Bluff, and the Passion for Evidence

It was an impressive performance by the secretary of state while commanding the world's attention. Powell had deployed to the fullest the "secrecy/threat matrix" at the core of the counterterror state (Masco 2014, 144). Soon the United States invaded Iraq; the expectations for finding the concealed weapons of mass destruction were high. Anyone reading a liberal newspaper such as the *New York Times* could only have an unmistakable sense that Hussein possessed or was about to possess a frightening arsenal of weapons of mass destructions. The paper was so convinced that a front page piece by Judith Miller was entitled "U.S. Experts Find Radioactive Material in Iraq."[1]

Except that there were no weapons of mass destruction to be found in

Iraq. The long list of facts brought by Powell, as well as all the media's feeding into the imminent expectations of finding such weapons, amounted to no evidence whatsoever. The false narrative had all been based on fantasy. But by then the United States had committed itself to an "asymmetric warfare" in which for years it would spend in each single hour in Iraq the equivalent of the total of al Qaeda financial resources (Singer 2009, 271). If the investment in nuclear weapons since 1940 is estimated in $5.8 trillion (Masco 2006, 336), the tag for the War on Terror, according to Brown University's Watson Institute, is $4.4 trillion.

The facts enlisted by Powell at the United Nations (the aluminum tubes, the vial of anthrax, testimonies by defectors, and so on) were real facts even if their value as evidence of WMDs was soon demolished. How was this "evidence" assembled and believed? One component that the intelligence services did not know at the time, and which was made known years later to the public on July 2, 2009, was that, based on CIA's interviews with him, evidence had in fact been planted by Hussein himself to keep his regional enemies at bay. Thus, a critical "evidence" was that Hussein actually had been *bluffing*. Such a hall of mirrors between real and pretended intentions is central to the murky semantic space created between terrorism and counterterrorism. The inability to sort out real threat from bluff makes those espousing counterterrorism vulnerable to be fooled into a catastrophic course of events.

The logical status of Powell's assertions about Hussein's future acts is reminiscent for the anthropologist of the one displayed by the Azande oracular revelations: "Oracular revelations are not treated as hypothesis and, since their sense derives from the way they are treated in their context, they therefore *are not* hypotheses. They are not a matter of intellectual interest but the main way in which Azande decide how they should act. We might say that the revelation has the logical status of an unfulfilled hypothetical" (Winch 1977, 88). Nor does Powell consider his projections about Hussein's future course of action hypotheticals but as about-to-happen unfulfilled certainties. In fact, a mantra constantly heard about nuclear terrorism is based on ruling out hypotheticals—"it is not if but when." Only actual events can be perceived by the senses, yet fantasy or magical thinking provides the explanation for future events. Since knowledge of the future evil of witchcraft or terrorism is hard to come by, one needs arcane and secret means for obtaining it.

Powell's evidence at the United Nations, and others we will examine below, in all their historic gravity, should be placed at the nexus of history and fiction. A model for such nexus can be found in Terry Castle's discussion of the famous ghost story *An Adventure* (1911), written by Charlotte Moberly and Eleanor Jourdain, two well-educated and proper women who recounted in great detail how they, while visiting Versailles as tourists, saw a lady who was none other than Marie Antoinette. She observes the following about the intense interest aroused by the book: "The prime symptom of Adventure-mania was a passion for invoking 'evidence'" (Castle 1991, 30). It is enough of a problem to explain how someone might see a ghost, but the issue gets multiplied when two see the same delusion, which leads Castle to investigate the nature of collective hallucinations and invoke Sigmund Freud's lament that we still possess "no explanation of the nature of suggestion" (quoted in Castle 1991, 12) and of ideological transference in general. Such "passion for invoking evidence," when there was none, is also evident in Powell's testimony and raises issues of how the "contagious folly" of a nonexistent threat could be shared by so many. Hence the deployment of the modern notion of fantasy becomes relevant to grasp counterterrorist culture and the risks it may entail to global security. In the opposition between dream and reality, fantasy is on the side of reality; in the way psychoanalysts understand it, fantasy is what gives consistency to what we call reality.

Sociologists and anthropologists have long studied the crucial role of the Durkheimian "collective representations": ideas, beliefs, values, and emotions elaborated and held collectively by a society. Historians likewise are used to speak "of the realm of imaginary representations, a realm that also has a history, fed not by 'facts' alone but also by 'interpretations'" (Vidal-Naquet 1991, 328). But while "representation" is the subjective mode of actual realities, imagination per se, in its inconstancy of form, may represent nothing and be just fantasy. This chapter's approach to terrorism—that most factual and traumatically realistic discourse in the current political discourse—examines the phenomenon as a case of collective representation and views its evidence as filtered through the framework of fantasy.

What Do You Want to Hear? Guantánamo Evidence

"Is the story true?," the torturer asks the Guantánamo inmate Mohamedou Ould Slahi about the confession extracted from him after months of torture. "I don't care as long as you are pleased. So if you want to buy, I am selling," Slahi replies (Slahi 2015, 292).[2]

Slahi is one of the hundreds of people who were taken to Guantánamo with no record of wrongdoing. A native of Mauritania and with an engineering degree from the University of Duisburg in Germany, Slahi proved to be one of the many instances of misplaced identity in which a supposedly big fish, after years of harrowing torture, provided no valuable information, his case ultimately dropped for lack of evidence. Lt. Col. Stuart Couch refused to prosecute him because his incriminating statements had been obtained through torture. Judge James Robertson granted Slahi habeas corpus and ordered his release in April 2010.[3] The Department of Justice appealed the decision, and Slahi was kept in custody until October 17, 2016. In 2005 Slahi wrote a Dantesque document, *Guantánamo Diary,* the narration of his years of torture in the hands of the United States.

After a lawsuit filed by the Associated Press for his transcripts and the pressure of his attorneys, Slahi's memoir was declassified by the U.S. government and finally published with many redactions in 2015. If the historian Carlo Ginzburg "learned to read witchcraft trials as texts, which provided direct evidence of the inquisitors and lay judges behind them, as well as some indirect and usually distorted evidence on the defendants" (1991, 321), similarly Slahi's diary provides extraordinary proof of what type of evidence counterterrorist knowledge and policy is based upon, but most important evidence of the level of fantasy and delirium of the torturers themselves.

Central to Slahi's experience is, in his own expression, the "endless catch-22" in which he is unbearably caught (214).[4] His interrogators want information, which he does not possess. Frequently he is unable to open his mouth because of the swollen lips; he finds himself bleeding from his mouth, ankles, wrists, nose; at times the superior orders the torturer to stop because, Slahi said, the superior "was afraid of the paperwork that would result in case of my death" (214). At one point a team takes him into a high-speed boat through the sea to simulate some kind of execution. He will have to be willing to tell them what they want to hear, but he will have to build a narrative that becomes credible. Slahi is most lucid in showing how difficult such task is: "Had I done what they accused me of, I would have relieved myself on day one. But the problem is that you cannot just admit to something you haven't done; you need to deliver the details, which you can't when you hadn't done anything. It's not just, 'Yes, I did!' No, it doesn't work that way: you have to make up a complete story that makes sense to the dumbest dummies. One of the hardest things to do is to tell an untruthful story and maintain it, and that is exactly where I was stuck" (232). It has to be a plausible lie that makes sense, and this requires an entire narrative, for "fantasy is the primordial form of *narrative*, which serves to occult some original deadlock" (Žižek 1997, 11). In order to placate the torturers, he has to dress his lie in a story that must look plausible, otherwise the catch-22 gets transferred to the torturers themselves, who will end up realizing in anger that he is "lying" when he is confessing and is "telling the truth" when he admits to his making up the evidence. Believing Slahi's tale was made more difficult because by then the interrogators knew that most of the Guantánamo inmates had no terrorist past.

The torturers were not getting the collaboration they wanted from Slahi, and at one point he was transferred to a special torture unit. This is how Slahi is providing his evidence: "I was literally in terror. For the next seventy days I wouldn't know the sweetness of sleeping: interrogation 24 hours a day, three and sometimes four shifts a day. I rarely got a day off. I don't remember sleeping one night quietly. 'If you start to cooperate you'll have some sleep and hot meals.' xxxx used to tell me repeatedly" (218). The interrogators allege that another top terrorist confessed that he had been recruited by Slahi for the September attack. After the seventy days and nights of torture, Slahi is taken to a "far faraway secret place" (267) to continue the interrogation—a place where no sleep was allowed and where "all the guards were masked with Halloween-like masks, and so were the Medics" (271). The guards keep their names secret from the inmates. All Slahi wants is to die. He starts to hallucinate and hear voices day and night. Slahi's "confession" will finally take place, and the torturers will be "happy" that they got the "evidence" they looked for.

"Confessions are like the beads of a necklace: if the first head bead falls, the rest follow" (275), Slahi notes in reference to the fact that an admission of culpability is the easy thing; what follows, establishing an entire detailed narrative that will satisfy the imagination of the torturer and incriminate people you don't know, is the hard part: "I had no crimes to confess to, and that is exactly where I got stuck with my interrogators. . . . But through my conversations with the FBI and the DoD, I had a good idea as to what wild theories the government had over me" (275). Slahi has to admit that "obviously there is no way out with you guys." The torturer replies: "I'm telling you how!" Slahi gives in: "Now, thanks to the unbearable pain I was suffering, I had nothing to lose, and I allowed myself to say anything to satisfy my assailants. Session followed session since I called xxxx" (278). The interrogators are "very happy" (). Slahi notes: "I answered all the questions he asked me with incriminating answers. I tried my best to make myself look as bad as I could, which is exactly the way you can make your interrogator happy. I made my mind up to spend the rest of my life in jail. You see most people can put up with being imprisoned unjustly, but nobody can bear agony day in and day out for the rest of his life" (278).

The false information could all be easily checked out and disproved, but ignorance of facts becomes a condition for the fantasy narrative. The torturers imposed an actual taboo about admitting ignorance: "Whenever I thought about the words, 'I don't know,' I got nauseous, because I remembered the words of xxxx, 'All you have to say is, 'I don't know, I don't remember, and we'll fuck you!' Or xxxx: 'We don't want to hear your denials anymore!' And so I erased these words from my dictionary" (280). He is asked to write his answers, which deserve congratulatory comments: "You're very generous in your written answers; you even wrote a whole bunch about xxxx, who you really don't know," xxxx accurately said, forgetting that he forbade me to use the words 'I don't know'" (280). There is no negative in the unconscious, Freud famously wrote. The difference between a factual narrative and a fantasy narrative is that there is no negative limit; everything is possible in the realm of fantasy. Demanding information, while forbidding the statement "I don't know," is the de facto ordering of a fantasy narrative.

The interrogators are happy with Slahi's cooperation. But they want the *whole* truth, and such guarantee presents real problems of certification. "I think you have provided 85 percent of what you know, but I'm sure you've gonna provide the rest" (289). He is told his story about Canada doesn't make sense:

"So what would make sense?" I asked.

"You know exactly what makes sense," he said sardonically.

"You're right, I was wrong about Canada. What I did exactly was . . ."

"I want you to write down what you've just said. It made perfect sense and I understood, but I want it on paper."

"My pleasure, Sir!" I said. (290)

Slahi writes down exactly what they have voiced to him for years now. "I came to Canada with a plan to blow up the CN Tower in Toronto. . . ." (290) [a tower he had never heard about before Guantánamo]. The interrogator is happy:

"This statement makes perfect sense."

"If you're ready to buy, I am selling," I said. (291)

But in the end Slahi's catch-22 gets transferred to the torturers themselves: how can they know that the confessed evidence is anything but the blowback of their own fantasy? If the interrogators really wants to know the facts, it should be relatively easy to prove that the fabricated narrative is false in many facts of substance and detail. Thus the process will require a further stage in which they will have to keep torturing Slahi to see if they can sort out when the man is lying and when not. "If we discover that you lied to us, you've gonna feel our wrath" (288), they tell him. After he gives false testimony against a Canadian, the torturer comes back to him: "I talked today with the Canadians and they told me they don't believe your story about xxxx being involved in drug smuggling into the U.S." (282) [Two years later he is relieved to learn that the man incriminated by him was in fact released].

Slahi is the incarnation of the famous Lacanian "Che vuoi?" (What Do You Want?). He provides them the tale they want to hear. But not everyone is happy with buying the confession extracted under torture; one of the torturers "doubted the truthfulness of the story" (291). He is asked whether the story he is telling is true: "if you want to buy, I am selling." The torturers find this disconcerting: "But we have to check with the other agencies, and if the story is incorrect, they're gonna find out." At this point, since he has already "sold" them whatever information they wanted, and knowing his fate has been sealed, Slahi is even willing to sell them the truth: "'If you want the truth, this story didn't happen,' I said sadly" (292). This provokes the fury of the torturers: "xxxx came back harassing me and threatening me with all kinds of suffering and agony." Not only do the torturers have to believe the story they are hearing from Slahi; he himself has to pretend to believe it or else "the radically intersubjective character of fantasy" (Žižek 1997, 8) gets lost. Slahi and his tormentors had to come to some kind of agreement by which, while he plays the role of "the-one-who-knows," the torturers have to be "the-ones-who-believe" his stories.

As if to reassure themselves they didn't hear "the truth," Slahi is ordered to write more about his Canadian plot. After all, "You know, nobody really knows what we're doing here. Only a few people in the government know about it. . . . The President reads the files of some detainees. He reads your case" (318). The torturers want to believe that the confession reflecting their own fantasy will become a true narrative that can hold up for everyone, including the president. As to Slahi, in his answers to his torturers—Che vuoi?—making up the tales was not the hardest part; it was having to believe them *himself* in order not to ruin the intersubjective nature of the fantasy narrative.

Confronted with their doubts, at one point the torturers take the strategy of hypothesizing:

"Let's talk hypothetically. You understand hypothetical?" xxxx said.

"Yes, I do."

"Let's assume you've done what you confessed to."

"But I haven't."

"Just let's assume."

"Okay." I said. . . .

"Between you and xxxx, who was in charge?"

[Slahi adopts the frame of "let's assume this is true" and makes up a reply.] "'It depends: in the mosque I was in charge, and outside he was in charge," I answered. The question assumed that Hanachi and I are members of a gang, but I didn't even know Mr. xxxx, let alone conspire with him as part of a corps that never existed. But anyway I could not tell something like that to xxxx. I had to tell him something that made me look bad.

"Have or haven't you conspired with those individuals as you admitted?"

[Slahi shifts to the frame "this is true."] "You want the truth?"

"Yes!"

"No, I haven't," I said. (294–95)

The torturers are enraged to be caught up in the schizophrenic mirror of made-up truth/lie Slahi offers them in reflection of their own fantasy. The torturers "tried to play all kinds of tricks on me. . . . They drove me into the infamous catch-22: If I lie to them, 'You'll feel our wrath.' And if I tell the truth, it will make me look good, which would make them believe I am withholding information because in their eyes I AM A CRIMINAL and I wasn't yet able to change that opinion" (295). Now that after years of torture he has agreed to tell them what they wanted to hear, they'd like their fantasy to be *true*. The search for truth reaches its surreal climax when they subject him to a lie detector test. *Slahi's lie* is what the torturers wanted in order to confirm the truth of their own fantasy; *Slahi's truth* (his total innocence) was the ultimate blow to the torturer's fantasy framework. Could it be that a lie detector might get them out of their own catch-22 by proving beyond doubt that in fact Slahi did take part in all the terrorist plots he confessed to, that his confession is after all true, that he himself believes his own confession? The answers Slahi provided are erased in the book.

The interaction between Slahi and his torturers conforms to the semantic situation studied by Gregory Bateson in his seminal essay "A Theory of

Play and Fantasy." His argument is that a paradoxical frame similar to Epimenides's paradox (the Cretan who said "All Cretans lie"—if he was telling the truth he was lying, and vice versa) obtains in play and fantasy, situations that he diagrams as ruled by the premise "All statements within this frame are untrue" (Bateson 1973). The self-contradictory nature of the premise forces that if a statement is true, then it must be false, and if it false, then it must be true, which was Slahi's predicament. Tyranny could be defined as a situation in which the tyrant is allowed to "play" with the laws while imposing his own fantasy over the objective facts.

The catch-22 in which Slahi is caught extends to his emotions; he suffers the Stockholm Syndrome regarding his own torturers. As one of them leaves Guantánamo, Slahi finds himself crying in the cell "as if I'd lost xxxx, and not someone whose job was to hurt me and extract information in an end-justifies-the-means way. I both hated and felt sorry for myself for what was happening to me" (320). Such emotional attachment surprised the interrogators, who made sure to remind him, despite his emotions, that he is a "criminal" after all (320). Among the many redactions in each page of *Guantánamo Diary*, there is one that surprised its editor Larry Siems: the deletion by the army of the word "tears" in Slahi's statement, tears provoked by the mention of his family (229). But deleting "tears" makes perfect sense, for such emotional expression humanizes Slahi in stark dissonance with the treatment they gave him as an animal. Slahi was repeatedly told: "Looks like a dog, walks like a dog, smells like a dog, barks like a dog, must be a dog" to which he adds the comment: "I know I am not a dog, but yet I must be one" (276). In a replica of Pier Paolo Pasolini's *Saló*, the photos of tortured people at Abu Ghraib showed them on a leash and making them walk like dogs. And once you have turned the prisoner into a terrorist beast, not only are you free to torture him indefinitely but also, why not, practice bestiality with him, a caged and defenseless animal, while others watch the session from a monitoring room. Slahi narrates how two female officers take off their blouses and force him "to take part in a sexual threesome in the most degrading manner" (230), something that is "hurtful" to his sex. Once Slahi had been turned fully into an animal to be hunted, tortured, fucked, and executed, put a tear in his face and such *evidence* breaks the entire fantasy narrative based on his bestiality. The censor of the *Diary* is willing to allow the reader know that they abused the dog physically and sexually, but never that Slahi could feel pity and shed a tear. William Blake wrote: "A tear is an intellectual thing";

counterterrorism could be defined as the prohibition of the statement "A tear is a terrorist thing."

In the end, as Morris D. Davis, a retired air force colonel and the chief prosecutor of the military commissions at Guantánamo from September 2005 to October 2007, put it in a piece entitled "Guantánamo's Charade of Justice," it is not just al Qaeda leaders but the American legal system that is on trial, his conclusion being that "Guantánamo has come to symbolize torture and indefinite detention, and its court system has been discredited" by the evidence of a "litany of failure" (Davis 2015). Eleven years passed by since Slahi wrote his *Diary* and six years since Judge Robertson ordered his release in April 2010. And yet Slahi was still in Guantánamo, still guilty of his torturers' deliriums, until October of 2016. Slahi's case shows the true *body of evidence*—the ultimate indictment of the counterterror state's framework of delusional fantasy. As John le Carré put it with rigorous precision, "A vision of hell, beyond Orwell, beyond Kafka: perpetual torture prescribed by the mad doctors of Washington."[5]

Guantánamo as Counterterrorism's Fundamental Fantasy

Secretary Powell's chief of staff and the man who helped Powell prepare his speech at the United Nations, Col. Lawrence Wilkerson, wrote in a sworn statement that, by the end of August 2002 President Bush, Vice President Cheney, Secretary of Defense Donald Rumsfeld, and others knew that of the initial 742 inmates, "the vast majority of Guantánamo detainees were innocent . . . [and] that there was a lack of any useable evidence for the great majority of them" (Wilkerson 2010). A study by Seton Hall University Law professors profiling 517 Guantanamo inmates found that 8 percent of them were characterized as al Qaeda fighters and "that U.S. forces 'purchased' 95 percent of those in Guantánamo from Afghan warlords and others who turned in alleged al Qaeda and Taliban for a bounty" (Wright and Dixon 2008, 133).

How can we grasp the stark fact that the U.S. counterterrorist security state willingly subjected hundreds of innocent prisoners it knew were innocent to the harshest of tortures for a period of years while providing a charade of military justice? President Obama promised to close it as soon as he took office but was unable to do so in eight years as president. Why the *necessity* of Guantánamo? A key answer is: Guantánamo offered the *fundamental fantasy* necessary to provide consistency to the U.S counterterrorist culture and security state. It was proof that "the worst of the worst" were being kept under control and punished. The general public, impervious to news that by and large the inmates had been apprehended for bounty and were innocent, overwhelmingly approved of it and continues to do so. Dismantling Guantánamo as a tyrannical farce would imply that counterterrorism was left bereft of its enemy's core fetish.

The obscenity of innocent inmates knowingly kept in Guantánamo while interrogators put on a show of searching for "evidence" of terrorism can be illustrated with another equally Dantesque Guantánamo diary, Murat Kurnaz's *Five Years of My Life* (2007). Born in Bremen, Germany, Kurnaz married a Muslim woman from Turkey and decided to go for two months to the Masura Center in Lahore, Pakistan, to learn what he needed to be a good Muslim husband. As he was to return to Germany on December 1, 2001, he was arrested in Peshawar, Pakistan. He was taken first to Kandahar and then Guantánamo. Like most prisoners in Guantánamo, he had been sold for a bounty of three thousand dollars. Kurnaz writes of grisly images of inmates with legs and fingers amputated as well as people killed in Kandahar and Guantánamo as the result of torture; he describes in harrowing detail how close he came to death on several occasions. The hope for him was that he would find an interrogator who would listen to his evidence; in the end it should have been quite easy to check the facts of his life in Germany and verify he had conducted an ordinary life and was by no means a terrorist.

The stark fact was that, in the words of his attorney, "the U.S. government knew of his innocence as early as 2002 (just six months into his detention), even as it continued, cynically, to argue that Murat was an 'enemy combatant'" (Azmy 2007, 240). For five years of interrogation the United States would pretend to be either in search or in possession of "evidence" to subject him to the most extreme, life-threatening forms of torture. Survival at all costs was Kurnaz's goal, and for this he held on to his faith and to the hope that someone would check the bare facts of his life. One day he comes to the realization that "they had known everything about me from the very beginning. They weren't interested in the fact that I had never been to Afghanistan and was innocent. I didn't stand a chance" (Kurnaz 2007, 144).[6]

But the pretense of the search for evidence has to continue in order to make sense of the torture, and the questions become more and more absurd: the color of his shoes in Bremen, what brand of shirt he preferred, confirmation of his birth certificate, the correct spelling of his name. German interrogators, who must have known of his innocence, arrive in Guantánamo in search of "evidence they could use to accuse me of some crime" (173). The interrogators accuse him of lying; "you know everything about me," he protests. "We have our own evidence," they reply (175).

In September 2004, after almost three years of living literally in a cage of six feet by seven, and two years after U.S. officials knew he was innocent, Kurnaz was taken to a tribunal that is going to determine whether he is an enemy combatant. Two weeks later the judge read his ruling that he was a dangerous enemy combatant on the grounds that he belonged to al Qaeda, the evidence being his friendship with a friend from Bremen, Selçuk Bilgin, who allegedly became a suicide bomber; a second charge was that he belonged to Jama'at al-Tablighi because he had lived with that group (the Tablighi are an avowedly pacifist and apolitical group). As if the absurdity of blaming Kurnaz for his former friendship with a suicide bomber whose attack took place eighteen months after he was in Guantánamo was not enough, the reality was that Selçuk Bilgin lived in Bremen and had not immolated himself. A phone call would have been enough to check these facts. But that would imply the military tribunal had to give up their fantasy narrative that the man they had tortured to the extreme for years could be anything but a terrorist.

Later in 2005 and 2006 the Administrative Review Board would take another look at his case and conclude that "the defendant was captured in Tora Bora in Afghanistan where he was leading a group of Taliban guerrillas. He is considered an enemy combatant and will be kept in Guantánamo." When he replied that they had known for five years that he was arrested in Pakistan, not Afghanistan, the head of the tribunal stood his ground: "That's what we've concluded from the evidence" (217).

In January 2005 Judge Joyce Green ruled that the Guantánamo detainees were entitled to due process rights and could challenge their detention. She mentioned in particular Kurnaz's case, her conclusion being that his detention was unlawful (Azmy 2007, 248). But the government appealed Judge Green's decision, which was later upheld by the Supreme Court. In the meantime Kurnaz's attorney, Baher Azmy, found himself in the position of having to go to Germany in March 2005 to shame the government into negotiating his release by publicizing his Guantánamo torture. Kurnaz, who though he was born and lived all his life in Germany was not technically a German citizen, would find out not only that the Americans had been willing to release him in 2002 when they decided he was innocent, but also that "the German government apparently didn't want to let me reenter the country, and claimed that my residency permit had expired" (234). It would take another fifteen months before the new Chancellor Angela Merkel would plead with President Bush and obtain his release.

Kurnaz's innocence was a *known* fact that the U.S. officials and interrogators had to render into an *unknown* in order to continue with their search for evidence in their show of justice. The ultimate evidence was that to give consistency to their counterterrorist reality they had to stick to their fantasy regarding Guantánamo and the terroristic and beastly nature of their inmates. President George Bush released 532 detainees; Obama released 161, and of the 61 remaining in August of 2016, 20 were cleared for transfer if there were countries willing to take them. The prospect of closing Guantánamo created an alarm among the Republicans in the House, who in September passed a bill with 244 votes in support of representative Jackie Walorski's view that "Americans are safer with these dangerous detainees securely locked up."[7] The very prison that became internationally an emblem of American lawlessness and brutality, its orange jumpsuits adopted by the Islamic State while depicting the execution of Westerners, is also the emblem that is needed to sustain the fundamental fantasy of safety from terrorism.

"Like Sheer Fantasy": Intentionality as Evidence

Terrorism is by now the most routine of news. Take the recurrent thwarted terrorist plot opening up the afternoon cable newscast. We have been informed about dozens of terrorism plots foiled in the United States and elsewhere since 9/11.[8] No one can take lightly these frightening news; and yet, are these arrests *evidence* that reveal the existence of actual terrorism plots? Take the Washington Metro bombing plot, the New York subway plot, the plot to blow the Sears Tower, the one to bomb a Portland Christmas tree lighting: what they all have in common with dozens more across the nation is that they were in fact organized and led by the FBI—they were sting operations. What the frightened viewer doesn't know is that in fact there was no real risk in the alleged plot, that it was essentially an elaborate ploy by the FBI to catch some al Qaeda sympathizer. Having examined all the high-profile terrorism plots of the decade from 2001 to 2011, Trevor Aaronson found that, "of the 508 defendants, 243 had been targeted through an FBI informant, 158 had been caught in an FBI terrorism sting, and 49 had encountered an agent provocateur" (Aaronson 2013, 15). With the exception of three cases, most of them were small-time criminals, people who made some false statement (72 cases) or were prosecuted for immigration violations (121 cases). The Human Rights Watch report of 2014 observed that there was no single terrorist attack linked to Islamic organizations between 2001 and 2013, yet there were dozens of manufactured terrorist plots that resulted in hundreds of people going to jail. The report quotes the former FBI agent Michael Germano: "When the FBI undercover agent or informant is the only purported link to a real terrorist group, supplies the motive, designs the plot and provides all the weapons, one has to question whether they are combating terrorism or creating it" (Gessen 2015, 245–46). The report goes on to say that "the FBI may have created terrorists out of law-abiding individuals" and that the informants and agents "often chose targets who were particularly vulnerable—whether because of mental disability, or because they were indigent and needed money that the government offered them" (246). Leaders of Islamic organizations have denounced the fact that informers infiltrated in their mosques "have helped promote plots" (Vitello and Semple 2009). These informers are usually experienced criminals, such as Shaded Hussain, "an accused murderer and con artist who in less than ten years has become one of the Bureau's most valuable terrorism informants" (Aaronson 2011, 223).

What body of evidence does the journalist present to support the scary news about foiled terrorist plots? He simply repeats the statements offered by the counterterror officials, unconcerned they are "creating crimes to solve crimes so they can claim a victory in the war on terror" (Aaronson 2011, 33). The *news* of the foiled plot, given as an unquestionable document that provides direct proof of terrorism, becomes the ultimate evidence of the ubiquitous terrorism threat. Aaronson shows in abundant detail the media's lapdog approach since 9/11 in covering terrorism cases in the United States; they operate "in an information vacuum, as most, if not all, of the initial information comes from the police or prosecutors," thus providing "the government with a public suspension of disbelief" (Aaronson 2011, 71); it will take weeks and months before they can interview the defendants and get a more nuanced view, but by then the story is old and no longer makes the front pages. The public will not find out that, case after case, "the only terrorist involved . . . was an imaginary one on the FBI payroll" (Aaronson 2011, 73). But, having abdicated any definition of terrorism to the counterterrorist state, the media goes along with the theater of sting operations rather than cast a critical eye as to who the real terrorists are (as opposed to the people on the margins entrapped by the FBI). Thus, "in sting after sting, from Miami to Seattle, the FBI and its informants have provided the means for America's would-be terrorists to carry out an attack, creating what a federal judge has called a 'fantasy terror operation'" (Aaronson 2013, 234).

As several FBI and Justice Department agents admitted, "chasing terrorists is like chasing ghosts—you'll only see them if you're willing to let your eyes play tricks on you" (Aaronson 2013, 207). Which brings us back to the historic ghost story *An Adventure* with which we began and which aroused such public interest during the first decades of the twentieth century; "a passion for invoking 'evidence,'" we were told, was "the prime symptom of *Adventure-mania*" (Castle 1991, 30). Such passion for evidence, when there was none, was also the hallmark of Powell's testimony at the UN. The "contagious folly" of a shared vision of Marie Antoinette, or the fear of terrorist "ghosts" by such a wide public, required that we deploy the notion of fantasy. Arthur Cummings, an ardent supporter of sting operations as a former assistant director of the FBI's National Security Branch, put it best when he argued that one needed to understand that "the FBI's true enemies weren't so much Al Qaeda and Islamic terrorism but rather the idea of Al Qaeda and Islamic terrorism." His emphatic assertion that "we're at war with an idea" (Aaronson 2013, 226) should be stated as "we're at war with a fantasy"—a fantasy of a fetish Terror that overpowers both terrorists and counterterrorists.

Sting operations are about the intentionality of potential terrorists for carrying out future acts. What type of evidence is this—about events that have not yet taken place? As law professor Mark Kelman put it, "answering questions about the 'probability' of a future event poses even more than typically difficult epistemological problems compared, for instance, to questions about whether a particular event in the past occurred" (1991, 171). It is not that there is lack of evidence that terrorism has a past and present replete with heinous violence. And yet, what seems most terrifying and defining of contemporary terrorism is what is yet to come—most critically, as prophesized by so many commentators, the specter of "it is not if but when" of nuclear terrorism.

Time is the defining axis that differentiates fantasy from historic reality. In the waiting for terror defined by the imminence of a threat, what *could* happen is actually the case *now* as collective representation and fear. What takes place in real time is a small part of terrorism; its future anticipation, its fantasy, is as a critical component of the counterterrorism culture. One could argue that the distortion of temporality implicit in such waiting and fearing of terror can become self-fulfilling (Zulaika 2009), that is, a false definition of reality provokes a behavior that later makes it true; in its perverse logic the course of events becomes "proof" of the correctness of the prophecy (Merton 1968, 477).

Nothing has been more consequential in the War on Terror than the Bush administration's doctrine of preemption that led the United States to the war in Iraq. By definition, "the logic of pre-emption entails action *before* the event, and relies upon an imaginary of extreme threats, which justify otherwise unthinkable actions" (Stampnitzky 2013, 168). Sting operations illustrate counterterrorism's need to act before the crimes have been committed—its primary evidence is concerned with having clues about *non*-events that might reside in the intentionality of potential terrorists. Preemption continues to justify the imposition of a State of Exception on American politics, including the continuing existence of Guantánamo. The judges naturally partake of this same ideology of preemption against the ghosts of terrorism, and thus in case after case "these men, some broke, others with mental problems, couldn't have committed even small-time offenses on their own, and yet the FBI and Justice Department have convinced courts and the public that they *are* terrorists, even though it was government informants and agents who provided the plans and weapons that allowed them to become terrorists in the first place" (Aaronson 2013, 235).

There is one sting operation that deserves particular attention because it preceded the first attack on the Twin Towers in February 1993. It took place against the group associated with the blind Sheik Omar Abdul-Rahman. The key figure to the operation was the informer Emad Salem, who received in compensation two million dollars. With Salem's testimony, the Sheik was condemned to life in prison. What type of evidence did Salem have? Salem "began his testimony by admitting that he had lied to just about everybody he ever met," the *New York Times* reported; that he was "always ready with another believe-or-not exploit"; and that his testimony sounded "like sheer fantasy" (MacFarquhar 1995, A9). An editorial added that the indictment of the Sheik "only required to prove *the intention* to wage a terror campaign" and concluded that "only the sketchiest connections [were] established between Sheik Omar Abdul-Rahman and the alleged mastermind of that crime, Ramzi Ahmed Yousef."[9] And yet it was evidence enough for counterterrorism to condemn the man, considered by many Muslims their supreme spiritual leader and legal authority, to life in prison. Two of those Muslims closest to him were Osama bin Laden and Ayman al-Zawahiri.

How is it that a mercenary's "like sheer fantasy" testimony became key evidence to condemn Sheik Rahman to life in prison? The answer rests in good part in Kelman's observation that, "Questions of how we claim to know the things that we know and whose claims to knowledge are treated as authoritative are inescapable in reaching legal judgments" (1991, 169). Sheik Rahman's moral and judicial authority couldn't have been higher for the Muslims (some commentators have compared him with the status a pope has for the Catholics); the CIA had used his high authority and his services for years when they brought him to the United States to help recruit jihadists against the former Soviets. But obviously the claims that mattered in his trial were those of the informer Salem. The fact is that "we believe that the defendant we favor has produced differentially convincing evidence to bolster a claim" (Kelman 1991, 170). Blind and frail, Sheik Rahman is a learned and holy man for his community, but in the United States he is Muslim—in the eyes of the counterterror state law, his moral authority was no match with the mercenary Salem, who admitted "that he had lied to just about everybody he ever met." In a culture in which the figure of the Terrorist embodies absolute Evil, it was enough to associate the blind Sheik with such a tabooed figure to condemn him. In the framework of "like sheer fantasy" assumed by his counterterrorist handlers, Salem's fabrications were solid evidence.

Drones from Area 51

The drone program is the latest development in counterterrorism, "the only game in town" in the words of ex-CIA director Leon Panetta. Drones are the tragic proof that even under President Obama, terrorism continued to be the fundamental fantasy of U.S. policy. Obama was critical of the rhetorics of the War on Terror as candidate, but once in power he basically continued his predecessor's policies, vastly expanding drone warfare. Ten thousand feet above in the sky, and seventy-five hundred miles away at Creech Air Force Base, the drones are a further step in the sensorial distancing from the targeted enemy. The enemy is no longer a real body but a mere image in the computer screen. The belief is that the flying robots will soon be "in the position to take the initiative against the enemy on a battlefield" and that "the pressure to let robots take the shot will be very hard to resist" (Caryl 2011, 58). The scenario is a Nintendo-like war in which subject-less machines, praised for "their ability to see and think" (Caryl 2011, 58), and while mimicking all sorts of animals, will on their own identify and eliminate the terrorists. The drones can do all the warring operations, they can program a target and follow it for days while flying on their own, and they can make irrelevant the human participation. Such nonhuman component appears to be in fact the most marvelous aspect of the drones: the unmanned machines have no desires of their own, are not subjectively responsible for their killings, cannot commit war crimes or kill themselves.

The new robotic military industry has developed in close association with science fiction. The drones are operated to a large extent from Creech Air Force Base in the Nevada dessert, forty-five miles north of Las Vegas, known by the soldiers as "the home of the hunters." It is close to other secretive and restricted places in the Nevada Test and Training Range such as Area 51, also known as Dreamland and Paradise Ranch. Given the secrecy around the facility, whose very existence was denied for decades, Area 51, while developing and testing new weapon systems, became also the site of intense fantasy, famed for all sorts of unidentified flying objects and conspiracies. Area 51 has been the setting for more than sixty movies, TV shows, and video games (Singer 2009, 138). There is a Science Fiction Channel with a TV series about Eureka, the town set up by the Pentagon for scientists to work and live in. In short, Area 51 conflated during the Cold War the development of the latest weapon systems with the fantasy supplement of extraterrestrial sightings and conspiracy theories.

If the atomic bomb tested mostly in Nevada's desert became "the national fetish" (Masco 2006, 17) during the Cold War, the counterterror state has weaponized drones in the same test site with a similar fetishistic goal. The conspiracy epicenter is no longer populated with extraterrestrial aliens; they have been replaced with the terrorist aliens also seemingly belonging to an entirely strange world. The Bureau of Investigative Journalism estimates that drones have killed between six and eight thousand people. This is the Real of the drone effects. But, given that there is complete ignorance as to who the vast majority of these victims are, fantasy plays a key role in determining who they are and justifying why they should be killed. The estimates as to how many of them are combatants and how many civilians are starkly different depending on which sources you pay attention to. Cian Westmoreland, in a talk he gave at the University of Las Vegas Law School in March of 2016, claimed that as a drone technician he had directly participated in the killings of 359 innocent civilians just in the year 2009. In August 2011 the counterterrorism chief John Brennan stated that not a single noncombatant had been killed in a year of strikes; the Conflict Monitoring Center, a private organization that collects Pakistani and foreign news reports, estimated on their web page that of the 609 killed in 2011, only four were al Qaeda leaders. According to the *Drone Papers*, in 2012 over a period of four months drones killed 155 people in the tribal areas of Afghanistan: nineteen were people they intended to kill; the rest were missed targets (Scahill 2016, 53). The stark contrast in numbers results ultimately from how you define "terrorist." Potentially everyone is a terrorist if he/she conforms to the "signature strike" of a certain life pattern in a given territory observed from a drone ten thousand feet above. As an example, most adult males traditionally carry guns in Pakistan or Yemen, a "pattern of life" that makes them all potential targets. But guns might not be necessary as the ultimate evidence, for, as a CIA officer told Jane Mayer of the *New Yorker*, "no tall man with a beard is safe anywhere in Southwest Asia" (Ahmad 2011). This results in a method that "in effect counts military-age males in a strike zone as combatants, unless there is explicit intelligence posthumously proving them innocent" (Becker and Shane 2012). You must be a "terrorist" if you are in a zone where there are terrorists and if you conform to my fantasy framework by which you look like one.

The strategic fantasy about the unilateral combat conducted with drones is the belief in warfare without any risk for our side. From Achilles to Siegfried to Hercules to Ajax, "The great myths of invulnerability are almost all accounts of failure" (Chamayou 2015, 73). The ultimate instance of such intolerance to risk was Vice President Cheney's famous 1 percent theory: if Saddam Hussein had a 1 percent chance of obtaining weapons of mass destruction, the United States had to act to prevent it (Suskind 2006). Ruling out chance from a terrorist scenario, a type of warfare in which deception is the sine qua non at all levels, is like ruling luck from poker: only a traumatized player would adopt such a self-defeating inflexibility.

In the opinion of many legal scholars (e.g., Cohn 2015), drones have removed all boundaries between legitimate combat and assassination. If we follow Michael Walzer and Grégoire Chamayou (Chamayou 2015, 13) in recalling the history of ethics of warfare—that you cannot kill if you are not ready to die—the drone, by ruling out real combat, "destroys the very possibility of any clear differentiation between combatants and noncombatants" (147). This is at the heart of the hotly debated issue of whether the victims are overwhelmingly combatants or civilians. If you completely ignore who the people you are killing are, as is the case in most instances, the need to claim a fantasy-based "evidence" that they are actually terrorists becomes imperative—the fantasy sustains the belief whether you are engaged in assassination or not.

What Does the Terrorist Want?

Che vuoi? What do you want? What is bothering you? In psychoanalytic theory, "fantasy is an *answer* to this *'Che vuoi?'*; it is an attempt to fill out the gap of the question with an answer. In the case of anti-Semitism the answer to 'What does the Jew want?' is a fantasy of 'Jewish conspiracy': a mysterious power of Jews to manipulate events, to pull the strings behind the scenes" (Žižek 1989, 128). In the case of suspect Muslim migrants in a rich European country, the answer to "What do Muslims want?" is the fantasy of a terrorist plot, the fear that they are going to take over Western culture. This provokes reactions such as the one in Switzerland—a referendum to deny them permission to build two minarets. Or the more recent one of France's prohibition of the burkini or full swimsuit because, as Prime Minister Manuel Valls put it, it symbolizes Islam's "enslavement of women." In Slavoj Žižek's words, "The crucial point that must be made here on a theoretical level is that fantasy functions as a construction, as an imaginary scenario filling out the void, the opening of the *desire of the Other*: by giving us a definitive answer to the question 'What does the Other want?,' it enables us to evade the unbearable deadlock in which the Other wants something from us, but we are at the same time incapable of translating this desire of the Other into a positive interpellation, into a mandate with which to identify" (Žižek 1989, 128). It is not only that the torturer answers to Slahi's "What do you want?" with his own construction of a fantasy narrative; it is also that the coordinates of the counterterrorists' desires are not simply satisfied but constituted by the fantasy-scene: "through fantasy, we learn 'how to desire'" (Žižek 1989, 132). Something becomes the object of our desire "by entering the framework of fantasy, by being included in a fantasy-scene which gives consistency to the subject's desire" (Žižek 1989, 133). The tabooed figure of the Terrorist is an individual in possession of that unknown quality that is "in it more than it," an X that provokes for both followers and opponents intense fear and desire.

The U.S. defense budget has almost doubled since the Cold War when it emerged as the only superpower; it currently surpasses the budgets of most other countries combined. Such staggering military reality can hardly be understood unless we grasp as its indispensable supplement the figure of the Terrorist. The point is not to deny the existence of violence in many countries or that there are people who fit a standard definition of actual or potential terrorists; it is rather the imminent expectation of the terrorist with the WMDs (a possibility that security experts such as Robert Mueller [2006] have ruled out as extremely improbable). Such configuration of a worldwide terrorist threat operates much in the way that collective representations have worked in the past at the confluence of history and fiction.

The drone war has been described as "sheer fantasy, if not literally science fiction" (Sluka 2011, 72). Michael Ignatieff wrote that virtual war "as a surgical scalpel and not a bloodstained sword" is a seductive illusion, adding: "We need to stay away from such fables of self-righteous invulnerability" (2000, 214–15). These "fables," turned into the current hegemonic culture, require a valid theory of fantasy, one that does not render it into the "not-real," but considers that fantasy "constitutes a dimension of the real" (Butler 1990, 108). Reality is masked by fantasy and "the two become compellingly conflated" (Butler 1990, 107). But fantasy, in its semantic excess, can also interrogate and contest the claims of the real. Fantasy's own power of fragmentations implies that the mastery the subject claims over it is already undone and that the very identity of the subject of fantasy is put into question by the multiple identifications available to the fantasy setting.

Journalists Dana Priest and William M. Arkin (2011) have described a new counterterrorism industry of thousands of government organizations and private companies with the mission of studying and catching subjects whom they have never met and whose primary cultural or subjective contexts they utterly ignore. The basic working premise for this staggering security industry with over a million private contractors and public officials with top-secret clearances would seem to be never to let us be in touch with a terrorist body or project ourselves into a terrorist subject; never to let us mess up our fantasy relationship with the tabooed Terrorist by actually having a really meaningful contact with the feared/desired Monster.

Whether it is Hussein's bluffing or the FBI's counterterrorist sting operations, deception and the planting of false evidence are crucial to terrorist warfare. In such a game the problem facing the counterterrorist is what type of evidence to accept as valid. This is reminiscent of classical detective fiction, a genre in which misinformation and lack of evidence are central to the plot. The detective is aware of his ignorance and knows that there is more to the evidence than meets the eye, that there is a gap between the evidence and what it hides. "There is a gap, a distance, between the evidence and that which the evidence establishes, which means that there is something that is *not* visible in the evidence: the principle by which the trail attaches itself to the criminal" (Copjec 1994, 176). In detective fiction, the detective's skill for spotting unsuspected evidence emerges typically in opposition to the figure that serves as his foil—the proverbially dumb policeman. Both the police and the detective are looking for evidence, but the detective knows that the evidence per se cannot account for the way it reveals itself. Both are in search of "evidence," yet it is the Colombo-esque detective, irritating in his rumpled and apparently absentminded manners, who shrewdly resolves the case by binging the decisive evidence, while making a fool of the policeman. What was wrong with the policeman's approach is that he ignores the criminal's subjectivity in its complex interaction of cultural premises and unconscious desire. In his search for "objectivity," the policeman will take seriously every piece of evidence, including those deliberately planted by the criminal to fool him. The detective's knack, on the contrary, is his ability to read literally the murderer's desire in the traces he left hidden or in the very evidence that is *not* there.

If "after the bombings of Hiroshima and Nagasaki [the Cold War] was fought incessantly at the level of imagination" (Masco 2014, 16), this is not less true of the current War on Terror. But if the framework of fantasy is a necessary supplement to the counterterror culture, such reliance may turn out to be its Achilles heel as well. Masco's work provides a groundbreaking analysis of the cultural and imaginary continuities between the Cold War and the War on Terror—the recognition that the 'new' counterterror state in 2001 was actually a repetition, modeled in language and tone on the launch of the national security state in 1947" (2014, 5). From the beginning, the security state exploited nuclear fear to create a docile citizenship. "A key innovation of the counterterrorist state," Masco adds, "is . . . [the] commitment to using the imaginary to locate danger" (2014, 11). Another way to state the transition is that the War on Terror rejects deterrence to embrace preemption. The shift entails a change in the imaginary from the symbolic fiction of world hegemony based on nuclear power (fantasy as stabilizing dream) to the spectral reality of a world disorder under the ubiquitous menace of terrorism (fantasy as unconquerable chaos). In deterrence the security state is engaged in securing defense systems never to be used—the threat is based on ritual display and symbolic meaning, including the dream that atomic weapons would make war obsolete. In preemption one has to endlessly fantasize future acts of war based on current nonevents. In deterrence the state uses collective fantasy to produce evidence—of an already existing state of terror, whereas in preemption the public is fed fantasy to sustain the evidence—for what does not yet exist but is to come. Careful analysis as to how "overblown" the threat posed by terrorists is will not diminish the assumption that they are in possession of an apocalyptic power—something that can only be explained by their accessing the general public's framework of fantasy. Nothing seems more critical for exorcising the media and the public from the terrors of the current post-9/11 security state than to unveil the evidentiary role of fantasy in underpinning it.

The psychoanalytic cure for the traumatized subject consists in awakening the subject from the spell of fantasy: "The final moment of the analysis is defined as 'going through the fantasy': not its symbolic interpretation but the experience of the fact that the fantasy-object, by its fascinating presence, is merely filling out a lack, a void in the Other. There is nothing 'behind' the fantasy; the fantasy is a construction whose function is to hide this void, this 'nothing'—that is, the lack in the Other" (Žižek 1989, 133). Counterterrorist culture, we have argued in this chapter, in all its traumatic fear and trembling, is also dependent on a fantasy construction that serves as supplement to the real of violence. "Traversing the fantasy" regarding terrorism doesn't mean confronting the reality as it is; it implies accepting the inconsistencies inherent to the figure of the Terrorist itself. How to gain a distance from this spectral framework, how to unhook enjoyment from the pursuit of the hunted terrorist—that becomes the critical issue.

Notes

1   *New York Times*, May 4, 2003.
2   Parenthetical citations to Slahi's account refer to this edition throughout.
3   During this period the U.S. government lost thirty-four out of forty-six habeas corpus cases.
4   Slahi had been first arrested and interrogated in January 2000 as he returned to his home country Mauritania from Canada, where he felt watched by the U.S. intelligence services. Two months after 9/11, Slahi turned himself in to the Mauritanian authorities for questioning; he was arrested and rendered for eight months to a "black site" in Jordan, then taken to the infamous Bagram Base, and from there to Guantánamo in August 2002.
5   Back cover copy of Kurnaz's book.
6   Parenthetical citations to Kurnaz's book refer to this edition throughout.
7   "The Latest Bad Idea for Guantánamo," *New York Times*, Editorial, September 20, 2016.
8   According to Heritage Foundation, sixty plots have been foiled in the United States (see Zuckerman, Bucci, and Carafano 2013.) The home secretary for Great

Britain claimed on November 2014 that British security services had foiled forty terror plots since the London attacks of 2005 (Topping 2014).

9   *New York Times*, March 19, 1995, A14.

References

Aaronson, Trevor. 2011. "The Informants," *Mother Jones*. September–October, 30–43.

Aaronson, Trevor. 2013. *The Terror Factory: Inside the FBI's Manufactured War on Terrorism*. New York: IG Publishing.

Ahmad, Muhammad Idrees. 2011. "The Magical Realism of Body Counts." *Al Jazeera*. June 13.

Azmy, Baher. 2007. "Epilogue." In Kurnaz, *Five Years of My Life: An Innocent Man in Guantánamo*, translated by Jefferson Chase, foreword by Patti Smith, 239–55. New York: Palgrave Macmillan..

Bateson, Gregory. 1973. "A Theory of Play and Fantasy." In *Steps to an Ecology of Mind: Collected Essays in Anthropology, Psychiatry, Evolution, and Epistemology*, 150–66. New York: Ballantine.

Becker, Jo, and Shane, Scott. 2012. "Secret 'Kill List' a Test of Obama's Principles and Will." *New York Times*. May 29.

Butler, Judith. 1990. "The Force of Fantasy: Feminism, Mapplethorpe, and Discursive Excess." *Journal of Feminist Cultural Studies* 2(2): 105–25.

Caryl, Christian. 2011. "Predators and Robots at War." *New York Review of Books*. September 29, 55–58.

Castle, Terry. 1991. "Contagious Folly." In *Questions of Evidence*, edited by James Chandler, Arnold I. Davidson, and Harry Harootunian, 11–42. Chicago: University of Chicago Press.

Chamayou, Grégoire. 2015. *A Theory of the Drone*, translated by Janet Lloyd. New York: New Press.

Copjec, Joan. 1994. *Read My Desire: Lacan against the Historicists*. Cambridge, MA: MIT Press.

Davis, Morris D. 2015. "Guantánamo's Charade of Justice." *New York Times*. March 28.

Gessen, Masha, 2015. *The Brothers: The Road to an American Tragedy*. New York: Riverhead Books.

Ginzburg, Carlo. 1991. "A Rejoinder to Arnold I. Davidson." In *Questions of Evidence*, edited by James Chandler, Arnold I. Davidson, and Harry Harootunian, 321–24. Chicago: University of Chicago Press.

Ignatieff, Michael, 2000. *Virtual War: Kosovo and Beyond*. Washington, DC: Cato Institute.

Kelman, Mark. 1991. "Reasonable Evidence of Reasonableness." In *Questions of Evi-*

dence, edited by James Chandler, Arnold I. Davidson, and Harry Horootunian, 170–88. Chicago: University of Chicago Press.

Kurnaz, Murat. 2007. *Five Years of My Life: An Innocent Man in Guantánamo.* Translated by Jefferson Chase, foreword by Patti Smith. New York: Palgrave Macmillan.

MacFarquhar, Neil, 1995. "In Bombing, a Deluge of Details." *New York Times.* March 19.

Masco, Joseph. 2006. *Nuclear Borderlands: The Manhattan Project in Post–Cold War New Mexico.* Princeton, NJ: Princeton University Press.

Masco, Joseph. 2014. *The Theater of Operations: National Security Affect from the Cold War to the War on Terror.* Durham, NC: Duke University Press.

Merton, Robert K. 1968. *Social Theory and Social Structure.* New York: Free Press.

Moberly, Charlotte, and Eleanor Jourdain. 2014. *An Adventure: A True Story about Time Travel.* San Francisco: White Rabbit Press.

Mueller, John. 2006. *Overblown: How Politicians and the Terrorism Industry Inflate National Security Threats, and Why We Believe Them.* New York: Free Press.

Powell, Colin. 2003. "Remarks to the United Nations Security Council." *Washington Post.* February 5.

Priest, Dana, and William M. Arkin. 2011. *Top Secret America: The Rise of the New American Security State.* New York: Little, Brown and Company.

Scahill, Jeremy, et al. 2016. *The Assassination Complex: Inside the Government's Secret Drone Warfare Program.* New York: Simon and Schuster.

Singer, Peter W. 2009. *Wired for War: The Robotics Revolution and Conflict in the 21st Century.* New York: Penguin.

Slahi, Mohamedou Ould. 2015. *Guantánamo Diary,* edited by Larry Siems. New York: Little, Brown and Company.

Sluka, Jeffrey A. 2011. "Death from Above: UAVs and Losing Hearts and Minds." *Military Review.* May–June, 70–76.

Stampnitzky, Lisa. 2013. *Disciplining Terror: How Experts Invented "Terrorism."* Cambridge: Cambridge University Press.

Suskind, Ron. 2006. *The One Percent Doctrine: Deep Inside America's Pursuit of Its Enemies since 9/11.* New York: Simon and Schuster.

Topping, Alexandra. "Theresa May Claims 40 Terror Plots Have Been Foiled since 7/7 Attacks." *Guardian.* November 24, 2014.

Vidal-Naquet, Pierre, 1991. "Atlantis and the Nations." Translated by Janet Lloyd. In *Questions of Evidence: Proof, Practice, and Persuasion across the Disciplines,* edited by James Chandler, Arnold I. Davidson, and Harry Harootunian, 325–51. Chicago: University of Chicago Press.

Vitello, Paul, and Kirk Semple. 2009. "Muslims Say FBI Tactics Sow Anger and Fear." *New York Times.* December 18.

Wilkerson, Lawrence. 2010. "Declaration by Lawrence B. Wilkerson in the Case of Adel Hamad." March 24. Testimony published by The Guantánamo Testimonials Project, Center for the Study of Human Rights in the Americas, University of California at Davis.

Winch, Peter, 1977. "Understanding a Primitive Society." In *Rationality*, edited by R. Wilson, 78–111. Oxford: Basil Blackwell.

Wright, Ann, and Dixon, Susan. 2008. *Dissent: Voices of Conscience.* Kihei, HI: Koa Books.

Žižek, Slavoj. 1989. *The Sublime Object of Ideology.* London: Verso.

Žižek, Slavoj. 1997. *The Plague of Fantasies.* London: Verso.

Zuckerman, Jessica, Steven P. Bucci, and James Jay Carafano. 2013. *60 Terrorist Plots Since 9/11: Continued Lessons in Domestic Counterterrorism.* Special Report #137 on terrorism. Washington, DC: Heritage Foundation.

Zulaika, Joseba. 2009. *Terrorism: The Self-Fulfilling Prophecy.* Chicago: University of Chicago Press

CONCLUSION

Discontinuities and Diversity

MARK MAGUIRE AND URSULA RAO

Bodies as Evidence emerged over several years from a series of informal conversations and formal workshops. The editors and contributors, working in ethnographic field sites from India to the United Kingdom and Argentina to the United States of America, noted that many contemporary matters of great consequence are now recognized and discussed as matters of evidence. On the one hand, calls for evidence-based policies and practices seem to be heard everywhere; on the other hand, previously taken-for-granted evidential relations are being tested and teased apart. Of course, as we stated in the introduction to this volume, the history of philosophy has witnessed the rise and fall of numerous evidential regimes, but discussions of evidence are by no means confined to epistemology or scientific discourse. Rather, most professions recognize and gather evidence in particular ways and operate their own systems of "veridiction." Indeed, it is possible to argue that deep transformations in professions, disciplines, and institutional divisions of labor are part of the contemporary problematization of evidence. For example, anthropologist Helen Lambert (2009) describes the rise of "evidence-based medicine" alongside the increasing prominence of similar discussions in the domains of welfare, housing, and public policy. In short, our discussions based on ethnographic knowledge of diverse field sites suggested to us that much could be said about the contemporary by engaging directly with contested bodies of evidence.

Bodies as Evidence also emerged from the recognition that discussions of evidence in anthropology have thus far been limited. Lambert's (2009) excellent discussion of evidence-based medicine turns to focus on ethnography, questioning the lack of "evidence" in, of, and from the discipline's favored method. Her work is illustrative of recent writing that takes anthropological evidence as its primary focus (e.g., Csordas 1994; Hastrup 2004; Engelke 2009; Chua, High, and Lau 2009; cf. Cull 1854). These anthropologists insist upon the relational qualities of evidence—in Thomas Csordas's (1994, 475) elegant formulation, "Evidence has to be of or for something." However, this position clearly presents a two-sided challenge. First, ethnographic understandings of evidence must be sufficiently open to account for the numerous evidential regimes found in the world. Anthropology, as Mary Douglas once put it, is classically about our "provincial logic" encountering "native thought." Thus, "two different sets of hypotheses about the nature of reality and how it is divided up are exposed, each carrying the ring of self-evident truth so clearly that its fundamental assumptions are implicit and considered to need no justification" (1972, 27). Second, however—and this is the inspiration behind several recent writings on evidence in anthropology—ethnographic engagements with relational evidence-making, causation, and doxastic attitudes are still expected to be "evidence based" in the contemporary moment. Regardless of the varieties of so-called native thought, a certain provincial logic seems to be prevailing.

Bodies as Evidence is not a series of essays on anthropological methods; it is, rather, a response to the contemporary focus on evidence, the tremendous weight placed upon evidence today, and the simultaneous erosion of trusted sources of evidence. In this volume, then, the editors and contributors have focused on evidence in security contexts, one of the contemporary domains in which relations of cause and effect, truth and falsehood, doxastic and affective attitudes and reason all seem to be coming apart and reforming. Although security is often regarded as a natural requirement of human life, the semantically vacuous term is better understood as denoting processes that naturalize themselves differently depending on cultural factors and the particular historical moment. In other words, "security" and "insecurity" are names for processes that are highly variable. For instance, in *The Spirit of*

Laws Montesquieu proposes that security and justice are foundational to liberty, but he concedes that "there are cases in which a veil should be drawn for a while over liberty, as it was customary to cover the statues of the gods" (1914, 102). In this analysis, however, one does not govern primarily through security; one does not permanently govern in the darkness behind a veil. Note, then, the historical discontinuity between Montesquieu's philosophy and the post-9/11 "securitarian" reason of U.S. vice president Dick Cheney:

> We do, indeed, though have obviously the world's finest military. . . . We also have to work sort of the dark side, if you will. We're going to spend time in the shadows in the intelligence world. A lot of what needs to be done here will have to be done quietly, without any discussions, using sources and methods that are available to our intelligence agencies if we're going to be successful. That's the world these folks operate in. And so it's going to be vital for us to use any means at our disposal, basically, to achieve our objective. (Cheney 2001)

The contrast here is between the eighteenth-century reason of the state (*raison d'état*) and the contemporary reason of the counterterrorist apparatus.

Today's "security" thus seems to name a permanent process of following a potentially dark path to an unreachable future free from terror, deprivation, and injustice. To begin to study the processes and pathways of such security measures, one must attend to discontinuity with the past, to ruptures in the relations of evidence with the world, and to the production of doxastic and affective attitudes, moral and ethical relations, and even reason. In short, neither security nor evidence offers us unbroken lines that stretch back into the past. Michel Foucault points directly to the modern rupture in evidence that uncoupled the "truth" of morality and ethics from scientific rationality:

> Descartes . . . said, "To accede to truth, it suffices that I be any subject which can see what is evident." Evidence is substituted for ascetics at the point where the relationship to the self intersects the relationship to others and the world. The relationship to the self no longer needs to be ascetic to get into relation to the truth. It suffices that the relationship to the self reveals to me the obvious truth of what I see for me to apprehend that truth definitively. Thus, I can be immoral and know the truth. I believe that this is an idea which, more or less explicitly, was rejected by all previous culture. Before Descartes, one could not be impure, immoral, and know the truth. With Descartes, direct evidence is enough. After Descartes we

have a non-ascetic subject of knowledge. This change makes possible the institutionalization of modern science. (Foucault 1983, 252)

While some anthropologists have sought to provincialize Foucault's approach to relations of truth, knowledge, and power (e.g., Tambiah 1990), others recognize that the orientations available in his work pointed to problematizations worthy of sustained anthropological attention (e.g., Rabinow 1996, 161). Indeed, it is noteworthy that Foucault emphasized the highly specific and mundane forms of knowledge that accompanied the birth of modern institutions such as the asylum, the clinic, and the prison—forms of knowledge that would later assume the mantle of scientific rationality. "The birth of the sciences of man," he tells us, "is found in . . . ignoble archives, where the modern play of coercion over bodies, gestures and behaviours had its beginnings" (Foucault 1995, 191). Today, the always unstable and unfinished walls dividing key societal institutions such as the military, the police, the prison, and the factory have crumbled; disciplines have blurred; and divisions of labor have broken down and reformed.

Security discourses and practices now traverse many societal domains. Disciplining is achieved not only in mainstreamed institutions but through the micromanagement of populations in contexts of welfare, urban governance, policing, and the war against terror. The discussion of Ieva Jusionyte, Daniel M. Goldstein, and Carolina Alonso-Bejarano on the penetration of the national boarder into the inner space of the nation-state makes painfully obvious the multiple threatening presences of portals in the lives of migrants. To survive, draw benefits, and be granted citizens' rights, people must regularly evidence their compliance with multiple rules. Nikolas Rose (1996) argued that government in advanced liberal democracies downloads onto citizens the responsibility of caring for themselves and their lives. Security regimens ensure that citizens comply. They also create shadow worlds, the characters of which have been at the center of several chapters in this volume. Hypervisibility of those aspects thrown up by indicators hide the human experience of living in an age of (in)securitization. They create instead the worlds of "illegal" migrants rendered increasingly insecure, worlds where, despite the fantastical promises of forensic knowledge, some dead bodies are identified and others remain Other. Then there's the illusion of "evidence" from the tortured body. Thus, while contemporary security regimes often claim scientific rationality, they remain rooted in ignoble and provincial forms of knowledge production.

Security clearly has a problem: *bodies as evidence*, or the desire for and fascination with technologies that promise to provide evidence-based and thus neutral knowledge by tracking, understanding, and tracing the human body. But, as the contributions to this volume show, while technoscience promises neutral knowledge about human bodies it generally delivers only partial knowledge about social categories and persons. In short, (in)securitization produces and reproduces the poor, the migrant, the victim, the criminal, or the terrorist enemy. Indeed, in *The Quest for Certainty* (1930, 51), John Dewey proposes that modern scientific rationality has failed to acknowledge or digest an ancient philosophical problem, namely, "that certainty, security, can be found only in the fixed and unchanging." But security has also become a matter of regulating the "changing course of events" (1930, 96) and even the risk-filled future. Security now labels regulatory efforts to specify, fix, lock into place, verify, and make certain a world that often refuses to cooperate. Thus, in the gaps, interstices, and shadows of security-modernity one finds tricksters, fakes, and frauds; occult economies; and the malevolent operations of terrorist enemies. Like the counterfeit modernities that Jean and John Comaroff (e.g., 2006) address, security exposes a double conceit at the core of modernity, namely, that bodies, signifiers, and identities can be fixed and that security discourses and practices have somehow acquired a magical formula that will enable that fixing to occur. One can give numerous examples to illustrate, but perhaps the most obvious example comes yet again from U.S. counterterrorism. Since 2001, the U.S. government has invested hundreds of millions in technologies that can search the human body for signs of "malintent" or the intent to cause harm. The theory of malintent substantiates technoscientific efforts to read the body, from eye movement to fleeting facial expressions. In other words, theory decides what counts as evidence. But scientific rigor has to take a back seat, because the theory is classified in order to maintain security (see Maguire and Fussey 2016).

But how do we anthropologically investigate the production of knowledge, and evidence, in the realm of security? In this volume we have emphasized conceptual work on body-knowledge, as well as the mimesis and magic that can be found tangled within the roots of the great contemporary drive to secure individual identities, bodies, boundaries, and borderless conflicts. It is clear to us that security and insecurity are interfused in the sense that fear is both a target and outcome of security discourses and practices. As Jean Comaroff put it during one of the workshops that inspired this volume, late modernity is stalked by "the perfectly ordinary person who turns out to be someone, something, dangerously different from whom they say they are—by the spectre of the counterfeit citizen, the imposter immigrant, the bogus asylum seeker, the inscrutable terrorist" (Comaroff 2013). Our efforts herein have shown the play of truth and falsehood, seen and unseen, the elevated claims and "ignoble archives" (Foucault 1995, 191). We have not, however, succumbed to the temptation to see power as always coercive or alterity as an always-available source of alternatives. Rather, through its diverse contributions, this volume shows us the enormous and active production of knowledge and evidence in the realm of security, bodies of evidence that are never as coherent as they present themselves, forms of knowledge that are forever shadowed by insecurity and doubt, for both the observer and the observed.

This volume began with contributions on the topic of biometric security. Today's registration efforts ongoing in India are part of the largest biometric capture project in human history. But such efforts have a particular history, one rooted, according to Michael Taussig, in the use of fingerprints to prevent people from impersonating others in order to collect pensions and other benefits. Biometrics became signatures and fetishes, used to make people legible and to scare them with the power of mysterious signs. This was, in essence, the "modernizing sorcery [of] colonial bureaucracy" (1993, 222). But modern biometric systems emerged in multiple locations, from the Hooghly River in India to metropolitan heartlands of empire, and drew new lines connecting colonial administrations to policing institutions and scientific racists to social reformers. Simply stated, biometrics was not and is not a series of targeted interventions to solve problems of identification. Rather, what we are investigating here is a coalition between practical problems and solutions and much broader visions of human life itself. The evidence presented by the human body to verify individual identity is evidence of a unit within a human population that is pockmarked by unknown spaces and forever ringed by an outside. Again, we must attend to discontinuous histories in order to understand the ways in which error-prone technoscience imagines and targets human life, which is itself, "never completely in the right place, that is destined to 'err' and be 'wrong'" (Foucault 1994, 15).

Of course, the point here is not that the human body cannot be read or that all technical and scientific efforts are doomed to failure; rather, we have attended to particular contemporary ways of reading the human body and looked to the contemporary drive to do so in an expanding number of domains. The new bodies of evidence create new power-knowledge regimes and with them novel ethical dilemmas. They result from the confrontation of power with the fleshy condition of human existence. Insecurity is written into the body. For example, the deployment of biometric registration reveals the intimate link between moral order and body inspection. The technological upgrading of the multilayered international borders causes innumerable physical and mental injuries and even death. The use of forensic evidence for recovering the stories of victims of specific political orderings, such as illegal border crosses or victims of mass killings, individualizes and sentimentalizes the memory of suffering. It offers avenues for families to mourn and cope with untimely death at the cost of sidelining broader political debates about ethical failure and unjust orders. Counterinsurgency tactics and the use of drones are defended by a discourse that celebrates death as achievement of intelligence. The rhetoric of the War on Terror justifies killing suspected bodies before they can articulate an alternative truth. The effort to fix and settle opens the search for security and play of evidence to its Other. Thus, questions of difference come into sharp focus in contemporary policing and counterterrorism. When one reads Gregory Feldman on how an undercover police team translates intelligence into "evidence," one is left wondering about the status of both. Do police, those charged with the provision of security, recognize shifts in security discourses and practices; do they see contemporary bodies of evidence as pockmarked by unknown spaces and forever ringed by a troublesome outside?

It seems that anthropology needs to be better engaged with "evidence-based" institutions and assemblages where security is produced, and thus better able to offer insights and critique. To date, many of the efforts to study evidence in the discipline of anthropology have been methodological, reacting to a sense that anthropology will lose its relevance among evidence-based fields if it does not agree to become more transparent about its own data-gathering techniques. Thus far, these efforts have not gained traction, and the discipline has not engaged with evidence as a problem of the contemporary. *Bodies as Evidence* is an effort to highlight the problem of evidence today, rather than an effort to fold anthropology and ethnographic approaches into contemporary power-knowledge. Herein, we do not valorize anthropology or the ethnographic; rather, we are unified by a concern with evidence in security contexts: if we can grapple with and pin down the problem of evidence in contexts where security is produced then engagement, reflexive analysis, and even critique are possible. If not, the truth will be produced by others, elsewhere, uncritically.

References

Cheney, Dick. 2001. "Vice President Cheney on NBC's 'Meet the Press' with Tim Russert." *Washington Post*. September 16. http://www.washingtonpost.com/wp-srv/nation/specials/attacked/transcripts/cheney091601.html.

Chua, Liana, Casey High, and Timm Lau. 2009. *How do We Know? Evidence, Ethnography, and the Making of Anthropological Knowledge*. Cambridge: Cambridge Scholars Press.

Comaroff, Jean. 2013. "The Truth about Crime." "Bodies of Evidence" workshop, December 10, Maynooth University, Ireland.

Comaroff, Jean, and John L. Comaroff. 2006. *An Excursion into the Criminal Anthropology of the Brave Neo South Africa*. Berlin: LIT Verlag.

Csordas, Thomas. 2004. "Evidence of and for What?" *Anthropological Theory* 4(4): 73–80.

Cull, Richard. 1854. "Remarks on the Nature, Objects, and Evidences of Ethnological Science." *Journal of the Ethnological Society of London* 3(1): 103–11.

Dewey, John. 1930. *The Quest for Certainty: A Study of the Relation of Knowledge and Action*. London: George Allen and Unwin.

Douglas, Mary. 1972. "Self-Evidence." The Henry Myers Lecture. *Proceedings of the Royal Anthropological Institute of Great Britain and Ireland*, 27–43.

Engelke, Matthew, ed. 2009. *The Objects of Evidence*. London: Wiley-Blackwell and the Royal Anthropological Institute.

Foucault, Michel. 1983. "On the Genealogy of Ethics." In *Michel Foucault: Beyond Structuralism and Hermeneutics*, edited by Hubert L. Dreyfus and Paul Rabinow, 229–53. Chicago: University of Chicago Press.

Foucault, Michel. 1994. "Life: Experience and Science." In *The Essential Foucault: Selections from Essential Works of Foucault, 1954–1984*, edited by Paul Rabinow and Nikolas Rose, 6–18. New York: New Press.

Foucault, Michel. 1995. *Discipline and Punish: The Birth of the Prison*. New York: Vintage Books.

Hastrup, Kirsten. 2004. "Knowledge and Evidence in Anthropology." *Anthropological Theory* 4(4): 455–72.

Lambert, Helen. 2009. "Evidentiary Truths? The Evidence of Anthropology through the Anthropology of Medical Evidence." *Anthropology Today* 25(1): 16–20.

Maguire, Mark, and Pete Fussey. 2016. "Sensing Evil: Counterterrorism, Technoscience, and the Cultural Reproduction of Security." *Focaal* 75(3): 31–45.

Montesquieu, Charles de Secondat. 1914. *The Spirit of Laws*. London: G. Bell and Son.

Rabinow, Paul. 1996. *Essays on the Anthropology of Reason*. Princeton, NJ: Princeton University Press.

Rose, Nikolas. 1996. "Governing 'Advanced' Liberal Democracies." In *Foucault and*

Political Reason, edited by Andrew Barry, Thomas Osborne, and Nikolas Rose, 37–64. Chicago: Chicago University Press.

Tambiah, Stanley J. 1990. *Magic, Science, Religion, and the Scope of Rationality*. Cambridge: Cambridge University Press.

Taussig, Michael. 1993. *Mimesis and Alterity: A Particular History of the Senses*. New York: Routledge.

CONTRIBUTORS

CAROLINA ALONSO-BEJARANO teaches in the Latino and Caribbean Studies Department at Rutgers University. Her research interests lie in the intersection of decolonial feminism and migration studies, particularly as it relates to interethnic immigrants' rights activism in the United States. She absolutely loves teaching and believes it is an important form of activism, and in her spare time she works as a DJ in New York City.

GREGORY FELDMAN teaches in the Department of Sociology, Anthropology, and Criminology at the University of Windsor. His previous books include *The Migration Apparatus: Security, Labor, and Policymaking in the European Union* (2011) and *We Are All Migrants: Political Action and the Ubiquitous Condition of Migrant-hood* (2015).

FRANCISCO J. FERRÁNDIZ is a tenured researcher at the Spanish National Research Council (CSIC). He received a PhD in social and cultural anthropology from the University of California, Berkeley. He is the author of *El pasado bajo tierra: Exhumaciones contemporáneas de la Guerra Civil* (2014), and has co-edited (with Antonius Robben) *Necropolitics: Mass Graves and Exhumations in the Age of Human Rights* (2015).

DANIEL M. GOLDSTEIN is Professor in the Department of Anthropology at Rutgers University. He is the author of three monographs: *The Spectacular City: Violence and Performance in Urban Bolivia* (2004); *Outlawed: Between Security and Rights in a Bolivian City* (2012); and *Owners of the Sidewalk: Security and Survival in the Informal City* (2016).

ELIDA K. U. JACOBSEN is Senior Researcher at the Peace Research Institute Oslo (PRIO). She is also academic coordinator of the semester course in Peace and Conflict Studies by Oslo and Akershus University College, which takes place in Pondicherry, India. Her research concentrates on governance and local practices in India and Europe.

IEVA JUSIONYTE is Assistant Professor of Anthropology and Social Studies at Harvard University. Her research on statecraft, borders, crime, and security lies at the intersection of legal and political anthropology, and multidisciplinary approaches to space and terrain. She is the author of *Savage Frontier: Making News and Security on the Argentine Border* (2015) and *Threshold: Emergency and Rescue on the U.S.-Mexico Border* (forthcoming in 2018).

MARK MAGUIRE is Dean of Maynooth University Faculty of Social Sciences. His research explores counterterrorism training and operations in several European jurisdictions. He is coeditor of *The Anthropology of Security* (2014) and of *Spaces of Security* (2018).

JOSEPH P. MASCO is Professor of Anthropology at the University of Chicago. He is the author of *The Nuclear Borderlands: The Manhattan Project in Post-Cold War New Mexico* (2006) and *The Theater of Operations: National Security Affect from the Cold War to the War on Terror* (2014).

AMADE M'CHAREK is Professor of Anthropology of Science in the Department of Anthropology, University of Amsterdam. Her laboratory ethnography of human genetic diversity has been published with Cambridge University Press (2005). She is the principal investigator of the ERC-consolidator RaceFaceID project, on face-making and race-making in forensic identification.

URSULA RAO is Professor of Anthropology at the University of Leipzig in Germany. Her current research focuses on e-governance and the social consequences of biometric technology in India. She has also written on Hindi and English journalism, urban space, and ritual theory. She is the author of *News as Cultures: Journalistic Practices and the Remaking of Indian Leadership Traditions* (2010).

ANTONIUS C. G. M. ROBBEN is Professor of Anthropology at Utrecht University. His books include *Political Violence and Trauma in Argentina* (2005) and *Argentina Betrayed: Memory, Mourning, and Accountability* (2018). His most recent edited volumes are *Necropolitics: Mass Graves and Exhumations in the Age of Human Rights* (2015; coedited with Francisco Ferrándiz), *Death,*

Mourning, and Burial: A Cross-Cultural Reader (2017), and *A Companion to the Anthropology of Death* (2018).

JOSEBA ZULAIKA is Professor and researcher at the Center for Basque Studies, University of Nevada, Reno. His books on political violence and terrorism include *Basque Violence: Metaphor and Sacrament* (1988); *Terror and Taboo: The Follies, Fables, and Faces of Terrorism* (1996; coauthored with William Douglass); *Terrorism: The Self-Fulfilling Prophecy* (2009); and *That Old Bilbao Moon* (2014).

NILS ZURAWSKI is a senior researcher and visiting professor at the Institute for Criminological Research at the University of Hamburg. He has published widely on surveillance, security, and control. He is coeditor of *The Anthropology of Security* (2014) and author of the monograph *Space-Control-Worldview* (2014; published in German).

INDEX

affect, 17, 31, 55, 81, 118, 125, 173, 176–77, 180, 183, 190–91, 229–30
Agamben, Giorgio, 1, 11, 162
algorithms, 16–17, 38, 144, 147
Andersson, Ruben, 96, 105
Apartheid, 7; funerary apartheid, 124–25
apparatus, 4, 17, 58–59, 72, 132, 139, 142, 143, 161, 176, 188, 230
Arab Spring, 89–91
Arizona, 12–13, 43–47, 49–52, 55–56, 58–60, 61n1, 73–74, 76, 80
atherosclerosis, 10–11

Bateson, Gregory, 137, 154–55
biometric security, 2, 4, 9–14, 92–93, 107n5, 163, 166, 233–34; in India, 24–42; iris recognition, 25–32; and surveillance, 67–88; 91
Blake, Robert, 2
Blake, William, 210
border security, 2, 7, 9, 11–15, 32, 43–60, 61n2, 61n3, 61n4, 61n5, 61n6, 67–69, 71–72, 75, 82–83, 90–101, 105–6, 107n1, 107n4, 163–64, 166, 173n1, 234; EUROSUR, 92; E-Verify, 13–14, 67–84;

FRONTEX, 91–94; Joint Operation Hermes, 91; Schengen, 91, 93, 163; Schengen Information Service (SIS), 91, 93, 163; Secure Border Initiative, 46, 55
Bourdieu, Pierre, 58
Brown, Michael, 16, 137–38, 153, 154n2
Bush, George W., 181, 192, 195, 196n2, 196n3, 196n10, 202, 211, 214, 217

Campesi, Giuseppe, 91
Canguilhem, Georges, 20n6, 34
Capa, Robert, 110–12
Capehart, Jonathan, 138
Cattaneo, Christina, 100–1, 103–4, 107n10, 107n11
Cheney, Dick, 192, 196n10, 211, 220, 230
classification, 11, 26, 31, 33, 35, 37, 113, 177, 181–82, 184, 186–89, 196n2, 196n7
Clifford, James, 5
Cold War, 7, 17, 175, 177–80, 184, 186, 191, 195, 219, 221, 223
Comaroff, Jean and John, 7–8, 20n4, 232; Jean, 232–33; John, 104
crime, 4, 7–8, 20n4, 79, 92, 100, 147, 151–52, 171, 206, 213, 215, 217;

crime (*continued*)
crime-scene analysis, 138; future, 16, 149–50; data on, 20n4, 142–43, 145–47, 149; against humanity, 15, 113–15, 120–26, 129, 131–33, 219; mapping of, 139, 143, 148, 150, 155n3, 156n8; organized, 153, 164

Csordas, Thomas, 5–6, 229

databases, 11, 20n4, 25, 38, 72–73, 79, 93, 97, 103, 163; data double, 29. *See also* statistical data
De Genova, Nicholas, 55, 67–68
De León, Jason, 47, 50, 69, 96
dental evidence, 15, 99–100; forensic dentistry (odontology), 100
Descartes, René, 230
DNA, 10, 15, 99–101, 103, 107n8, 115, 126–27, 130–31, 133, 138
Douglas, Mary, 11, 229
drones, 14, 46, 90, 92, 106, 184, 186, 194, 202, 218–22

Egypt, 89
emergency responders, 13, 43–60, 61n1, 61n5; firefighters, 44–45, 49, 51–52, 54–57, 60, 61n3, 61n4
Engelke, Matthew, 5, 229
errors, 3, 11–12, 24, 28–29, 31, 34–39, 233; failure, 3, 12, 34, 37, 59, 94, 126, 190, 211, 220, 233–34; failure to enroll, 12, 26
ethnographic methodology, 4–5, 7, 9, 12–14, 16, 19, 45, 47, 58, 61n1, 75–76, 139–40, 142, 145, 152, 155n2, 173n1, 228–29, 234
European Commission, 92–93
Evans-Pritchard, E. E., 6
evil, 203, 218

families, 22; relatives, 103–4, 127, 130–31, 188–89, 234; undocumented, 74, 77, 81, 83

Fassin, Didier, 57–58, 147, 153
Feldman, Gregory, 4, 17, 57, 141, 162, 173n2, 234
Ferguson, Missouri, 137–39, 142, 146, 154
fingerprints, 15, 25–29, 36, 100, 122, 163, 233
forensic science, 2, 9, 11, 14–16, 90–91, 95–96, 99–106, 107n8, 110–15, 119–22, 124, 126, 129–33, 231–34; CSI effect, 14, 16, 126, 133; exhumations, 112–13, 115, 122–23, 125, 130
Fortes, Maximilian, 3
Foucault, Michel, 3, 10, 20n6, 34, 139–43, 151, 153, 155n4, 172, 190, 230–31, 233
Franco, General Francisco, 113, 124–25, 128–29; Francoism, 126–27, 128–31
fraud, 2, 8, 11–12, 24–28, 35, 38, 189, 232; identity theft, 75
Frazer, James, 5, 18

Geographical Information Systems (GIS), 16, 148, 150
Goffman, Alice, 153
Goldstein, Daniel M., 4, 20n5, 76, 140; Carolina Alonso-Bejarano and, 13–14, 33, 231
governance, 12, 19, 27, 32, 34–38, 147, 154, 155n3, 155n4, 180, 195, 231; smart cards, 25
Graeber, David, 170
gray zone, 162, 165, 169–70, 173, 161–62
Greece, 2, 94, 97, 103
Guattari, Félix, 13
Gulf War, 2

Hart, Keith, 5
Hetherington, Kevin, 96
Homeland Security, 13, 45–46, 57, 59, 67, 72, 75, 181, 196n5
hospitals, 10–11, 31, 44–45, 49–52, 56–57, 59, 61n6, 101–2

preparedness, 57, 79
prison, 34, 58, 154, 190, 217; Guantánamo Bay, 204–7, 210; prisoners, 11,
17, 116, 119–21, 182, 190, 207, 210–12,
214, 217, 231
profiling, 16, 52, 93, 99–100, 139, 156n8,
211

Rabinow, Paul, 6, 19n1, 24, 34, 231
Rao, Ursula, 4, 11, 26, 32, 36–37, 99,
106; Elida K. U. Jacobsen and, 12–13,
25
Red Cross (International), 103, 130;
Red Cross (Mexico), 44
refugees, 68, 89–92, 94, 96, 98, 100, 106,
106n1, 113; refugee camps, 96, 106n1;
refugee crisis, 105
Robben, Antonius C. G. M., 4, 15–16,
100, 115, 118
Rose, Nikolas, 156n9, 231
Rove, Karl, 2
Rumsfeld, Donald, 211

science fiction, 147, 222
secrecy, 17–18, 175–96, 202, 219
securitization, 13, 44, 47–50, 68, 83;
(in)securitization, 19, 231–32
Solzhenitsyn, Aleksandr, 6
South Africa, 2, 7–8
Soviet Union, 6, 112, 177–80, 186, 190,
218
Spanish Civil War, 110, 124
statistical data, 16, 37, 46, 73, 97, 126, 139,
142–43, 149, 163, 190; Big Data, 147,
155n3. See also databases
Stocking, George W., 5
Strathern, Marilyn, 5
surveillance, 14, 26–27, 32–33, 38,
45–46, 55, 68, 70–71, 90–94,
107n5, 140, 151, 154, 156n7, 159,
163–72, 182, 189–90; surveillance
studies, 26
Syria, 92, 97, 105

taboo, 11, 207, 218, 221–22
Taussig, Michael, 15, 124, 233
technoscience, 11–12, 14, 16, 232, 233
terrorism, 45, 201, 203–4, 214–19,
223–34; counterterrorism, 2, 4, 10,
182–83, 196n2; 211–12, 219, 232, 234
Thucydides, 2
torture, 11, 16–18, 114, 118–19, 132, 214,
231
totalitarianism, 7, 14–15; dictatorships,
113–14, 124–26, 128
Trump, Donald, 3
truth telling, 11, 34
Tunisia, 90, 95, 97–98, 101, 107n9
Turkey, 94–95, 140, 212

uncertainty, 1, 7, 10, 19n1, 81, 83, 114,
167
undocumented migrants, 13, 26, 27, 45,
47, 51–53, 60, 61n5, 61n6, 61n8, 67–83,
83n1, 84n7, 84n8; deportation, 44,
52, 69–72, 75, 78–79, 81–83, 84n6, 97;
illegal immigrants, 11–13, 26, 31, 33,
43–44, 52–53, 55–56, 60, 68, 71, 77, 91,
96, 102, 160–61, 165, 171, 231, 234
Unique Identity (UID), 11, 24–25, 29
United Kingdom, 3, 32, 107n8, 114,
139–40, 147–51, 156n7, 178, 195, 228

Vietnam, 20n2; Vietnam War 2, 43,
112, 187
violence, 2, 8, 13, 45, 47–48, 55, 55–59,
90, 124, 132, 138, 140, 146, 151, 153, 186,
216, 221, 224; structural violence, 31,
153
visual security, 10–12, 27, 39, 139,
142–43

Wacquant, Loïc, 58
war on drugs, 45, 55; drug trafficking,
13, 17, 46–48, 53, 59, 96, 167, 172,
173n1
war on terror, 11, 17–18, 57, 68, 180, 182,

9 781478 002949